BARGAINING

Power, Tactics,
and Outcomes

Samuel B. Bacharach
Edward J. Lawler

BARGAINING

▼▼

Power, Tactics,
and Outcomes

Jossey-Bass Publishers
San Francisco • Washington • London • 1981

81-1104

BARGAINING
Power, Tactics, and Outcomes
        by Samuel B. Bacharach and Edward J. Lawler

Copyright © 1981 by: Jossey-Bass Inc., Publishers
                      433 California Street
                      San Francisco, California 94104
                                &
                      Jossey-Bass Limited
                      28 Banner Street
                      London EC1Y 8QE

Library of Congress Cataloging in Publication Data

Bacharach, Samuel B.
        Bargaining, power, tactics, and outcomes.

        Bibliography: p. 215
        Includes index.
        1. Negotiation. 2. Collective bargaining.
I. Lawler, Edward J. II. Title.
HD38.B17   302.3   81-8197
ISBN 0-87589-498-4   AACR2

Manufactured in the United States of America

JACKET DESIGN BY WILLI BAUM

FIRST EDITION

Code 8112

The Jossey-Bass
Social and Behavioral Science Series

▼▼

Preface

▼▼▼

When two or more individuals, groups, or organizations experience a conflict of interest, and when they wish to resolve their differences because it would be mutually beneficial to do so, they decide to *bargain*. Each party comes to the bargaining table with a certain power base, with the wherewithal to concede or refuse conditions desired by the opponent. Whether the conflicting parties are nations, corporations, or unions, the bargaining is a process of social interaction through which each party tries to maximize its gains and minimize its losses. Each party uses various tactics to accomplish this goal, to manipulate the other party in the desired direction. Those tactics may include bluffing, argumentation, concessions, threats, strikes, and so forth. In short, bargaining arises from conflict, and it is *action* shaped by the *tactics* used to gain desired ends.

For too long bargaining theory has neglected or assumed away the calculative thought pattern of actors in bargaining.

This volume treats bargaining actors as conscious decision makers who think about what they are doing and act in accord with their perceptions. *Bargaining* is based on the premise that bargainers analyze any bargaining setting in terms of bargaining power. That is, in bargaining, each party analyzes his or her bargaining power in juxtaposition to the bargaining power of the opponent. Bargaining power in turn determines the tactics that each party will adopt. Our primary objectives in this book are to examine the determinants and consequences of bargaining power and link bargaining power to the use of particular tactics.

We begin by demonstrating that previous theories of bargaining either neglect bargaining power or treat it simply as a description of the bargaining context. We then propose a framework for bargaining power and examine the role of power in decisions on concessions, the use of threats, how to define the issues of bargaining, what arguments to present in bargaining, and conflict resolution. In some chapters we present original data from social psychological experiments to illustrate and develop ideas. Our basic premise is that bargaining power can be used to analyze virtually all critical features of bargaining, thereby facilitating an integrative analysis of bargaining context, bargaining process, and bargaining outcome.

Chapter One critiques bargaining theory and gives special attention to theories of collective bargaining offered by Zeuthen, Hicks, Pen, and Chamberlain. Their theories suffer from inadequate analyses of bargaining power, which in turn lead to a neglect of the tactical nature of bargaining. The consequence is that bargaining theory offers little of use to practitioners faced with making calculations and tactical decisions or to scholars attempting to understand tactical decisions at the bargaining table. The chapter ends by pointing to the need for a framework on bargaining power.

To fill this void in bargaining theory, Chapter Two develops a framework on bargaining power based on the notion of dependence. The framework identifies the dimensions that bargainers consider when judging each other's bargaining power and when making decisions about particular tactics; it emphasizes the tactical, subjective nature of bargaining power. Once simply a characterization of the bargaining environment, or context, or a predictor of bargaining outcome, bargaining power becomes the central element of bargaining, pervading all facets of the bargaining relationship. To understand bargaining, therefore, is to understand how bargainers perceive, use, and manipulate power.

Chapter Three applies the framework on bargaining power to concessions. The basic choice confronting bargainers is how large or small, tough or soft their concessions should be. Toughness may extract more concessions from an opponent, but it also has the drawback of increasing the chance of an impasse. Chapter Three examines how bargainers use dimensions of bargaining power to make decisions on how tough to be in the bargaining. With the use of some illustrative social-psychological data, the chapter indicates how different images of bargaining power result in different levels of concession.

Bargainers also must decide whether (and when) to build up their capabilities of doing damage to each other and whether (and when) to use these resources in a punitive way. Chapter Four develops and contrasts two viewpoints. On the one hand, a theory of deterrence suggests that building up punitive capabilities reduces the tendency of parties to use punitive tactics and facilitates concession making. On the other hand, a theory of conflict spiral indicates that building up of punitive capabilities increases the likelihood of parties using punitive tactics in a way that inhibits serious bargaining. Chapter Five relates the deterrence and conflict spiral theories to the bargaining power framework and demonstrates, through the use of original social-psychological data, how bargainers can maximize the positive consequences of punitive capabilities, specified by deterrence theory, while minimizing the negative consequences delineated by the theory of conflict spiral.

Chapter Six examines tactics of argumentation at the bargaining table. How parties define issues is critical to their efforts to gain advantage and reach the best possible solution; this chapter treats the definition of issues as negotiable and looks at the consequences of different ways of defining the issues at hand. Much of the argumentation at the bargaining table can be construed as power arguments or normative arguments. The bargaining power framework identifies the major types of power arguments, the most critical, and estimates the success of different kinds of arguments. Normative arguments are grouped into equality, equity, and responsibility categories. Different normative arguments are likely to be effective under different conditions of power and the chapter suggests that bargainers select normative arguments by evaluating the bargaining power relationship.

The role of bargaining power in conflict resolution is treated in Chapter Seven. The chapter suggests a qualification of the old adage, "It is best to bargain from strength" and indicates that parties with nonconvergent, or unequal, power are less likely to reach an agreement and more likely (if they do agree) to construct settlements that depart from various principles of "split the difference." Convergent, or equal power, facilitates conflict resolution at settlement points that are generally more satisfactory to bargainers after the conflict has been resolved. Original data from social-psychological experiments support these conclusions.

Chapter Eight elaborates the theory of bargaining power. A key point is that bargainers can choose to analyze their own and their opponent's bargaining power in various ways. Different ways of analyzing power lead to different images of bargaining power that bargainers in turn act on in the bargaining process. Their image of bargaining power determines how they use concession tactics, punitive tactics, and arguments at the bargaining table. The framework emphasizes the subjective side of bargaining power, the tactical nature of the bargaining process, and the emergent quality of bargaining outcomes. The authors hope that the volume will encourage practitioners and students of collective bargaining to think more critically about traditional ways of analyzing power and that it will facilitate efforts to deal more systematically with this critical dimension of bargaining relationships.

The conceptual framework is flexible and broad enough to guide empirical analyses of bargaining and provide insights for practitioners. *Bargaining* illustrates the theoretical framework primarily with reference to and implications for labor-management relations, but the theory extends beyond any particular context. Transcending traditional disciplinary boundaries and offering a social-psychological perspective on bargaining, the book should be of interest to those in the fields of collective bargaining, industrial relations, organizational behavior, and international bargaining. It should also be of interest to social psychologists, sociologists, and political scientists concerned with power and interdependence in conflict relationships.

Acknowledgments

This work was partially funded by the National Science Foundation (SOC 78-26768). In writing this volume, we have received assistance from many people. Rose Malanowski provided excellent editorial and substantive suggestions. Jae-On Kim, Stephen Mitchell, and David Wagner gave us helpful comments on some chapters. The following people assisted with the collection and analysis of the data in Chapters Three, Five, and Seven: Dwayne Ferguson, Marcia Radosevich, Joyce Moeller, and Derek Mason. Pamela Kline provided invaluable typing and clerical services. Jan Wood did a superb job of typing the final manuscript. Above all, we would like to express our special gratitude to Joseph B. Shedd, who gave unselfishly of his time and made extensive comments on nearly all of the chapters. We also have our personal debts. Edward J. Lawler thanks his wife, Joan, for making most everything possible and his son, Michael, for tolerating another summer in Ithaca and for understanding the time pressure. Samuel B. Bacharach is especially indebted to Wendy Campbell for both her intellectual inspiration and personal support. He would also like to thank Pamela Kline for bringing organization and harmony to his nine-to-five world.

Finally we want to emphasize that this was a joint work in every respect.

July 1981   Samuel B. Bacharach
                                                Ithaca, New York

                                                Edward J. Lawler
                                                Iowa City, Iowa

Contents

▼▼▼

xv

Contents

The Authors

▼▼

Samuel B. Bacharach is associate professor in the Department of
Organizational Behavior, New York State School of Industrial
and Labor Relations at Cornell University. He received his B.S.
degree in economics from New York University and his Ph.D.
degree in sociology from the University of Wisconsin in 1974.
Bacharach was a visiting associate professor in the Jerusalem
School of Business of the Hebrew University in Spring 1981. He
serves as a book review editor for *Administrative Science Quarterly,* on the editorial board of the *Industrial and Labor Relations Review,* and as editor of an annual review, *Sociology of
Organizations: Theory and Research.* He is the author of *Organizational Behavior in Schools and School Districts* (1981)
and of numerous articles that have appeared in *Administrative
Science Quarterly, Journal of Personality and Social Psychology, Administration and Society, Industrial and Labor Relations Review, Academy of Management Journal,* and *Social*

Forces. He is doing a study of union politics with a grant from the Spencer Foundation.

Edward J. Lawler is associate professor in the Department of Sociology at the University of Iowa. He received his B.A. degree in sociology from California State University, Long Beach, and his Ph.D. degree in sociology from the University of Wisconsin in 1972. Lawler was a visiting associate professor in the Department of Organizational Behavior, New York State School of Industrial and Labor Relations at Cornell University during 1978-79 and 1981-82. He has served on the editorial board of *Social Psychology Quarterly* (formerly *Sociometry*) and has published articles in such journals as the *Journal of Personality and Social Psychology, Journal of Conflict Resolution, Industrial and Labor Relations Review, Social Psychology Quarterly,* the *Journal of Applied Social Psychology,* and *Social Forces.* He is presently studying bargaining and coalition processes.

The authors previously published *Power and Politics in Organizations* (1980) and are continuing their collaborative efforts in several areas, including political mobilization in collective bargaining, bargaining tactics, and power and authority in organizations.

BARGAINING

▼▼▼

Power, Tactics,
and Outcomes

1

Critique of Bargaining Theory

▼▼

Bargaining receives attention in a variety of disciplines including economics, industrial relations, applied mathematics, political science, and social psychology. However, it was originally and remains closely identified with the field of economics. The identification of bargaining with economics can be attributed, in large part, to the rise of trade unions during the latter part of the nineteenth century. Trade unionism posed a problem for economics: To explain how unions could persist and affect wage rates without inducing substantial unemployment within the atomized, perfectly competitive markets assumed by economic theories.

Most of the first successful unions were craft organiza-

Note: Joseph B. Shedd is a coauthor of this chapter.

1

tions, able to exercise some control over the supply of labor. Consequently, theorists defined unions as monopolies and treated union-management bargaining as a bilateral monopoly. This approach was adequate to explain the persistence of union-management bargaining, but it could not predict the wage rates generated by union-management bargaining. Theorists such as Edgeworth (1881) and Pigou (1938) argued that imperfect competition would foster a range of indeterminateness, the lower end of which would be whatever wage the employer would have to pay in order to retain a labor force of acceptable size, and the upper end, the maximum wage the union could demand without inducing an unacceptable level of unemployment. According to this formulation, economic theory could predict the range of possible bargains, or the contract zone, within which the parties would settle, but not the precise wage rate within this range.

That an economic problem could have an indeterminate solution dissatisfied many economists, however, and two other approaches to wage rates were considered. First, scholars associated with the emerging field of industrial relations rejected the notion of a contract zone and offered a variety of market and institutional explanations for the wage rates established by collective bargaining. Two attitudes characterize this tradition: Suspicion of theories that are not firmly grounded in or derived from empirical investigation—that is, a skeptical view of deductive theorizing; and emphasis on the environmental determinants of bargaining outcomes with little or no attention to the bargaining process. This environmental tradition has generated a rich body of historical, context-specific information, but because of its emphasis on isolating the predictors of bargaining outcome, it has generated little theory designed to integrate that information. As our understanding of factors that affect bargaining outcomes has grown, so has our need to understand how the relationships among such factors are mediated by or manifested in the bargaining process. As some scholars have recently indicated (for example, see Kochan, 1980), theorists should no longer treat the bargaining process as a black box whose content resists analysis.

The second response to the bargaining problem was to retain the notion of a contract zone and to search for a determinate solution within that range. This effort has been led by economists and game theorists (many of them applied mathematicians). The nature of these solutions varies as much as the empirical analyses of scholars in the environmental tradition, but two general features characterize this approach: The solutions are deductive, based on stringent assumptions about the bargaining problem; and the assumptions essentially collapse environmental conditions into static parameters of bargaining. The basic strength of this approach lies in its effort to develop general theories of bargaining that transcend, at least to some extent, institutionally specific elements of bargaining. The weakness is that the deductive mode of theorizing is used in a way that renders practical application difficult if not impossible.

In this book, we offer a general theory of bargaining that can be used to integrate research on the environment of bargaining and research on the bargaining process. In that sense, our work bridges the two theoretical traditions. It falls within the second tradition in that our approach is deductive; however, our basic focus is the interaction of the bargainers. In one sense, our work falls within neither tradition. We are not particularly concerned with finding determinate solutions to the bargaining problem, as economists have defined it. We are convinced that there is more regularity to bargaining than many theorists have suggested, but we are also convinced that the regularity is often obscured when the ultimate test of a theory is its ability to predict the bargaining outcome. We are more interested in anticipated bargaining outcomes, as an independent or intervening variable, than in actual bargaining outcome as a dependent variable. We are more concerned with demonstrating predictability in the process of bargaining than with establishing a direct connection between the context and the outcome of bargaining. We focus on how the bargainers themselves might make such a connection.

Since our approach is more closely identified with the deductive tradition than with the environmental tradition, let us review the work of four theorists in the deductive tradition—

John Nash, John Hicks, Frederik Zeuthen, and Jan Pen—and a
fifth, Neil Chamberlain, who spans the environmental and deductive traditions better than any theorist to date. Our intention is to elucidate the basic approach embedded in these theorists' classic works. Before discussing their efforts, however,
we must specify in broad terms the bargaining problem addressed
by such theories.

The Bargaining Problem

Virtually all theories of bargaining begin with a common
image of the bargaining problem—namely, that bargainers need
to reach some settlement but, at the same time, wish to settle
on terms favorable to themselves. This image captures the
mixed-motive nature of bargaining relationships. Bargainers
have some incentive to reach an agreement and, therefore, to
cooperate with each other; they also have some incentive to
push for a settlement consistent with their own interests and at
least somewhat inconsistent with the other's interests and,
therefore, to compete with each other. If they had no incentive
to cooperate, they would not bargain at all; if they had no incentive to compete, they would not need to bargain. Theories
of bargaining begin with the simple and obvious notion that bargainers compare the costs and benefits of no agreement with
the costs and benefits of particular settlements. These costs and
benefits ostensibly determine the concession behavior of the
parties and also the nature of the ultimate settlement. This basic
proposition underlies all the theories treated in this chapter.
The manner in which particular theorists treat this general
proposition depends partly on how they conceptualize the bargaining problem. The theories of concern to this chapter include
most, but not necessarily all, of the following elements in their
definition of the bargaining problem:

A bilateral monopoly. There are two bargainers who are
virtually stuck in their relationship. Neither has other parties
with whom to negotiate a comparable or better settlement, and
each is highly committed to the outcomes at issue. In other
words, there is a high level of mutual dependence in the bargain-

ing relationship. Nash (1950) and Zeuthen (1930) explicitly adopt this focus, and it is implicit in Hicks's (1963) approach. Pen (1959) and Chamberlain (1951, 1955) also adopt this focus, but they are more sensitive to possible variation in each party's dependence on the other.

An issue or set of issues. The issue confronting the parties is conceptualized as the division or distribution of some quantitative resource. This distributive quality of issues accounts for the incentives of parties to compete with one another as an increase in benefit to one party necessarily implies a decrease in the other's benefit. The prototypical focus of bargaining theories is the wage rate in a labor-management bargaining, and this issue is typically treated in isolation from other issues.

A contract zone. The issue or set of issues to be negotiated contains a range of possible bargains. The outer limits of this range are the minimum demands that each party will expect a settlement to satisfy. These minimum demands represent the payoffs that a party expects to receive in the event of no agreement. Consequently, offers outside the contract zone would not produce an agreement, because one or the other party would be better off without an agreement. The limits of such a zone constitute the bargainers' incentives to cooperate, because any settlement within those limits would make both of them better off than would nonagreement. Nash (1950), Zeuthen (1930), and Pen (1959) all make explicit use of such a concept, and Hicks (1963) does so implicitly. Chamberlain (1951, 1955) argues that such a concept is misleading, but he acknowledges that his model can be used to characterize such a zone.

Convergence of offers and counteroffers. The bargaining process can be characterized as the convergence of offers and counteroffers over time. Of those we discuss, Zeuthen (1930) is the only theorist who actually traces this process from start to finish, but the process of offers and counteroffers is central to the analyses of Pen (1959) and Chamberlain (1951, 1955) as well. Hicks (1963) focuses on the logic that dictates the parties' final, prestrike convergence, and Nash (1950) collapses each party's successive offers into the selection of a particular strategy (with only one move) that it will pursue in bargaining.

While Hicks's and Nash's models are formally static, both make assumptions that presuppose such a convergence process.

A determinate solution. There is a single, predictable settlement that the bargainers will agree upon. Chamberlain (1951, 1955) is the only one of these five theorists who does not claim to have specified a determinate solution, but Nash (1950, 1953) is the only one to have made such a claim without reservations. Hicks (1963) and Zeuthen (1930) generate such solutions, given certain assumptions, but both note that the logic of their models suggests why those assumptions might not be fully satisfied in the real world. In effect, they claim to have demonstrated determinate tendencies rather than strictly determinate solutions. In contrast, Pen (1959) merely specifies conditions that must be satisfied by a solution.

Perfect information. Bargainers have complete and perfect information on their own and the other's situations and on possible outcomes of the bargaining. The extent of parties' information about one another is a critical element in all the theories, but Nash (1950, 1953) and other game theorists are the only ones who make this a categorical assumption. The determinateness of Hicks's (1963) solution depends upon such an assumption, but he acknowledges its restrictiveness. Zeuthen (1930) originally indicates that his solution depends on such an assumption, but he later acknowledges that it is inconsistent with his basic framework (Zeuthen, 1955). Pen (1959) and Chamberlain (1951, 1955) reject the perfect-information assumption.

The foregoing six elements define the nature of bargaining in the broadest possible terms and provide bases for drawing initial distinctions among the major theorists. The last two elements—the determinateness of a theorist's solution and the extent of bargainers' knowledge—provide a clear continuum that serves to order our discussion. In order to identify and contrast basic approaches to bargaining, we first discuss the work of Nash, and then Hicks, Zeuthen, Pen, and Chamberlain.

John Nash: Game Theory and the Structure of Bargaining

The game-theoretical approach to bargaining represents the most thorough search for a determinate solution to the bargaining problem. Game theorists place bargaining in the context of a more general theory of individual choice. They seek to determine how a rational party attempting to maximize individual gain chooses between alternative lines of behavior, given that the payoff from the choice is contingent, in part, on the choice of another party. Given this mutual dependence, choice becomes a strategic issue, that is, a party must assess how to maximize its own gain in the context of potential interference from the other. The major purpose of game theory is to offer a set of rules that describe how rational actors choose the best strategy.

The nature of the player's reasoning varies with the structure of the game or nature of the interdependence relationship. In bargaining relationships, bargainers have reason to cooperate with one another, to reach an agreement and avoid the costs of conflict or impasse, but they also have reason to compete with one another for the scarce commodities at stake. Consequently, neither a strategy of total cooperation nor a strategy of total competition will maximize individual gain; some mixture of these pure strategies is necessary. Game-theoretical approaches to bargaining attempt to identify determinate solutions that reflect the mixed strategies most consistent with bargainers' conflicting interests.

A review of game theory is beyond the scope of this book (such reviews are offered by Harsanyi, 1977; Rapoport, 1966; Stahl, 1972; and Young, 1975). We are concerned only with illustrating the basic approach of those game theorists who have addressed the bargaining problem. For this purpose, we focus on the theory of John Nash, whose determinate solution is the foundation for virtually all other game-theoretical models of bargaining.

Nash's theory was a response to von Neumann and Morgenstern (1944)—the founders of the game-theoretical tradition —who held that there is no determinate solution for variable-sum or bargaining games. In variable-sum games, such as bargaining, the product of the parties' payoffs or utilities is not constant or fixed because different outcomes can specify different total amounts of payoff to be distributed by the parties. As long as one potential outcome of bargaining (for example, non-agreement) would leave both parties with poorer outcomes than other potential outcomes, there is a variable-sum element to the bargaining problem. The only prediction that von Neumann and Morgenstern offered about the solution to such games was that it would lie on an agreement frontier. The agreement frontier is "Pareto-optimal," which means that it includes all of each party's best possible outcomes, given any possible outcome for its opponent. That is, neither party will accept a solution that does not give it at least as much as it would get from nonagreement, and neither will accept a solution if another solution would give it a higher payoff without requiring the other party to accept a lower one.

Nash (1950) was dissatisfied with the indeterminate nature of von Neumann and Morgenstern's solution and sought to specify a determinate solution for two-party bargaining games. The only way he could do so was to add a number of assumptions about the structure or elements of the bargaining relationship. He began, however, with a number of assumptions that virtually all game theorists make:

1. Actors are rational and expect the other to be rational.
2. Actors attempt to maximize their own gain or utility.
3. Actors have complete information on the utility of alternative settlements to themselves and their opponent.

The first assumption means that both parties are aware of logic or rules that purportedly dictate their choice of strategies, and both are prepared to accept them. The second means that each party's choice of strategies is dictated by its own immediate interests. The possibility that longer-range interests might make it advisable for a party to accept somewhat poorer payoffs is excluded from its decision making. The third assumption means that the parties have no opportunity to influence each other's choice of strategies by the information they control, and they have all the information they need to anticipate each other's choices. By implication, it also means that the parties have no opportunity to create new outcome combinations, for example, by suggesting that the outcomes in this game be linked with outcomes in some other game. If qualitatively different issues or resources are potentially at stake, that possibility is already reflected in the outcome possibilities of which the parties are already aware. Their only option is to select one of these outcomes. In the case of bargaining games, the following assumption is added (see Nash, 1950; von Neumann and Morgenstern, 1944):

4. Neither party will settle for an agreement that is not Pareto-optimal.

The most central idea in game theory is that solutions are based on the utility functions of each party. The utility functions represent that party's relative preference for payoffs from all potential outcomes. In bargaining games, whatever influence the bargaining context or environment might have on a party is assumed to be reflected in these relative preferences. Nash's solution, like those of other theorists, is deductively derived from assumptions about the nature of these utility functions. Such reasoning holds that a different solution would imply different assumptions and, hence, somewhat different environmental conditions; and that the interaction in bargaining must not play a role in the prediction of a determinate solution. This reasoning implies the need for more assumptions. Nash (1950) adds the following:

5. "Good faith" bargaining—once a bargainer makes an offer it cannot be retracted, and an agreement, once reached, is enforceable.
6. If their final demands or offers are incompatible, bargainers get the utility associated with a failure to reach agreement (0, 0 payoff in Nash's basic model).
7. If the set of possible settlements is limited to a more restricted range on the agreement frontier, the determinate solution remains the same as long as the original solution, based on the complete agreement frontier, is included in the more restricted set.
8. The only significant differences between the parties are those reflected in their utility functions.

9. An order-preserving linear transformation of the utilities does not change the solution. That is, if the utility values of a party's potential outcomes are multiplied by a positive constant or are increased or decreased by a positive constant, the same outcome (now represented for that party by a new utility value) still represents the solution.

These additional assumptions have several implications. First, assumptions 5 and 7 indicate that the initial offer of the parties, concession patterns, and so forth within the bargaining process have no effect on the solution. If one bargainer makes a larger initial concession than the other, the operative contract zone becomes that part of the agreement frontier between the two initial offers, but the solution remains the same as long as the original solution remains in this restricted subset. Second, the addition of assumption 6 to assumptions 5 and 7 transforms bargaining into a one-move game. This characterization is consistent with the notion of strategy in game theory. Strategy is essentially the choice of the one move that will generate the maximum payoff. Tactical moves and countermoves (what game theorists call the game in *extensive form*) are transformed into one strategic move (the game in *normalized form*) that dictates or collapses the more specific round-by-round behavior.

Assumption 8 is often called an assumption of symmetry, but by that Nash (1950) does not mean to suggest that there are no significant differences between the parties, for example, in their resources or in their need to reach an agreement. The assumption merely specifies that if there are such differences, they will be completely reflected in each party's relative preferences for different outcomes. Assumption 9, however, gives Nash the ability to impose symmetry on the parties. This assumption dictates that the important feature of a party's preferences for different outcomes is its relative preferences for those outcomes. This property gives Nash the prerogative of adjusting each bargainer's utility scales to assign each a utility of zero at "no agreement" and to assign each of them the same utility score for their maximum conceivable payoffs even though their objective payoffs or their satisfaction with them might differ at these points. Assumptions 8 and 9 are the major ones that underlie Nash's determinate solution. Together they indicate that one party's choice of strategies will not be affected by its knowledge that it values a particular agreement or fears non-agreement either more or less than its opponent. Interpersonal comparisons of utility values are irrelevant, and efforts to influence each other's utility values have no effect on the ultimate solution.

Nash (1950) demonstrates that the only solution that satisfies the foregoing assumptions is one in which each party's utility is exactly half of what it would be if each achieved its most desired outcome. More technically, the only solution that meets all the assumptions is that point on the agreement frontier that maximizes the product of the differences between each party's utilities for agreement and nonagreement. Figure 1 illus-

Figure 1. Nash's Solution

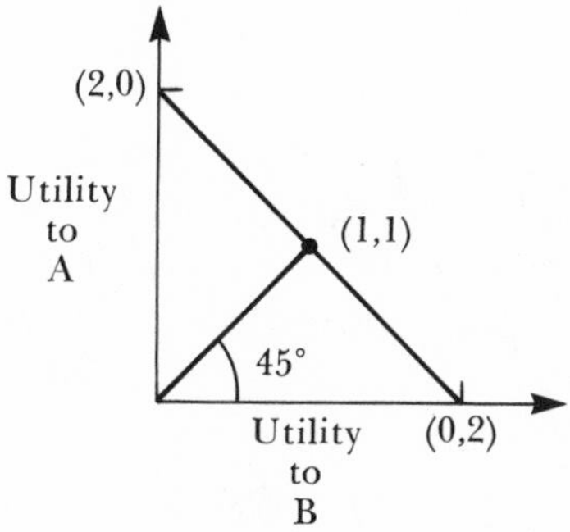

trates Nash's solution. The solid line in the graph is the Pareto-optimal agreement frontier, and the axes represent the utilities for bargainers A and B at each settlement point on this agreement frontier. In Figure 1, both parties prefer a distribution of payoff giving themselves two utility units and the opponent no utility units. Under these symmetrical circumstances, the solution is identified by a line at a 45° angle to the point of origin. This is the only point that creates an equal and proportional net gain for each bargainer (a solution of one utility unit for each party).

While Figure 1 is the most basic illustration of Nash's theory, the theory can also be applied to cases involving asymmetry in the actors' utility functions. Consider a case in which the most favorable agreement for A is two units of utility and none for B, while B's most favorable outcome would give it four and A none. Bargainer B has somewhat more utility at stake in the bargaining. Despite this asymmetry, Nash's original theory would still suggest a proportional net gain in utility for both bargainers and, therefore, a solution giving each party half the utility attached to its most preferred outcomes (that is, a solution of one unit for A and two units for B). This generalization of Nash's model is made possible by the linear-transformation assumption, which allows us to "stretch" bargainer B's most favored position to (0,4) because this simply involves the multiplication of B's original utilities (Figure 1) by a constant.

Both of these examples assume that the utility received by parties who do not reach agreement is zero. In the real world, however, the failure to reach agreement need not leave parties with a net gain or loss of zero utility. For example, each party might have the ability to go elsewhere to conclude an agreement; each might derive some satisfaction from keeping the resources it would have had to give up in order to reach an accord; or, each might be able to reduce the other's gain to below the zero-utility point through some form of punishment. The linear-transformation assumption permits the maintenance of the (0,0) conflict point by adjusting the utilities to take such factors into consideration. Nevertheless, there may be situations in which it would be important to represent these factors as "threat points," symbolizing the relative (and perhaps unequal) costs that parties incur as a result of no agreement. It would be particularly important to represent this element if the parties have an opportunity to influence each other's payoffs at the nonagreement point, as they clearly do in labor-management bargaining.

Nash (1953) demonstrates that his original solution can also be generalized to this type of situation, which he calls a *threat game.* Since the theory contends that parties will settle at the point where the product of the differences between their utilities at agreement and nonagreement is largest, it can generate a solution for any point of origin. The point of origin or nonagreement payoff in threat games is determined by the punitive strategies of the bargainers. Environmental conditions will dictate the strategies available to each party and the nonagreement payoffs produced by any combination of strategies. Each party will have an interest in maximizing its own nonagreement payoff and minimizing its opponent's, and different strategies may be required to accomplish each result. Nash side-steps this problem by assuming that each party will evaluate its threat options with reference only to the agreement payoff that any combination of nonagreement payoffs would dictate in the bargaining game. With a known (potential) agreement frontier, and the possibility of bluffing eliminated by assumption, Nash demonstrates that each party will have an optimal threat that is a best response to its opponent's optimal threat. There will be a determinate point of origin and, thus, a determinate solution to this bargaining game.

Nash's solutions to bargaining games are the best-known and most widely accepted game-theoretical treatments of the bargaining problem, but they are not without competitors. We will not discuss the details of these alternative approaches, except to note that each modifies one or more of the assumptions underlying Nash's solutions.

Raiffa (1953) offers two alternative solutions based on different assumptions about the effects of a nonlinear agreement frontier. Nash (1950, 1953) assumes that if a linear agreement frontier is bent or curved toward the origin, the solution remains the same as long as the midpoint of the original frontier is still on the agreement frontier. That assumption requires bargainers to act as if they were dividing up the linear frontier, even if each can claim only a limited amount of that frontier; for example, employers who cannot claim all their profits for themselves because they are required by law to provide workers a minimum wage. Raiffa suggests a different rule, which would have the parties split the difference between their maximum feasible demands while taking account of such limitations. Alternatively, they might adopt an agreement that yields each the same proportion of their maximum feasible demands. The latter requires an ad hoc comparison of their utility functions. Such an ad hoc comparison calls Nash's transformation-invariance assumption into question, however, since one party is likely to object when it discovers that the other has been assigned a larger objective payoff simply because its own maximum feasible demand has been arbitrarily assigned a smaller utility score.

Shapley (1953)—see also Luce and Raiffa (1957)—specifies a different solution for threat games in which the point of origin for the bargaining game is determined not by anticipated movement from it to the agreement frontier but by the separate payoff values that each party could be sure of getting if the other were completely malevolent and prepared to do its opponent the greatest possible damage, regardless of costs to itself. Once that (hypothetical) origin is established, movement to the agreement frontier is the same as in Nash's model.

Braithwaite (1955) also addresses the threat game, specifying optimal threats and movement from the origin to the agreement frontier as Nash does, but only after assuming that the parties have adjusted their utility scales to account for the different strategies each bargainer has available in the event of nonagreement. That is, if the parties fail to reach agreement, then both could adopt a defensive strategy of securing the best possible payoff for itself, a punitive strategy designed to keep the other party's payoff to a minimum, or each could adopt a different strategy. Braithwaite argues that the party that stands to gain the most by choosing between a defensive and punitive strategy will have an advantage over the other—an advantage that is reflected in the distribution of payoffs at the agreement point.

This proliferation of different solutions would seem to be rather devastating for those game theorists who present their models as predictive theories of bargaining outcomes. However, there is considerable disagreement among game theorists about whether their theories should be considered predictive or prescriptive. Nash is ambivalent on this point, but Harsanyi (1965, 1977), the foremost defender of Nash's set of assumptions, insists that those assumptions and their resulting solution describe the properties of actual bargaining. Others, like Raiffa (1953) and Braithwaite (1955), characterize their approaches and Nash's as arbitration schemes that provide alternative definitions of what might constitute a fair, equitable, or acceptable solution to the bargaining problem. Neither argument appears satisfactory. It is begging the question to assert that a particular approach can serve to define an acceptable solution if its proponents cannot first demonstrate that it has some predictive validity, and it is patently silly to assume that bargainers would necessarily accept the same set of ground rules if they perceive that different ground rules will yield different payoffs for themselves and their opponents.

The assumption that bargainers will accept a common definition of their situation, and hence, a common set of rules governing their behavior in that situation, is the most fundamental assumption in game theory and one that serves to underscore the costs of searching for a determinate solution. Those costs fall into five categories:

Realism. A determinate solution requires restrictive assumptions about the actors (that is, rationality, perfect and complete information, and so forth) and their underlying utility functions. Actual bargaining simply does not manifest the conditions required to treat such questions by assumption.

Application. Given the lack of realism, attempts to apply game theories require a modification or weakening of the assumptions underlying the models. Typically, tests of the models are not tests at all, but heuristic extrapolations from idealized models (see, for example, Bowlsby and Schriver, 1978; Hammermesh, 1973; Svejnar, 1980). The theoretical status of game theory is simply unclear, as exemplified by the predictive-prescriptive debate among game theorists.

Informativeness. A determinate solution requires a substantial loss in the informativeness of the theory. We did not need Nash (1950, 1953) to tell us that the midpoint of the contract zone is a likely solution, nor is Raiffa (1953) enlightening us by suggesting that bargainers might split the difference between their maximum feasible payoffs. What one needs to explain is not why actors will tend to split the difference but when they will choose to observe such a rule and how they will interpret that rule once they have decided to apply it.

Neglect of the bargaining process. A determinate solution requires that the tactical and manipulative nature of bargaining interaction be treated as either epiphenomenal or dangerously "noisy." The assumptions of game theorists specify a priori solutions that are possible only if the bargaining process has not interfered. The bargaining process is reduced to a ritual for bargainers to converge on an a priori outcome.

Inadequate analysis of environmental constraints. The external constraints on bargainers must be treated by game theorists as filtered through each party's utility functions. External constraints essentially dictate the values and shape of the agreement frontier and determine the utility of the conflict or no-agreement result. However, the relationship between these external constraints and the parties' utility functions is unspecified by the theories. A more systematic concern for the relationship of environmental conditions to the utility functions would add an element of indeterminacy that is simply unacceptable.

The constraints that must be imposed on a bargaining theory in order to generate a determinate solution lead to the neglect of issues and phenomena that are central to bargaining itself. As a consequence, we must reject game theorists' claims to have generated either a predictive or normative theory of bargaining. Game theory is not a dead-end street, but we cannot appreciate its contribution unless we face the right direction when looking down that street. The significance of game theory is best summarized by Rapoport (1966, p. 76), a noted game theorist: "The mathematician's elucidation of problems sometimes leads not to a solution but to a clarification, namely of what it is that the problem involves, what obstacles stand in the way of solutions, [and] what special cases of the problem can be treated by what methods."

Game theory is unable to tell us anything about the process of bargaining because its assumptions identify and remove all the obstacles that bargainers have to confront. While it is unrealistic to assume perfect or complete information, it is not unrealistic to propose that bargainers must gather information on each other, make subjective utility judgments, and attempt to manipulate each other's information and utility judgments. While it is unrealistic to assume that bargainers are rational, it is not unrealistic to assume that they are calculative, methodical, and utilitarian in their approach to the bargaining. It may be doubtful that bargainers have precise estimates of the utility of a given agreement or of nonagreement when they begin bargaining, but they certainly develop such perceptions and act on them in bargaining. It would be a mistake to assume that the parties are indifferent to the forces that affect the shape of the agreement frontier at the margins, that their preferences are unaffected by their knowledge of how much the other party values a particular outcome, or that they are confident that their agreement will be binding and enforceable. But it would be an even more serious mistake not to recognize that the parties have to deal with such considerations in one way or another.

Reconceptualizing game theory in this manner transforms its assumptions into variables. The contribution of game theory is that it identifies such variables and, more important, focuses on the relationships among them. In Rapoport's (1966) terms, game theory focuses on the logical structure of strategic conflict. Interestingly, the most striking feature of that structure is its cognitive nature. With the possible exception of Nash's assumption regarding the enforceability of agreements, the assumptions do not reflect environmental constraints, per se, but specify how the parties will address them. In game theory, the bargainers' perceptions about the structure of their relationship, and not some objective, externally imposed structure, determine the effect of external variables on the bargaining outcomes. Game theorists are unable to take advantage of such insights, because their method dictates that both parties' perceptions are identical and fails to account for the fact that the assumptions of game theory are subject to interpretation and manipulation by bargainers. The proliferation of game-theoretical solutions is an important reminder that there are many modes of rationality which bargainers, either individually or collectively, might use to orient themselves to bargaining.

John R. Hicks: Anticipating Changes
in Costs and Aspirations

Game theory is an approach to the bargaining problem that has generated a number of different solutions, while Hicks's theory of industrial disputes (1963) is a solution that has generated a number of different approaches. Hicks's theory has served as a point of departure for several models of labor-management bargaining and for analyses of bargaining power, strike frequency, strike predictability, and bargaining goals. His model is a "suggestive sketch" (Foldes, 1964) to which others have added so many lines that it is sometimes difficult to discern those of the original. The central notion of Hicks's solution is that bargainers anticipate changes in their own costs over time, and such anticipated change forms the basis of a party's concession behavior.

Hicks states his focus in a way that is not always appreciated in critiques of his theory. Commenting on some of these critiques, he notes, "Though it is called 'The Theory of Industrial Disputes,' its main object is not to make a theoretical analysis of the bargaining process. What it does seek to do is to answer the question: To what extent can trade union pressure compel employers to pay higher wages (or to grant more favourable terms to their employees in other respects) than they would have done if no such pressure had been exercised" (1963, p. 352). Unlike game theorists, Hicks is not concerned with bargaining in the abstract, but with bargaining between labor and management. More important, Hicks is not concerned with specifying a strictly determinate solution but with conditions that compel an employer to such a solution.

Hicks's answer is quite simple: An employer will grant an "excess" wage in order to "buy off" a strike, with the size of the excess being determined by the costs of the prospective strike. Assuming that strike costs are a function of strike length, the maximum concession that management is willing to make will depend on its estimate of the expected length of the strike. Hicks plots this relationship between strike length and wage concessions on what he calls the *employer's concession curve*, an example of which is provided in Figure 2. Each point on the concession curve represents the maximum wage rate manage-

Figure 2. Hicks's Solution for Labor-Management Bargaining

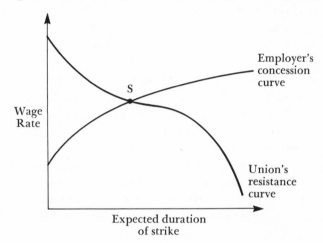

ment would offer (vertical axis) if it thought that such an offer could prevent a given strike duration (horizontal axis). The concession curve leaves the vertical axis at the wage rate the employer would be willing to grant without the prospect of a union strike, and it slopes upward as the length of the anticipated strike increases. The nonlinear shape of the concession curve reflects the fact that it "cannot rise higher than some fixed level, since evidently there is some wage beyond which no trade union can compel an employer to go. If wages are to swallow profits completely, he will prefer to close down the works and leave the industry" (Hicks, 1963, p. 142).

The concession curve, alone, represents a schedule of wage rate–strike length combinations, without saying anything about the strike length actually anticipated by the employer. To anticipate the strike length, the employer must estimate the resolve of the union at the various wage levels. Since a strike is also costly to the union, the employer will expect the resolve of the union to be inversely related to the length of the strike. Specifically, the *union's resistance curve* (see Figure 2) represents the employer's estimate of how long the union would be willing to "hold out" rather than concede to a low wage rate. Such a curve would leave the vertical axis at some arbitrarily high wage (selected by the union for internal political or tactical reasons) and slope downward in a manner that signifies that workers would be willing to endure more hardship (that is, a longer strike) the lower the wage rate. Hicks argues that the union's resistance curve is likely to be nearly horizontal over a considerable part of its length because there is some level of wages to which workers consider themselves to be entitled. To obtain this level they will strike for a considerable period, but "they will be less concerned to raise wages above it" (Hicks, 1963, p. 143). If the employer were unwilling to grant this minimum wage increase, the resolve of the union would eventually collapse, and its resistance curve would fall to or below the wage level the employer would have granted without union pressure.

The solution is at the point where the employer's concession curve intersects the union's resistance curve (point S in Figure 2). This is the highest wage that the employer will grant in order to prevent a strike. The employer will not offer more than point S because the costs of doing so would exceed the anticipated costs of a strike. The employer will readily offer a wage lower than point S because the costs of doing so would actually be less than the costs of a strike, but he or she will not expect the union to accept a wage rate that falls below that level. Thus, the solution point equalizes the cost of a strike and the cost of a given wage increase for the employer.

Hicks's determinate solution is a qualified one. First, the model applies only to bargaining *before* a strike and to anticipated, not actualized, strike costs. As Hicks readily admits, if a strike occurs, the costs that the employer actually experiences can no longer be bought off and the point of intersection depicted in Figure 2 is no longer relevant. Second, Hicks acknowledges that the curves are subject to tactical manipulation. If the union can convince the employer that its resistance curve is higher than depicted in Figure 2, then it can extract a larger concession than S from the employer. Hicks recognizes that manipulation is not only possible but quite likely, given the prospective benefits to the union. Third, the solution stipulated by Hicks is contingent on the ability of the employer to convince the union to accept S. This solution point constitutes the settlement the employer expects the union to accept after a strike of a given length, but it is unclear how or whether the employer could convince the union to accept this rate without a strike. The second and third points reflect the fact that Hicks's model does not treat the manipulative or tactical processes which establish the employer's concession and union's resistance curves or provide a foundation for understanding such tactical manipulation.

In order to interpret his solution as a determinate one, Hicks suggests (but does not state categorically) that we must accept the following: The employer's estimates of the two curves and intersection point are completely accurate; the union negotiators hold similarly accurate estimates; and the parties somehow convince each other that neither can do better than S with an actual strike. Several of Hicks's critics have argued that these assumptions are so restrictive that they drain his model of any possible value in the analysis of the bargaining process (see Pen, 1959; Shackle, 1957). But as Hicks points out, he did not intend to offer such a theory; like game theorists, he offers a definition of the problem that bargainers face without specifying the process by which the parties solve it.

There are grounds, however, for questioning the adequacy of Hicks's conceptualization of the bargaining problem confronting labor and management. Consider the asymmetry Hicks attributes to the labor-management relationship. Shackle (1957) argues that the union resistance curve in Hicks's model should have a positive, not a negative, slope because a union will consider longer strikes the higher the wage increase expected from a strike. This criticism, however, overlooks the direction of causality implied in Hicks's argument. Shackle's approach implies that a union will estimate the costs for a strike of a given length and then use those costs to calculate the wage rate that would compensate for sustaining such costs. Whereas Shackle proceeds from strike length to wage rate, Hicks moves from the wage rate to strike length. He assumes that a union has varying amounts of commitment to each of several wage rates, which determine the costs they are willing to bear in order to secure them. Hicks's argument is attractive because it avoids the assumption, implicit in Shackle's argument, that a union strikes in order to get a wage increase that compensates its members for the cost of striking. If this were the case, they would be just as well off accepting the employer's original offer and not sustaining any costs.

Nevertheless, Hicks's discussion indicates that he is not interested in capturing the union's decision making at a particular point in time. Hicks's two curves and their point of intersection should be interpreted only as elements of the employer's prestrike decision making. To apply these to the union's prestrike decision making would necessitate the assumption that a union's aspirations at one point in time are dictated by its impression of how those aspirations might change at a later time. It is unclear whether Hicks accepts the tautological implications of such an assumption, whether he is implying that a union has a separate (and perhaps differently shaped) set of curves underlying its decision making, or whether he is simply content to address only part of the bargaining problem. Given that he defines the bargaining problem in terms of considerations that lead the employer to grant wage rates higher than market forces dictate, the last explanation is probably most accurate. However, other theorists have been unwilling to accept this conclusion.

Many have offered theories that build from and add to Hicks's theory. Let us briefly review some of these theories and illustrate their common focus on how parties anticipate changes in their situation over time.

Ashenfelter and Johnson (1969) implicitly accept a single set of curves, one reflecting the employer's increasing costs and the other the union's declining aspirations over the course of a strike. They assume that those curves capture both parties' prestrike decision making. Bargaining is construed as an interaction between a profit-maximizing employer and union leaders who must contend with the political demands of maintaining their organization and getting themselves reelected. The basic purpose of Ashenfelter and Johnson's model is neither to describe the process of bargaining nor to predict the wage outcomes of such bargaining, but to predict the occurrence of strikes. In that sense, their theory falls outside the scope of our discussion. However, they suggest that the prestrike decision making of union leaders is affected by an expected decline in their members' aspirations over the course of a strike. This assumption is one way to side-step the otherwise tautological implications of applying Hicks's curves to union bargainers.

Foldes (1964) and Bishop (1964) offer models that base bargainers' concessions on their impressions of their own and each other's costs over strikes of varying lengths. Central to both theories is the calculation of the maximum strike length—the longest strike that parties are willing to endure—given perfect information about their own and the other's bargaining positions. They derive the maximum strike lengths differently, but the "concession mechanism" (Young, 1975) is similar. For any pair of wage demands, the party whose maximum strike length is shorter will give ground to its opponent. Both Foldes and Bishop demonstrate that, given such a concession mechanism, there is one and only one wage rate that either party could enforce against any alternative demand of its opponent. Their utility functions, and whatever environmental or personal properties underlie them, are givens not subject to real or perceived manipulation in the course of bargaining.

Cross (1965) focuses on the learning parameters of bilateral monopolists who do not possess perfect information about each other and who are bargaining over a fixed quantity of some resource. Bargainers use a differential calculus to determine the share of that quantity they can expect for themselves and to determine the concession rate that will maximize the total value of the settlement, given the most recent concession rate of their opponent and the costs the bargainer incurs for each unit of time that passes without a settlement. From Cross's theory, bargainers continually readjust their calculations, increasing, decreasing, or maintaining their own concession rate as they observe that of their opponent. The speed of their readjustment is governed by the magnitude of the error in their original estimates and by their "learning abilities." On the surface, Cross's perfect-information model appears altogether different from the static, institutionally specific model of Hicks. In fact, however, Cross derives from Hicks the basic notion that bargainers base their concessions on their own prospective costs and changes in their opponent's resistance over time.

Johnston (1972) presents a model of prestrike decision making that is much closer to Hicks. He addresses an apparent anomaly in Hicks's analysis—namely, that the employer in Hicks's theory calculates the wage-rate equivalents of anticipated strike costs as if certain that a strike will occur, but then makes an offer with complete confidence that doing so will prevent a strike. In contrast, Johnston develops a theory in which the employer fixes its prestrike offer so as to minimize the expected costs of what game theorists would call the combined event of going to strike with some probability p and not going to strike with the probability $1 - p$. The employer in Johnston's model considers strike costs as including the costs of granting a wage rate that may or may not be different from its prestrike offer. The intersection point of Hicks's curves, therefore, is irrelevant: Management's prestrike final offer might be higher than the one it thinks the parties might agree upon after the beginning of a strike if management believes there is a sufficiently high probability of the union's accepting the offer without a strike. However, management might hold something back from the prestrike final offer if there is a high probability that the union will not buy what management has to offer without the pressure of a strike.

Rabinovitch and Swary (1976) supplement Johnston's analysis of the employer's decision making with a parallel set of union cost and anticipation functions, and they examine the process of convergence at the bargaining deadline. They begin at the final prestrike negotiation session, at which each party announces a final position derived from its independent calculations of the costs or benefits of enduring or avoiding a strike. After receiving the other's final offer, each party recalculates these estimates, and agreement occurs (without a strike) if either party concludes that its prospects would be poorer with a strike. At each subsequent bargaining session, the parties announce new positions and then recalculate their anticipated gains or losses, based on the change in the other's position. The strike will continue until one or the other concludes that it would be better off accepting the other's most recent offer. Rabinovitch and Swary assume that bargainers treat each other's final, prestrike offers and any subsequent ones as straightforward evidence of each other's real positions.

The general approach of Rabinovitch and Swary to the bargaining process illustrates a problem common to all models associated with Hicks's theory. Bargainers may use information about the past and anticipated opponent's concessions to evaluate their own situations—that is, they are influenced by their opponent's concession behavior—but they are not viewed as using their own concession behavior to influence their opponent. If bargainers recognize that their own calculations will be used as new information in the next round of their opponent's calculations, however, bargainers will not focus only on objective cost-minimizing or gain-maximizing considerations. Each party will realize that it can manipulate the information that its opponent will use at the next stage and that its opponent may have intended a similar manipulation when it formulated its most recent position.

Here we have a serious theoretical weakness in Hicks's model. If we assume that bargainers base their decisions exclusively on what they *do* know about each other and themselves, then we may assume that over time bargainers organize their information and assess the advantages and disadvantages of accepting one set of terms or holding out for better ones. However, if bargainers are sensitive to what they *do not* know about each other—if they are concerned about the consequences of miscalculating each other's intentions—then to insist that they think in terms of constantly changing costs or aspirations is less persuasive. Bargainers will not divide the future into more than a handful of intervals unless they know or think they know what information applies to each interval. If they do not have such knowledge and confidence, the only intervals that are of much use to them are present and future, and the subjective concept of risk will have to be introduced into their decision making.

Frederik Zeuthen: The Risk of Conflict

In 1930, Zeuthen proposed his classic resolution to the determinacy problem. Zeuthen retains the concept of a contract zone, but argues that the economic forces which create the boundaries of that zone also create tendencies toward particular settlements. These tendencies are manifested in the bargaining process, and Zeuthen proposes to identify and account for these patterns within the bargaining process.

The tendencies that concern Zeuthen are embedded in the offers and counteroffers made by parties at the bargaining table. The bargaining process is conceptualized as a series of successive decision points that confront bargainers with the choice of reiterating their previous demand or making a concession—that is, reducing their demands. The problem for Zeuthen is to find the criterion that rational bargainers use to make these decisions. The criterion is the risk of conflict, or more precisely, the risk that a party subjects itself to when it rejects the other's offer and remains firm on its own most recent offer. Zeuthen's basic proposition is that bargainers will not yield or make concessions unless or until the risk of conflict becomes unacceptable.

The level of maximum acceptable risk is based on three pieces of information: the current offer of a bargainer, the current offer of the opponent, and the bargainer's conflict point. Assume a union has demanded a $1.00 an hour raise and management has offered $.25. Assume, also, that the bottom of the contract zone, and thus the conflict point for the union, is no raise. Zeuthen's theory indicates that the union's decision whether to make a concession depends on the prospective gains and losses of remaining firm on its demand of $1.00. If the union is certain that by standing firm it could eventually force management to acquiesce, it would gain $1.00 − $.25 = $.75. If the union is certain that management would never agree to its demand, then standing firm would prompt a breakdown in negotiations with a cost of $.25 − 0 = $.25. However, a union is seldom, if ever, certain about the response of management to a tactic of remaining firm. There is *some* possibility that management will accede to the union's demand and *some* possibility that it will not. The union's potential loss is weighted by its estimate of the probability that standing firm will provoke a breakdown in negotiations, and its potential gain is weighted by the probability that standing firm will eventually force the employer to concede to its position. The purpose of Zeuthen's theory is not to predict these probabilities, for they are inherently subjective. He simply assumes that a party will make such a probability estimate and then calculate whether its gain is more or less than its loss. If it concludes that its gain is greater than its loss, it will stand firm; if it concludes that its potential loss is greater, it will make a concession.

Although Zeuthen does not provide a basis for predicting bargainers' probability estimates in this first stage of their decision making, his argument does provide a basis for predicting the maximum risk that a rational bargainer would be willing to accept rather than make a concession. This probability can be portrayed as follows:

$$P_{\max} = \frac{Du - Dm}{Du - Cu},$$

where $P_{\max}$ is the maximum likelihood of risk acceptable to the union, Du is the current demand of the union, Dm is the current demand of the management, and Cu is the conflict payoff for the union. The maximum risk of conflict is a function of the ratio of the distance between the current demands of union and management and the distance between the union's current demand and its conflict point. The numerator is the gain to the union if the management eventually accepts Du; while the denominator is the total or maximum loss if there is a breakdown in the negotiations—Zeuthen's fighting costs. In our previous example, the maximum risk of conflict that would be tolerated by the union is ($1.00 - $.25)/($1.00 - $.00) = .75.

Zeuthen contends that a party's decision to stick with its previous demand or to make a concession at any given point in bargaining is a function of each party's $P_{\max}$. Both parties have a maximum risk of conflict, and the party with the higher tolerable risk can simply hold out longer, forcing the party with a lower acceptable risk to make a concession. Thus, if the union's P_{max} is greater than its estimate of management's P_{max}, then the union will expect management to make the next concession; if the union's P_{max} is lower than management's P_{max}, then the union will make the next concession; if the P_{max} of both are equal, both will make a concession. This process of concession and counterconcession is likely to be continued because a given party's concession manipulates the opponent's P_{max}. Looking back at the equation for the union, it is clear that a management concession will reduce the numerator and, hence, the union's maximum risk of conflict. Since both the union and management are subject to complementary equations, a concession by one party places the opponent in the position of having to make a concession (all other things being equal).

Zeuthen's theory predicts who will make a concession at a given point, but not the size of the concession. He simply assumes that a party will make the smallest concession necessary to make its opponent's P_{max} smaller than its own. It is quite conceivable that a given party will have to make more than one concession before the opponent's P_{max} becomes lower than the party's own. Thus, Zeuthen does not suggest that a union concession will invariably be followed by a management concession, but only that this will occur if the union's concession reduces management's P_{max} below that of the union. This process of concession and counterconcession continues until the maximum risk of conflict for both parties is zero, which is the settlement point. Bargaining, then, induces a process of convergence generated and maintained by each party's manipulation of its opponent's maximum acceptable risk of conflict. Concessions facilitate later concessions, and this process continues toward a settlement as parties mutually reduce each other's acceptable risk.

Zeuthen acknowledges several reasons why the determinateness of his model can be called into question—for example, the parties might miscalculate each other's willingness to sustain a conflict. One may be more or less cautious about accepting risk than suggested by its objective interests; the time required to conclude an agreement might exert unequal pressure on parties; the change in the value of a settlement might not be a linear function of the wage rate. Zeuthen suggests that some of these conditions could be handled by assuming that the parties transform the objective quantities into utilities; others might be treated as factors that influence the outer limits of the contract zone, but not the determinateness of the solution. Overall, Zeuthen argues that such factors do not undermine the *tendency* toward a determinate solution specified by the theory.

The major strength of Zeuthen's theory is its focus on the bargaining process. In contrast to many other theorists, Zeuthen insists that the influence of environmental forces on bargaining outcomes must be reflected in the process that produces those outcomes. His theory offers an explanation of why and when parties make concessions, ties a "molecular" analysis of the bargaining process to economic forces outside the bargaining relationship, and predicts the outcome of bargaining on the basis of the bargaining process. Zeuthen essentially attempted to integrate bargaining context, bargaining process, and bargaining outcome into a few simple theoretical principles. However, the inherent tension between his emphasis on the interaction of the parties and his intent on specifying a determinate solution is never satisfactorily resolved.

The failure to resolve this tension is reflected in the fact that Zeuthen's solution is dictated exclusively by the conflict points of the two bargainers. Regardless of parties' opening offers, who starts the bidding, or what values parties ascribe to their risk of conflict at any given point, Zeuthen's decision rules produce a settlement at the midpoint of the parties' conflict values. One can argue that Zeuthen's theory of bargaining process inadvertently makes the analysis of that process as superfluous as do game theories. In fact, Harsanyi (1965, 1977) demonstrates that Zeuthen's solution is identical to Nash's (1950, 1953)—that is, parties settle at the point that maximizes the product of the difference between what bargainers get from conflict and what each gets from the settlement point. Indeed, Zeuthen's theory implicitly or explicitly adopts stringent assumptions comparable to Nash's, although in his later work Zeuthen (1955) moves away from the assumption of perfect information. Nevertheless, Zeuthen's theory, with its general emphasis on the bargaining process, marks a useful transition between bargaining theories committed to the search for a determinate solution and those that reject this as a primary goal. Let us now consider several theories of the latter type.

Jan Pen: Uncertainty and Tactical Manipulation

If the information that bargainers have about each other is not perfect or complete, then uncertainty is a critical feature of bargaining. To overcome uncertainty, bargainers must observe and evaluate each other's behavior at the bargaining table. Bargaining essentially becomes a process of manipulating information, a process that may reveal certain patterns but not necessarily ones that yield a determinate solution. In the previous section, we suggested that Zeuthen's emphasis on a determinate solution is incompatible with his emphasis on the bargaining process. Game theorists have emphasized and refined his determinate solution while ignoring his emphasis on bargaining process. Pen (1952, 1959), among others, has developed Zeuthen's model of the bargaining process and discounted his determinate solution. Overall, an emphasis on bargaining process implies a theory that incorporates uncertainty.

Pen (1959) adopts Zeuthen's (1930) concept of acceptable risk but reconceptualizes it in a manner that builds uncertainty into his model. The first step in this reconceptualization involves the parties' preferences and conflict values. For both Pen and Zeuthen, bargainers are bilateral monopolists negotiating wage rates within a range of potential settlements. In contrast to Zeuthen, Pen's bargainers are not simple wage maximizers or minimizers. Their preferences for particular outcomes within the range of settlements are influenced by psychological, market, and political considerations that also affect the outer limits of that range. Consequently, the preferences attached to various wage rates are likely to have a nonlinear relationship to the monetary value of those wages. Pen (1959) characterizes these preferences as *ophelimity values,* rather than as utility values, to convey the notion that they have peaks which reflect intensities of preference for particular settlements. These ophelimity values are subjective and, therefore, one cannot assume that bargainers have anything but incomplete and imperfect information about them.

Like Zeuthen, Pen indicates that the maximum risk a party will tolerate is based on the expected gain from holding out (and getting its preferred settlement) and the expected loss if holding out provokes a conflict. However, since bargainers' ophelimity functions have peaks, bargainers will calculate these gains and losses with reference to their most-preferred outcomes (that is, target points), rather than with reference to their current demand or offer. This notion of targets represents a major difference between Pen and Zeuthen. Zeuthen's bargainers do not have a goal or target point against which to compare the opponent's current offer—they are simple wage maximizers whose risk calculations are grounded from below by a conflict value but have no target or upper reference point. Given Pen's (1959) reconceptualization, the maximum acceptable risk is:

$$P_{\max} = \frac{U(Wu) - U(Dm)}{U(Wu) - U(C)},$$

where $U(Wu)$ represents the ophelimity value that the union associates with its most preferred outcome, $U(Dm)$ is the ophelimity value it associates with management's current offer, and $U(C)$ is the ophelimity value it associates with a conflict. Pen treats $P_{\max}$ as a more or less objective calculation of the probability of conflict the union would be prepared to risk, given its most-preferred outcome, its conflict value, and the employer's current offer. This calculation is determined by the ratio of the difference between the party's target (goal) and the opponent's current offer to the difference between the party's target and conflict payoffs.

Pen argues that the maximum risk, thus defined, is not sufficient to explain concession behavior, because the actual risk of bargainers is also affected by their attitude toward risk taking. Some bargainers are more daring than suggested by objective calculations, while others are more conservative. What Pen (1959) terms a bargainer's *risk valuation function* leads it to adjust the maximum risk it is willing to accept at a particular point, producing its *propensity to fight*.

The final step for Pen's bargainer is to compare the propensity to fight with the immediate risk of conflict faced at a given moment in the bargaining. For Zeuthen, this is simply a matter of a party's comparing its own P_{max} with the other's P_{max}. Pen argues that the propensity to fight specifies the importance of continuing to press for better terms than currently offered by the opponent, assuming there is room for further bargaining. Knowing an opponent's propensity to fight tells a bargainer whether its opponent is prepared to abandon its own offer and accept the bargainer's demand, but it does not tell the bargainer how close the opponent might be to breaking off negotiations, which is the information that the bargainer needs to decide whether to press for still better terms from its opponent.

To acquire information on the inclination of the opponent to break off negotiations, a bargainer must try to estimate how much distance there is between the opponent's current offer and the opponent's conflict point; the latter marks the point where the opponent ceases negotiations. If a bargainer knows the opponent's conflict point with certainty, then the bargainer would assume that the immediate risk of conflict is zero as long as there is some distance between the opponent's current demand and that point. A bargainer with such knowledge continues to pressure the opponent until that limit is reached, at which point the immediate risk of conflict is equal to one, or until it secures its own most-favored outcome, at which point its own propensity to fight is zero. However, a bargainer is not certain about such judgments, so estimates of probability become necessary. The magnitude of the probability estimate is inversely proportional to the bargainer's estimate of the distance between the opponent's current offer and the opponent's conflict point. A bargainer's decision is based on a comparison of this probability estimate with its own propensity to fight. Overall, this analysis marks the sharpest contrast between Pen's theory and the theories discussed in previous sections. From Pen's theory, if bargainers possess the perfect information assumed by other theorists, they know each other's conflict points, and they will have a deadlock or abandon negotiations immediately. It is uncertainty that makes bargaining possible.

There is another important difference between Pen's theory and those discussed in previous sections. Unlike other theorists, Pen does not specify a mechanical decision rule dictating when a party will make a concession. Each bargaining party feels increasing pressure to make concessions, the more its propensity to fight declines and the more its perception of the risk of immediate conflict grows; but neither party is constrained in how it responds to such pressure—so long as its immediate risk of breakdown is not greater than its own propensity to fight. Pen's basic prediction is that a union will not stop bargaining and accept a contract until its risk of immediate breakdown equals or exceeds its propensity to fight, and management will not be prepared to stop bargaining until its risk of immediate breakdown equals or exceeds its propensity to fight.

Pen's theory raises the most general tactical dilemma confronting bargainers: How to manipulate the opponent's strategic thinking to induce the greatest concessions without provoking the opponent to break off negotiations. The easiest, but most costly, way to manipulate an opponent is to make a concession. A concession reduces the maximum risk acceptable to the opponent and may also affect the opponent's perception of the immediate risk of conflict (depending, of course, on how the opponent links the concession to the conceder's ophelimities). Overall, Pen's theory suggests that concession behavior is a critical form of tactical action, because a bargainer can manipulate both the opponent's propensity to fight and the subjective processes underlying the elements of risk.

The elements of bargaining that Pen identifies are likely to be subject to different kinds of tactical manipulation. The element most sensitive to manipulation is the opponent's estimate of the immediate risk because it is based on cues provided by the bargainer. Each party strives to convince the other that the distance between its current offer and its conflict point is quite small. The risk valuation function is probably vulnerable to the least manipulation since it is the most personal element in the model. A bargainer's most-preferred solution and minimum acceptable solution may be vulnerable to some manipulation, but Pen suggests that such manipulations are limited because they attempt to "persuade [the other party] that he does not see his own interests clearly and that he should therefore listen to the well-meant advice of his opponent" (1959, p. 140). Thus, Pen's theory identifies potential targets for tactical manipulation.

However, Pen's model does not provide a theory of tactical action. While it identifies points that are more or less vulnerable to manipulation, it does not predict which elements a bargainer will attack, which tactics will be successful, or when bargainers will use concessions in a tactical manner. This is a serious weakness for a theory that, on the surface, puts so much emphasis on the subjective and tactical elements of bargaining. A related weakness is Pen's treatment of the environment of bargaining. We agree with Pen that market and other environmental conditions "play their part only via the way in which the bargainers take them into account" and that "the play with which subjects can discount the fundamental [environmental] factors . . . is very considerable" (1959, p. 162). However, Pen's ophelimity values represent filtered data, while the ophelimity function which performs that filtering is left unexplained. Pen overlooks the possibility that elements of his theory should be particularly sensitive to information about the environment and that such information can be manipulated in various ways by the bargainers.

A third weakness in Pen's theory concerns his concept of uncertainty. When Pen argues that a bargainer's most-preferred outcome and conflict ophelimity are not subject to much manipulation by the opponent, he is implicitly assuming that bargainers have information that is almost perfect regarding the environmental conditions that directly affect them. Thus, uncertainty in bargaining results primarily from the bargainers' uncertainty about each other's situations.

The three weaknesses suggest that Pen severely restricts the extent to which his bargainers can use each other's uncertainty to their own advantage. These weaknesses are not unique to Pen's theory. They also apply to the other theorists who implicitly or explicitly assume the importance of uncertainty and manipulative action in bargaining. For example, consider the work of Shackle, Stevens, and Walton and McKersie. Shackle

(1957) contends that the goals and conflict estimates of bargainers reflect the perceived likelihood of different outcomes resulting from a particular strategy. He argues that it is inappropriate to conceptualize risk as a probability estimate based on a comparison of such potential outcomes. In Shackle's (1949) theory, bargainers have disposed of their probability estimates before they begin to consider the advantages and disadvantages of alternative strategies. His main emphasis is on each bargainer's selection among alternative strategies, and the bargaining process is characterized as a clash of these strategies. It is also noteworthy that Shackle is one of the few theorists who suggest that bargainers may consider a breakdown in bargaining as a rational strategy. His explanation for this is not fundamentally different, however, from Pen's (1959) explanation of why the limits of a bargainer's acceptable bargains might change in the course of bargaining or from Hicks's (1963) notion that unions sometimes strike to prevent that weapon from getting "rusty."

Stevens (1963) examines the tension between the desire to avoid an impasse and the desire to obtain favorable terms as a conflict between two "avoidance tendencies." The strength of each tendency is inversely related to the distance (in terms of wage rate being considered) from that goal. At the equilibrium point the strengths of a given bargainer's avoidance tendencies are equal, and this point corresponds to the wage rate that a bargainer would accept at that particular time. Stevens' emphasis is on tactical maneuvers that affect the opponent's avoidance tendencies and thus the opponent's equilibrium point. However, as Stevens indicates, his approach, like Pen's, treats tactical manipulation as having only an ad hoc, unpredictable relationship to the elements of his theory.

Walton and McKersie (1965) relate bargaining tactics to four subprocesses of bargaining: distributive bargaining, integrative bargaining, attitudinal structuring, and intraorganizational bargaining. Their treatment of the relationships among these subprocesses generates more insight into the interaction of bargainers than other theories; however, these discussions are almost always postscripts to their detailed classifications of what one bargainer might do to influence the other. They have probably done more than any other theorists to extend bargaining theory beyond its traditional focus on bilateral monopolists' dividing of a fixed sum of resources. However, while Walton and McKersie suggest that the use of one or a combination of the subprocesses will be determined by the nature of the issue or situation facing the parties, they devote little attention to the underlying forces that cause the parties to enter into bargaining, that dictate the scope of their common or conflicting interests, or that provide them with the leverage necessary to extract concessions from an opponent.

The major deficiency in Walton and McKersie's theory and others within the tradition of Pen is the neglect of bargaining power. These theorists fail to specify dimensions of the bargaining relationship, relate these to the environment, and use them to analyze tactical action in bargaining. The theories treat bargainers as if they were insulated from their environment and thereby deprived of bargaining power. Pen (1959) introduces his approach with a discussion of such matters and even organizes his discussion around the concept of bargaining power, but ignores this concept as he develops his model. Nevertheless, Pen's introductory remarks on bargaining power, in combination with Chamberlain's (1951, 1955) more explicit treatment of it, offer the foundation for the concept of bargaining power we develop in Chapter Two.

Neil W. Chamberlain: Bargaining Power

Few concepts in the labor-management field have been used in as many different ways as that of bargaining power (see Lindblom, 1948; Chamberlain and Kuhn, 1965; Somers, 1969). Some use it as a general label for all those competitive and noncompetitive forces that affect bargaining outcomes. Others treat bargaining power in terms of the observed difference in wage rates across different sectors. Still others attach the concept to particular resources or capabilities available to a party—the ability of a union to withhold its services, control its membership, and so forth. In Chapter Two, we will more generally examine the concept of bargaining power. At this point, our purpose is to briefly discuss the widely used conception of bargaining power proposed by Chamberlain and his associates.

Chamberlain and his associates broadly define bargaining power as the capacity of a party to produce an agreement on its own terms. This capacity is ostensibly equivalent to the opponent's *inducement* to agree to the party's terms. The inducement of the opponent to agree, in turn, is based on the ratio of the opponent's costs of disagreeing on the party's terms to the opponent's costs of agreeing on those terms. Thus, party A gains more bargaining power as B's costs of disagreement increase or as B's costs of agreement decrease. The costs of concern include both pecuniary and nonpecuniary ones, and such costs can be manipulated prior to or during the actual bargaining. These costs take account of the total bargaining situation, "not only the striking or resistance capacities of parties, but the economic, political, and social circumstances" (Chamberlain and Kuhn, 1965, p. 172). In other words, the concept of bargaining power encompasses any condition or variable that may alter the costs of agreement or disagreement for an opponent. Bargaining power represents the "effective force behind the whole collective bargaining relationship" (p. 170).

Chamberlain's approach rejects the assumption of a contract zone, common to most bargaining theories. Specifically, Chamberlain and Kuhn (1965) suggest that the notion of a contract zone is very misleading as it implies that conditions which determine the outer limits of the zone are different from those that determine how bargainers act within a given range—that is, conditions that make disagreement more costly than agreement are different from the conditions that might make agreement equally or more costly than disagreement. The concept of bargaining power subsumes the outer limits and range within the contract zone, such that it is no longer appropriate to separate these conditions. Furthermore, a fixed contract zone is inconsistent with Chamberlain's tactical and cognitive approach to bargaining power. He implicitly treats bargaining power in cognitive terms because the costs of concern are those perceived by the opponent, not necessarily the objective costs. These costs are not fixed by the environment but can be and are subject to tactical manipulation within the bargaining process. Thus even if there were a contract zone, it would be unstable and fluid given the cognitive and tactical aspects of Chamberlain's concept of bargaining power. Although all the theorists discussed in this chapter concede at least some influence to environmental conditions within the limits of a contract zone, Chamberlain's approach differs in that it attempts to grapple with the complexity and ambiguity ignored by other theories. With the exception of Pen (1959), other theorists assume that bargainers treat environmental conditions as givens and that departures from this assumption unnecessarily complicate the bargaining problem. Chamberlain's approach assumes that bargainers treat the interpretation of the costs and underlying conditions as problematic. In fact, this complexity and ambiguity actually allow bargainers to influence each other's thinking and thereby solve the bargaining problem.

Another basic contrast between Chamberlain's approach and others is that Chamberlain attempts to deal with both qualitative and quantitative differences in bargaining. Bargaining outcomes have not only quantitative effects on each party but also different qualitative effects on each party, and bargainers must translate these qualitative differences into common terms—be they utilities, wage rates, dollars, ophelimities, or costs—that have meaning for both parties. In essence, that is the purpose served by Nash's (1950) assumption of transformation invariance, Hicks's (1963) concept of anticipated strike length, Zeuthen's (1930) and Pen's (1952, 1959) concept of risk, and Chamberlain's (1951, 1955; Chamberlain and Kuhn, 1965) concept of bargaining power. Chamberlain's concept of costs is the most ambiguous of these concepts, but that very ambiguity enables him to stress parties' opportunities to manipulate each other's cost calculations. He argues that "it is in part the very incommensurability of certain issues that permits minds to be changed that might be unpersuaded if all significant issues could be reduced by an economic calculus to a numerical balance or imbalance" (1951, p. 221). Chamberlain's insistence that bargaining theory address all the issues involved in bargaining, rather than just wages, yields a concept of costs that is necessarily ambiguous. Furthermore, he claims that there are many ways for a party to define its costs, and he is unwilling to specify a priori reasoning or logic for parties.

The basic problem with Chamberlain's approach to bargaining power is that he neglects the implicit foundation of his framework—which is quite similar to the foundation of Pen's (1959) theory. Specifically, both Chamberlain and Pen begin by conceptualizing bargaining as exchange. Consistent with related work by social psychologists (see, for example, Blau, 1964; Emerson, 1962; Thibaut and Kelley, 1959), bargaining is grounded in two conditions: a scarcity of resources that fosters competition among those that need the same resources and an uneven allocation of resources that creates the need for exchange between parties who need each other's different resources. Two parties are likely to enter a bargaining relationship to the extent that each perceives the other as able to provide resources more readily or completely than others with whom they might negotiate. In other words, bargaining is ultimately based on some level of dependence or interdependence in the social relationship. Dependence is not simply a defining characteristic of a bargaining relationship; it is a dimension along which there is variation within and across bargaining relationships. Chamberlain and Pen begin with this central point about bargaining relationships but leave it behind as they construct their specific theories. If bargaining is ultimately grounded in the mutual dependence of parties, then theories of bargaining power explicitly must address the dependence relationship.

The present book is directed at this problem of emphasis in the work of Chamberlain and Pen. We agree with Chamberlain's assumption that bargaining power is critical to a theory of bargaining and with his implicit casting of bargaining power in cognitive and tactical terms. However, we also believe that the concept of bargaining power must be explicitly tied to the dependence or interdependence relationship of bargainers. Somers (1969) has argued that the single most important task of industrial relations scholars is to integrate the work of those he called the "externalists" and "internalists": "the specific need is to utilize the common framework to trace the effects of environmental forces on the motives, behavior, organization, decision making, and rules of the parties in industrial relations and to analyze the processes by which the internal factors influence the environment" (p. 40). Somers suggests that the concept of bargaining power, based on related notions of exchange, might provide the theoretical link that is needed to integrate the concerns of externalists and internalists. Somers' concern and his answer capture the primary intention of our book. To this end, in the next chapter we develop a dependence approach to bargaining power.

Our basic conclusion is that a general theory of bargaining must examine the relationship between the bargaining context, parties' evaluation of each other's bargaining power, and tactical action. The theory should consider the context but recognize that parties will attempt to change that context, either objectively or subjectively, in order to enhance their position in the bargaining. Our premise is that bargaining is a dynamic interplay between power and tactics; this implies the need for a theoretical framework that integrates bargaining context, process, and outcome.

2

Bargaining Power

▼▼

When a representative of a union meets a representative of management at the bargaining table, both have resources and face constraints embedded in the social, economic, and historical circumstances surrounding the relationship. A critical task for bargainers is to translate the environmental resources and constraints into tactical action at the bargaining table. A major task for bargaining theorists is to develop an understanding of this translation process. To do so requires a recognition that, on the broadest level, bargaining is a process of developing tactical action from motives and intentions that are, in turn, grounded in the bargaining context. Motives and intentions are important because bargaining is goal-directed behavior.

A theory of bargaining must address two very general questions: How does the context of bargaining determine the motives, intentions, and action of the bargainers? and, How do bargainers adjust or relate their own intentions and actions to those of the opponent? These are not only theoretical questions but also practical questions confronted by bargainers themselves. In responding to these questions, bargainers undertake three "coding" operations. First, they must transform the resources and constraints of the bargaining context into objectives and actions to be pursued at the bargaining table. Second, they must decipher and interpret the motives, intentions, and actions of the opponent. Third, they must present their own motives, intentions, and actions to the opponent so as to maximize the achievement of their objectives.

We contend that bargaining power is the key to these coding operations and to the interrelationship of bargaining context, bargaining process, and bargaining outcomes. A theory of bargaining must place power at its center and offer a framework for analyzing how bargainers themselves come to understand and act within their bargaining situation. In Chapter One, we demonstrated the need for a framework that integrates the environmental, process, and outcome focuses of prior bargaining theory. In this chapter, we argue that a dependence approach to bargaining power, drawn from sociological, social psychological, and collective bargaining literature provides the basis for such a theory. This chapter presents the basic outline of a dependence perspective on bargaining power and contrasts it with other approaches; in later chapters, we expand and further develop the implications of this perspective.

First, we begin by presenting three assumptions or postulates that underlie our approach: that a theory of bargaining must begin with the notion of bargaining power, must treat both the subjective and objective sides of bargaining power, and must examine tactical action in the context of bargaining power. We then contrast attribution, control, and dependence models of bargaining power, arguing that a comprehensive and integrative general theory of bargaining requires us to cast bargaining power within a dependence framework.

We portray bargaining as a game of managing impressions or manipulating information. This conception of bargaining is hardly new, but few have taken it seriously. It implies an emphasis on tactical action, that is, on the manner in which bargainers bluff, argue for their positions, attempt to deceive or manipulate each other, and make power plays to gain advantage.

Our emphasis on tactical action requires us to establish the relationship between bargaining power and tactical action and to view bargaining power as a product of bargainers' specific actions and the bargaining context. This image of bargaining generates three basic assumptions.

Assumption 1: Power Is the Essence of Bargaining

We assume that bargaining power is the pivotal construct for a general theory of bargaining. Bargaining power is not simply a part of the bargaining context or environment; it is not just another variable to be included in predictive models; it cannot simply be equated with payoffs or utilities; it is not simply a heuristic device for the retrospective interpretation of empirical findings. Bargaining power pervades all aspects of bargaining and is the key to an integrative analysis of context, process, and outcome.

This first assumption further suggests that bargaining power is not just an analytic construct for scholars; it is a critical construct by which bargainers organize their experience in bargaining. Bargaining power is a central organizing device or rule within the phenomenological world of bargainers, although bargainers are not necessarily conscious of it or how they use it. The phenomenological status of bargaining power should be viewed as a "primary framework" or "schemata of interpretation" in Goffman's (1974) sense. The schemata of interpretation is the conscious and unconscious framework within which bargainers organize and interpret their impressions of the setting and the bargaining process. When bargaining, parties are often unable to reflect on the formal dimensions of their framework. Yet their behavior and cognitive processes are constrained by the parameters of the unobserved schemata that they apply to the bargaining situation. Arguments that bargaining is an art, not a science, illustrate ways of justifying the inability of those who engage in bargaining to delineate the parameters governing their behavior and cognitions. When practitioners stress the importance of practical experience to an understanding of bargaining, they are testifying to both the role of experience and the subtlety of the schemata of interpretation intrinsic to and emergent within bargaining relationships. Thus, beyond its theoretical value, bargaining power can serve as a schemata by which bargainers organize their phenomenological experience.

The obvious implication of our first assumption is that a theory of bargaining must place power at its center. Unfortunately, this is not a simple task. The concept of power has a muddled and confusing history. Various conceptualizations of power have been offered in the bargaining field (for example, see Chamberlain, 1951; Dunlop, 1950; Stevens, 1963; Tedeschi and Bonoma, 1972) and in the larger social science literature (see, for example, Bierstedt, 1950; Dahl, 1957; Gamson, 1968). Because authors seldom specify areas of overlap and contradiction between different conceptualizations, connections between power and its operationalization remain relatively loose and variable. As a result, some authors have suggested that the concept of power is virtually useless, and others have simply ignored it (Lindblom, 1948; Schelling, 1960).

Purging the concept of power from the social sciences, of course, is one way to deal with the confusion. However, we (Bacharach and Lawler, 1980) have offered a different kind of resolution to the conceptual problems, arguing that scholars have placed demands on the concept of power that are unsuited to its theoretical status. Repeated attempts to conceptualize power are based on the assumption that it can and should be a precise term—a term subject to unambiguous definition and measurement. In contrast, we argue that power is inherently a *sensitizing concept* or *primitive term* (see Bacharach and Lawler, 1980; Blumer, 1969; Hage, 1972 for an analysis of such terms). A sensitizing concept points to a series or range of phenomena but not in a manner that allows precise definition or measurement. Such ideas capture the complex multidimensionality of phenomena while implying more specific ideas that may be subject to more precise treatment. While sensitizing concepts are inherently ambiguous, they provide a starting point for developing more precise and measurable concepts. By conceptualizing power as a sensitizing device, we can identify three approaches (that is, types of sensitizing concepts) to power in social science and bargaining literature: power as an outcome, power as a potential, and power as tactical action.

Power as an Outcome. The concept of power as an outcome is essentially a tautological one that is most closely associated with the work of Dahl (1957). From this standpoint, power is the equivalent of successful influence, and power that is not successful is not power at all. One evaluates power, then, by examining the outcome or result of some sequence of events or interaction. Thus in bargaining relationships, power is indexed by the bargaining outcome or the nature of agreement, and, therefore, power can be determined only after the fact. The only way one can posit an a priori distribution of power in a bargaining relationship is to assume that the relationship reflected in the outcome of previous encounters applies to the current contract negotiations. From this approach, bargaining power is not embedded in the bargaining process or even in an identifiable element of the bargaining context; the only empirical manifestation of bargaining power lies in the outcome of the negotiations. According to this approach, the prime value of power is that it provides retrospective interpretations for the distribution of payoff embedded in a settlement.

Power as a Potential. One can remove the tautological element from power by more clearly distinguishing potential power from actual or successful use of power (see, for example, Bierstedt, 1950; Wrong, 1968). From this standpoint, power is a resource that may or may not be used, and if used may or may not be effective. Power is a structural element of the relationship within which parties act to influence each other; consequently, one can identify empirical indicators of potential bargaining power independent of the outcome of the bargaining. This approach to power enables one to predict the outcome from the resources lodged in the social relationship.

Conceptualizing power as a potential is generally consistent with bargaining theories that predict outcomes from environmental conditions, such as the labor market. With this approach, the outcome does not simply describe power, but power may precede and predict bargaining outcomes. That is, bargaining power and bargaining outcomes become empirically distinct but related phenomena. Bargaining power can have a small, large, or even no effect on bargaining outcomes. However, while this conception of power is quite a common theoretical one, it is not consistently applied in empirical analysis. For example, Dunlop (1950) distinguishes between potential and actual (successful) power, but then argues that the outcome of bargaining is the only empirical indicator of power. Overall, the nontautological implications of treating power as a potential have not been fully developed either in the social science or bargaining literature.

Power as Tactical Action. A tactical approach to power is found most often in the work of social psychologists (see, for example, Michener and Suchner, 1972; Rubin and Brown, 1975; Strauss, 1978; Tedeschi and Bonoma, 1972) but it is also apparent in the work of Walton and McKersie (1965). A tactical approach implicitly accepts the distinction between potential and actual power, but discerns a third dimension—the use of power. This approach views potential power in terms of power tactics and attempts to predict bargaining outcomes from tactical action. The focus is on the use and effectiveness of specific tactics, such as threats, bargaining toughness, and so forth.

This tactical concept of power is most consistent with our approach, for it emphasizes the active, manipulative quality of power relationships. Power is not simply a structural or contextual condition, and it certainly is not an abstract description of the bargaining outcome. A tactical approach assumes potential power and stresses the tactical use of the potential, rather than the specific dimensions that define the potential. Neglect of the underlying potential power sometimes leads to analyses of tactics divorced from any analysis of power (for example, Walton and McKersie, 1965) or to piecemeal treatment of tactics that are only loosely connected to a concept of power. The appropriate framework is one that emphasizes tactical action, embeds such action in the larger power relationship, and gives attention to the cognitive features of bargaining power. These issues are the basis for the next two assumptions.

Assumption 2: Bargaining Is a Process of Tactical Action

Potential bargaining power, tactical action, and bargaining outcomes are analytically and empirically distinct phenomena. Tactical action is based on potential bargaining power and can be viewed as the intervening link between potential power and bargaining outcomes. An analysis of bargaining power, therefore, requires a framework that (1) identifies the multiple dimensions constituting each party's potential bargaining power, (2) identifies the major types of bargaining tactics, (3) shows how the dimensions of bargaining power affect tactical action, (4) shows how tactical action can alter bargaining power, (5) examines the conditions under which given tactics affect the bargaining outcomes, and (6) examines how outcomes at any given time affect potential power at later times.

In Chapter One, we criticized theories of bargaining that ignore the relationship between power and tactics and their role in the bargaining process. Our second assumption stipulates that tactical action is the most critical component of the bargaining process. By treating bargaining power as a determinant of tactical action, we point to the need for a theory that places tactical action in the context of the power relationship. Our theory specifies a reciprocal relationship between bargaining power and tactical action, which implies that bargaining power is an integral part of the bargaining process. Potential bargaining power sets the stage for tactical choices, but the tactical choices can subjectively or objectively alter the power relationship and thereby lead to other tactics. The interplay of potential bargaining power and tactical action transforms the bargaining outcomes into an emergent product of the bargaining process. Finally, the reciprocal relationship of potential power and bargaining outcomes takes account of the fact that the bargaining outcomes on one issue can affect a party's power with regard to another issue and that the overall settlement at one point in time can affect bargaining power in future contract negotiations. By distinguishing facets of power that are deemphasized or neglected in other approaches, we attribute an active, fluid quality to bargaining power.

Assumption 3: Bargaining Power Is Subjective Power

Bargaining theory, for the most part, has failed to seriously consider the relation of objective to subjective, or real to cognitive, power. Most work on collective bargaining is based on an economic paradigm and most social psychological work operates from a behavioral paradigm. While economic and behavioral paradigms differ in important respects, both emphasize the objective character of power. Bargaining power is generally equated with the control of objective exchange commodities. More specifically, it is treated as the quantifiably verifiable possession of objective exchange commodities, such as jobs, time, salaries, services, and so forth. From this standpoint, bargaining power is a reified structural or contextual phenomenon. Cognitive or subjective power is implicitly viewed as a mere reflection of these objective conditions—unless, of course, bargainers are misinformed, irrational, or stupid.

In general, objective approaches overlook the bargainers' ability to manipulate the objective and subjective sides of power. The objective dimension of power becomes important only to the extent that bargainers translate it into tactical action. Any process that involves relationships among qualitatively different influences (weighing apples against oranges or fruit against dollars) necessarily involves subjective judgments. We can ignore such subjective judgments only if we are prepared to assume that both parties make the same subjective judgments about the same objective information. Such an assumption underlies—and weakens—game-theoretical approaches to bargaining, in which the parties' preferences are treated as utilities subject to manipulation by theoreticians but not by the bargainers themselves. Because bargainers' preferences do involve qualitative judgments, Zeuthen's (1930) emphasis on risk as a basis of recalculation between sets of qualitatively different considerations is important—and his argument that neither party is concerned about how the other "is getting on" is unconvincing. As suggested in the works of Pen (1959) and Chamberlain (1951, 1955), the translation process is a thoroughly cognitive construction, and this points toward a subjective approach to bargaining power.

A subjective approach is most consistent with assumptions 1 and 2 in that it accentuates the fluid, tactical flavor of bargaining power. Assumption 3 is not intended to deny that power has an objective component, but to assert that the subjective is more important than the objective in analyzing the bargaining process. Power has an objective facet in that, at any point in time, bargainers may be constrained by such environmental factors as market conditions, supply of labor, and so forth. The objective power relationship establishes broad parameters that at once offer opportunities and impose limitations on bargainers. However, objective power is only important to the degree that bargainers consider environmental conditions when manipulating, developing, and using bargaining power. Objective market conditions can be objective sources of labor's and management's power, but they are important only to the degree that they are cognitively interpreted and used at the bargaining table. A bargainer's awareness of the objective conditions does not imply slavish acceptance of them, and thus the objective facet of power does not strictly determine the subjective impressions of power at the table.

Objective power is brought to bear on bargaining through the actual interaction of the parties; in this sense, it is an emergent product of the bargaining process. Bargaining power can be construed as the common thread by which bargainers interrelate the bargaining context and bargaining process. When one speaks of the accumulation of real power, then, one is speaking of parties' ability to convince each other that they control important exchange commodities. The union must convince management that the services labor provides are such that management must deal seriously with issues of concern to workers. Likewise, management must convince labor representatives that it provides important services that may not be available elsewhere, at least not without substantial costs. The critical tactic, then, is the manipulation of perceptions of power. Through tactics such as bluffing and argumentation, bargainers attempt to create a mutually accepted definition of the power relationship that is of some advantage to themselves.

Many of the objective circumstances underlying bargaining are given and not within the immediate control of bargaining parties. For this reason, tactics that *actually* change the power relationship are not always available options. However, tactics that alter the opponent's *definition* of the power relationship are quite common. There are two specific ways an actor can change the opponent's perception of the power relationship: change the objective foundation of the opponent's definition (that is, actually change the environment or context) and hope that this change affects the opponent's definition of the power relationship; or, directly attack the opponent's definition of the power situation by manipulating information, bluffing, and so forth. Our approach to bargaining power emphasizes the latter —changing the subjective perception of power.

Obviously our third assumption makes the perception of power a crucial theoretical and empirical issue. In addition to the reasoning discussed earlier, other factors imply or justify such a concern. The major one is that bargaining, like any conflict situation, is riddled with uncertainty and ambiguity. Bargainers seldom, if ever, approach the complete or perfect information that is assumed by the economic and game-theoretical models of bargaining discussed in Chapter One. Bargainers continuously process information imperfectly, and this information forms the foundation for their tactical action. Parties can only estimate the degree of resources controlled by themselves and their opponent, the commitment of their opponent to the issues at hand, their own dependence on an exchange with the opponent, and the likelihood of the opponent's levying sanctions or using power in other ways. Yet these estimates are the only reasonable foundation for bargaining tactics, and they are infused with the idea of power. The result of such information processing is an image of bargaining power that forms the foundation for bargaining tactics.

A final reason for a cognitive approach to bargaining power is that it is consistent with—and essential to—a conception of bargaining as impression management. By managing impressions of bargaining power, parties can use uncertainties and ambiguities to their own advantage. Projecting an impression of power may have the same effect as possessing real or objective power, especially in the short run. A large gap between objective power and subjective power may catch up with a party in the long run; however, given that objective conditions are inherently ambiguous and subject to various interpretations, the long run is problematic only if subjective power violates the broadest parameters embedded in the objective situation. At a particular point in time, the skillful presentation of power, whether real or cognitive, has important consequences for the bargaining relationship and process.

To conclude, our third assumption indicates that a subjective approach to bargaining power is central to an understanding of power in bargaining. A theory of bargaining power should identify the dimensions of power bargainers use to interrelate, classify, and interpret specific contextual and environmental conditions and develop tactical action. In other words, a theory of bargaining power must facilitate an understanding of how bargainers classify, organize, and synchronize the diverse contextual parameters and how they translate these parameters into power and tactics at the bargaining table. The task of the bargainer is to transform the context into a cognitive presentation of bargaining power, and the task of theorists is to capture this activity. To be more specific, the task of a bargaining party is to convince its opponent that it controls resources, that the opponent needs the resources, and that it is willing to use power. These manipulative actions ultimately determine a party's bargaining power.

The three basic assumptions that underlie our approach to bargaining identify the most general points of contrast between our theory and most prior work on bargaining theory. To summarize, we have argued that power is the essence of bargaining, that power and tactical action go hand-in-hand and must be treated as such, and that an analysis of bargaining power and tactics necessitates a subjective approach to power. To us, these seem relatively obvious points, implied in part by the predominant image of bargaining as impression management.

Approaches to Bargaining Power

Any treatment of objective power implies something about the information bargainers use to infer power—that is, any objective concept of power implies a theory of power perception. By the same token, any theory of subjective power requires a concept of objective power as a reference point. Let us contrast three approaches to power perception by placing these approaches in the context of the underlying concept of objective power. The first approach is based on attribution theory (see Schopler and Layton, 1974). The second approach views outcome control as the foundation for power perceptions (see Michener, Lawler, and Bacharach, 1973). The third approach offers a dependence theory of power perceptions (see Bacharach and Lawler, 1976; Chamberlain, 1955; Lawler and Bacharach, 1979; Pen, 1959). The attributional approach stresses power as an outcome; the control approach stresses the tactical element of power; while the dependence notion offers a relational approach that can be extended to both tactical action and outcomes. The dependence approach is the only one that clearly accepts the analytic and empirical distinction of power potential, tactical action, and bargaining outcome.

Attribution Approach. Schopler and Layton (1974) offer an approach to the perception of power that is related to attribution theory in social psychology. Just as attribution theory posits that A will attribute qualities to B based on B's behavior and its consequences (or effects), Schopler and Layton propose that attributions *of power* to B are based on the effect of B's behavior on A's behavior. The theories differ in that attribution theory deals with how a person explains or finds reasons for B's behavior (Jones and Davis, 1965), while Schopler and Layton examine how a person explains A's behavior through attributions of power to B. Both attribution theory and the attribution approach to power perception begin with the assumption that people interpret and explain the behavior of others through the application of a naive idea of causality (Heider, 1958). The attribution theory of power perception suggests that observers make power judgments by inferring causal connections between the behavior of one party and that of another.

The idea of naive causality leads Schopler and Layton to use Dahl's (1957) conception of objective power as a starting point for their theory of subjective power. As noted earlier, Dahl's approach treats power as an outcome, equates power with successful influence, and fosters post hoc or tautological uses of the concept. These features are quite consistent with an attribution approach, because attribution theory is concerned with the post hoc judgments people make about another after observing the other's behavior and its consequences. Dahl's concept of power is based on the effect of a power wielder on some target, that is, on the action of a target that follows some action by the power wielder. The way to evaluate the power of A is to determine what effect A has on B. Such evaluations require three types of information: B's behavior on two occasions, actions by A between the two occasions, and changes in B's behavior that would not have occurred without the intervention of A. This is a straightforward application of J. S. Mill's method of difference—A's behavior has caused B's behavior if B's behavior follows A's and would not have occurred without A's behavior. In this sense, Dahl's concept of objective power has the same foundation as Schopler and Layton's theory of subjective power. In fact, our schema of Dahl's concept also describes the basic elements of the attribution approach to power perception.

Adapting Dahl's objective concept for subjective purposes, one discerns two cognitive steps when parties judge their own and others' power. First, parties compare B's behavior on two occasions to determine how much change has occurred. Second, parties determine the nature of A's intervention. Subsequent inferences regarding power rely heavily on a cognitive construct: to compare what did occur with what might have occurred. Since intervention and nonintervention cannot both occur, actors must analyze what did occur within a mental construct of possible action or behavior that did not occur.

This task for the attributor of power is reminiscent of Weber's (1949) discussion of the role of mental constructs in causal analyses of social phenomena. In his discussion of the battle of Marathon, he did not ask what the effects of the battle were but what would have happened had the battle not taken place. The attributor of power is in a similar situation. If A intervenes, a mental construct of what might have happened under nonintervention is essential to a causal attribution; similarly, if A does not intervene, the mental construct is what might have happened had A intervened. Thus, the attributor of power must combine an observation of what actually did happen with a cognitive image of some sequence that did not occur. These matters indicate that, upon close examination, Dahl's concept of power implies a complicated, post hoc reconstruction of observable and unobservable sequences of action. Dahl's theory of power fails to address the coexistence of the objective and subjective aspects of power.

While Schopler and Layton attempt to develop a subjective theory grounded in Dahl's work, they do little more than direct Dahl's approach toward subjective concerns. Their primary step is with regard to biases in power perceptions. They suggest that subjective power does not fully conform to objective power primarily because of self-enhancement biases that lead parties to make attributions of power that buttress their self-image. Targets of influence tend to overestimate their own control of their behavior and to deemphasize the role of another's intervention because they prefer to see themselves as independent, self-directed, and self-reliant. Similarly, influencers tend to overestimate their power, that is, exaggerate the extent to which their intervention affects the target's behavior. The two main implications of these ideas on bias are that parties are likely to disagree on the distribution of power and that third parties or observers are likely to make a more balanced estimate of who really does have power. Schopler and Layton treat these biases by combining Dahl's concept of power with attribution theories of naive causality.

Several problems emerge when applying the power-attribution approach to bargaining, most of which are related to the implicit treatment of power as an outcome. The attribution approach leads one to equate the bargaining power of one party with the concession behavior of the opponent. To the extent that B makes concessions and these concessions can be ascribed to A's intervention, A is said to have power. The strength of A's power is the difference between the probability of B making concessions with A's intervention and the probability of B making concessions without A's intervention. From this standpoint, concessions are a defining characteristic of power, and attributions of power are post hoc rationalizations or justifications for previous action. Thus, the attribution approach neglects to consider concession behavior in bargaining as tactical behavior that can overcome or manipulate the power relationship as well as reflect it.

We have argued that a cognitive approach to bargaining power implies that bargainers present (or even exaggerate) their own control of resources, try to make opponents perceive (or exaggerate) their own need for the exchange commodities at stake, and try to convey that they are willing to use the resources to apply sanctions. An attribution approach to bargaining power ignores these issues; it does not view bargaining power as a potential, a capability, or a resource underlying the ability of one party to extract concessions from its opponent. As such, an attribution approach does not provide the practitioner with information or cues for interpreting the resources, for distinguishing objective and cognitive power and the tactical dimensions of the bargaining process. One needs a conceptualization of bargaining power that integrates power, tactical action, .and outcomes.

The Control (Sanction) Approach. The control approach has a more tactical emphasis as well as a more explicit concept of potential power than the attribution approach. In brief, this approach contends that the resources (capabilities) that are relevant to bargaining power are those that represent the ability of parties to sanction or punish one another. These resources are of two basic types: offensive and defensive capabilities. Offensive capabilities refer to those resources that can damage or punish the opponent; defensive capabilities are those resources that enable a party to block or mitigate any damage attempted by the opponent. Thus, from a control or sanction approach, bargaining power is a function of offensive and defensive capabilities.

As with Dahl's (1957) approach, the concept of power in the control approach contains an implicit theory of power perception. The basic propositions implied in a control approach to perceptions of power are the following:

	Perception of A's Power	Perception of B's Power
A's offensive capability	+	—
A's defensive capability	+	—
B's offensive capability	—	+
B's defensive capability	—	+

The control or sanction model assumes that bargainers view bargaining power in zero-sum terms—meaning that a condition viewed as increasing one party's power will simultaneously be seen as reducing the other's power. An increase in A's offensive capability will increase the power attributed to A and decrease the power attributed to B; an increase in B's offensive capability will increase the power attributed to B and decrease the perception of A's power. Within the control approach, bargainers evaluate the offensive and defensive capabilities and infer their own and the other's bargaining power from these evaluations.

Social psychological research on conflict and bargaining provides some indirect evidence on the propositions of the control approach. Typically, this research examines a situation between a power initiator (source of influence) and a target of influence. Within this context, the clearest evidence exists for the offensive-capability (damage) dimension. Numerous studies report that greater damage potential for the initiator leads the target to attribute greater power to the initiator and lower power to itself (for example, Horai and Tedeschi, 1969; Johnson and Ewens, 1971; Michener, Lawler, and Bacharach, 1973; Teger, 1970). Other research indicates that beyond the damage capability, per se, the perceived probability that the offensive capacity will be used by the initiator increases the potency ascribed to the initiator (see Lindskold and Bennett, 1973; Tedeschi and Bonoma, 1972). Conveying a willingness to use power also creates an image of power.

There has been relatively little research on defensive capability. However, Michener, Lawler, and Bacharach (1973) conducted research that incorporates the distinction between offensive and defensive capability and approaches a complete test of the control approach. They examined a power altercation between an initiator and a target and discerned four dimensions of control, two available to the initiator and two available to the target. The initiator had a damage capability and conveyed a certain probability of using it. The target had a blockage capability and a retaliation capability, which is tantamount to or part of the target's offensive capability. The probability of damage is a dimension Michener, Lawler, and Bacharach would add to a model for the control approach. We will return to this shortly.

The basic propositions in Michener, Lawler and Bacharach are: The greater the control the initiator has over outcomes valued by the target (damage capability, damage probability), the greater the power attributed to the initiator and the lower the power attributed to the target; and, the greater the control the target has over outcomes valued by the initiator (blockage, retaliation), the greater the power attributed to the target and the lower the power attributed to the initiator. These hypotheses were tested in an experimental study in which subjects were the target of a prospective attack from an opponent. Hypothetical scenarios presented subjects with a range of situations, for example, a salesperson in conflict with a regional manager over a commission-based income, and a congressman in a dispute with another congressman over the passage of a bill. In each case, the scenario gave subjects information on the dimensions of control measured in the study. All subjects were placed in the target position, thus the data on perceptions of power are limited to the target's behavior.

The results of this study generally support the researchers' propositions. The power the target attributes to the initiator is greater when the initiator has a high rather than low damage capability, when the initiator conveys a high probability of actual damage, and when the target's blockage potential and retaliation capability are low rather than high. Similar findings occur for the target's perceptions of its own power, except that the damage probability reveals no effect on the target's perceptions of its power. Overall, these findings lend credibility to the control theory of power perception.

Michener, Lawler, and Bacharach's study is not a complete test of the control model, but it does suggest an addition to the model, specifically, that one should distinguish the magnitude of an offensive or defensive capability from the probability of actual damage or blockage. Thus, the four dimensions of power have two characteristics: magnitude and probability. The addition of probability heightens the cognitive underpinnings of bargaining power. Bargaining power, from this standpoint, is a function not solely of capabilities but also of the probabilities parties attach to these capabilities. This attention to probability makes the tactical focus of the control perspective even more apparent.

The control model is more useful than the attribution model because it distinguishes between potential power and successful power and implies that tactical action intervenes between potential power and outcomes. The idea of offensive and defensive capability gives bargainers a conceptual device for interpreting or evaluating the resources embedded in the bargaining environment or context, for translating the resources into tactical action at the bargaining table, and for identifying some dimensions along which bargainers might attempt to manipulate each other's perceptions of power. However, the treatment of these issues in the control model is implicit and rudimentary.

The major inadequacy of the control approach is that it does not specify how offensive and defensive capabilities relate to the context of bargaining. More important, the control approach assumes that the stakes of bargainers are constant, nonmanipulable, and high. Both parties ostensibly ascribe high value to the outcomes at issue, and both are assumed to be stuck in the relationship. These conditions imply a particular kind of bargaining relationship. The stakes of bargaining essentially refer to the nature of the dependence relationship, and the dependence relationship can be construed as the context within which the offensive and defensive capabilities are evaluated by bargainers. We can treat the dependence relationship as the bargaining context and the offensive and defensive capabilities as general tactical issues that mediate the effect of the dependence relationship on the more specific tactics at the bargaining table. A theory of dependence, therefore, allows us to analyze the bargaining context and achieve a better balance between the emphases on power potential and tactical facets of bargaining. In addition, a dependence perspective can integrate the insights of economists, who have studied the influence of the bargaining environment on bargaining outcomes within institutionally specific realms, with the insights of sociologists and social psychologists who have studied the tactical dimension of bargaining.

The Dependence Approach. A dependence approach offers a more relational and resource-based concept of bargaining power than either the attribution or control approach. On the most general level, dependence refers to the degree that parties have a stake in the bargaining relationship. High stakes indicate that bargainers attribute considerable importance to maintaining the bargaining relationship. The comparative and mutual stakes of bargaining parties are essentially grounded in the resource context. However, the dependence relationship is not constant; it is variable across and within settings and can be manipulated objectively or subjectively in the course of bargaining. The dependence relationship is inherently ambiguous, and the nature of that relationship is often an implicit or even manifest issue at the bargaining table. In other words, bargainers negotiate not only the specific issues at hand but also the nature of their dependence on each other. A theory of bargaining, therefore, must provide a framework that grasps the essential components or variables of the dependence relationship and also relates this ambiguous context to tactical action at the bargaining table.

Dependence is not the focal point of most analyses of bargaining. Social psychologists devote the most explicit attention to dependence (see Blau, 1964; Emerson, 1962, 1972b; Gergen, 1969; Kelley and Thibaut, 1978; Komorita, 1977; Thibaut and Kelley, 1959) but they do not fully recognize or develop the potential of a dependence approach to bargaining. In fact, social psychological research and theory on explicit bargaining all but ignore dependence (see Chertkoff and Esser, 1976; Hamner and Yukl, 1977). Much of the economic, institutional, and legal research on collective bargaining implicitly or explicitly examines conditions that affect the dependence relationship of parties; and while the connection between such dependence and bargaining power is sometimes noted (see, for example, Dunlop, 1950; Levinson, 1966), few researchers systematically relate the notions of dependence and bargaining power. The efforts of Pen (1959) and Chamberlain (1955) are unquestionably the most important, however, their earlier (and most widely read) work on bargaining makes only passing reference to the relationship between dependence and bargaining power (Chamberlain, 1951; Pen, 1952). In the following pages, we offer a more complete theoretical statement of this relationship, building on the work of Emerson, Blau, Chamberlain, and Pen.

The most complete theoretical treatment of dependence is offered by Blau (1964) and Emerson (1962, 1972a, 1972b). Their work is not explicitly concerned with bargaining or bargaining power but can be extended to such phenomena. Emerson and Blau begin with the assumption that the power of one party is based on the opponent's dependence on that party—that is, the power of A is grounded in B's dependence on A, while the power of B is based on A's dependence on B. Applied to bargaining power, this leads to a basic proposition:

Proposition 1. An increase in the dependence of bargainer A on opponent B increases opponent B's bargaining power.

For example, the bargaining power of a union is based on management's dependence on the union and its members, while the bargaining power of management is based on the union's (and its members') dependence on management. Note that a party's bargaining power is not based on its own dependence, but on the other party's dependence.

We can identify more specific implications of dependence if we specify the dimensions of dependence. Two dimensions are suggested by prior work (Bacharach and Lawler, 1976, 1980; Blau, 1964; Emerson, 1972b; Lawler and Bacharach, 1979): the degree to which parties have alternative outcome sources and the degree of commitment to the outcomes at issue. In two-party bargaining, therefore, four variables are essential to an analysis of bargaining power: A's alternatives, B's alternatives, A's commitment, and B's commitment. These dimensions of dependence are derived from a basic tenet of social-exchange theory—namely, that social relationships, of whatever type, are based on the degree to which the outcomes received in the relationship are highly valued and not available in alternative relationships (see, for example, Blau, 1964).

A party's alternatives are determined by the availability of similar or substitutable outcomes from other relationships. It is important to distinguish alternative outcome sources that can be secured only by severing the relationship, and others attainable within the particular relationship. A union and corporation may be highly dependent on each other but may differ significantly in their dependence regarding various bargaining issues. A cognitive approach to bargaining power accentuates this potential difference, because subjective interpretations of the objective conditions regarding alternatives can vary much more than the objective conditions in any given context.

Individual members of the groups in conflict usually have more alternatives than the groups themselves. For example, it is easier for a worker to quit than for a union to sever its relationship with a corporation. The potential for manipulating power perceptions is also greater at the individual level. When market conditions are unfavorable to workers, union representatives might still convince management that highly trained workers can and will leave if management fails to make certain kinds of concessions. Similarly, management might argue that it can reduce its need for workers through technological changes, by altering production priorities, or by developing new products that require fewer workers.

The other major dimension of dependence is the commitment of parties to the outcomes at issue. Prior work on dependence provides a rather confusing conceptualization of this dimension. It has been termed *motivational investment* (Emerson, 1962), the *value of a reinforcer* (Emerson, 1972b), the *need for the outcomes* (Blau, 1964) as well as the *value of the outcomes* (Bacharach and Lawler, 1976, 1980; Lawler and Bacharach, 1976, 1979). *Value,* defined as the *importance* ascribed to outcomes, is probably the most generic way to identify this dimension. However, the term *value* sometimes refers to the magnitude of outcomes rather than to their importance (which may or may not be related to magnitude); to some, it can even imply cultural values or normative principles. In part to avoid these misleading connotations, we offer the term *commitment,* which captures the implications of the value dimension for bargaining relationships somewhat better than other terms.

Commitment, as a dimension of dependence, is not normative in character, and it does not imply the tactics of commitment analyzed by Schelling (1960). Schelling and others have used *commitment* to denote a tactic whereby a party conveys irrevocable commitment to a particular line of behavior, exemplified by "burning the bridges behind you." More generally, there are three ways that the idea of commitment might be applied to bargaining relationships: commitment to the relationship, which often has normative connotations; commitment to a line of behavior or tactical position, which is Schelling's (1960) usage; or commitment to the outcomes or issues at stake in the bargaining. The third constitutes the commitment dimension of dependence.

Chamberlain (1951, 1955) and Pen (1959) offer a conceptualization of power that parallels—in fact, antedates—the work of Emerson (1962) and Blau (1964). There is a difference in focus in that Emerson and Blau are concerned with power in the abstract, while Chamberlain and Pen are concerned with *bargaining* power and focus most of their attention on a particular institutional context (labor-management relations). Despite some differences between Chamberlain and Pen, both portray bargaining as an exchange in which the parties need resources controlled by each other. The bargaining power of a party is grounded in the other's dependence on the party for certain resources. The other's dependence, in turn, is based on the alternative outcome sources and aspirations of the other. Specifically, this indicates that the bargaining power of A is positively related to B's aspirations and negatively related to the number and quality of the alternatives available to B. These ideas are virtually identical to ones suggested by the Blau and Emerson theory of power dependence.

Given the alternatives and commitment dimensions of dependence, we can elaborate on our first proposition. A party's bargaining power should be greater, the lower the opponent's alternatives and the higher the commitment of the opponent to the outcomes at issue in the relationship. Proposition 1 thus suggests four hypotheses regarding labor-management bargaining power.

Hypothesis 1. A decrease in the union's (or its members') alternative outcome sources increases management's bargaining power.

Hypothesis 2. A decrease in management's alternative outcome sources increases the union's bargaining power.

Hypothesis 3. An increase in the union's commitment to the outcomes increases management's bargaining power.

Hypothesis 4. An increase in management's commitment to the outcomes increases the union's bargaining power.

Hypotheses 3 and 4 warrant further comment. The justification for these hypotheses is that higher levels of commitment by a bargainer imply that the opponent controls the party's access to valued commodities. If, for example, management controls outcomes valued by the union, management can manipulate the union's behavior by manipulating those valued commodities. While this reasoning seems logical, there is another way to consider commitment. High commitment by a union may, indeed, give management greater potential power, but it may also motivate the union to act forcefully or work hard to exact concessions. High commitment, therefore, may generate greater tactical effort, energy, or motivation, which may make it difficult for an opponent who has high power on the commitment dimension to succeed at the bargaining table. In other words, commitment may engender power, but this may be counterbalanced or overwhelmed by the tactical effort motivated by the opponent's commitment. This possibility affirms the importance of distinguishing the tactical aspects of the different dimensions of bargaining power. We return to this issue later in this chapter and repeatedly in this book as we analyze the tactical implications of commitment. For now, proposition 1 and our four hypotheses constitute the core of a dependence theory of bargaining power.

Some recent work develops these core ideas of dependence theory. Komorita (1977) constructs a concept of bargaining strength based partly on the concept of alternatives but neglects commitment and fails to integrate his concept into a comprehensive theory of dependence. We elsewhere (Bacharach and Lawler, 1980, chap. 7) use the dimensions of dependence to develop a theory of power struggle that is quite compatible with the present exposition, although we do not fully develop the implications of a dependence approach to bargaining. Our primary concern (Bacharach and Lawler, 1980) is with intra-organizational relationships and, more specifically, with the long-term effects of tactical action designed to change the power relationship.

There are two classes of problems with dependence theory. First, two unresolved theoretical issues hamper its application to bargaining: prior analyses fail to distinguish the relative power of parties from the total power in the relationship and from the power of a given party, that is, "absolute" power; and prior treatments neglect the related point that a dependence perspective fosters a nonzero-sum or variable-sum conception of bargaining power. Elucidating these theoretical issues is the first step in resolving a second problem with the theory. Although the theory offers a framework for describing the bargaining context, it does not relate the context to the process. To give the theory a stronger tactical emphasis we must articulate a theory of subjective power within the dependence approach. We will first discuss the unresolved theoretical issues and then develop the subjective side of our dependence framework.

Absolute, Total, and Relative Power. The application of the dependence perspective to bargaining power suggests three distinct facets of power: absolute, total, and relative power. Absolute power is the power of an individual party irrespective of the other party's power. Since the power of an individual party is determined by its opponent's dependence on it, the absolute power of A is determined by B's alternatives and commitment, regardless of A's alternatives and commitment. Total power is the sum of the parties' dependence on one another, and relative power is the dependence of one party compared to the dependence of the other party. The relative power of A can be expressed either as the ratio of B's dependence on A to A's dependence on B or as the ratio of B's dependence on A to the sum of both parties' dependence—total power—in the relationship. The first characterization of relative power presents one party's relative power as the reciprocal of the other's, and it is useful for characterizing relative advantage. The second is more useful for expressing the proportion of a range of outcomes one party might expect to claim for itself. In either case, however, relative power is a derived concept, not subject to definition (or manipulation) apart from the parties' absolute power.

Most theorists either treat power exclusively in relative terms or are so intent on identifying the terms of the parties' ultimate settlement that they dismiss the importance of analyzing absolute power as a separate construct. This is especially true of those who use statistical models to relate environmental conditions to bargaining outcomes, without considering the intervening bargaining process, because such models afford no basis for distinguishing between the effects of such conditions on one party's power and their effects on the other party's power. There have been occasional references to total power in the social psychology literature (see Rubin and Brown, 1975; Tannenbaum, 1968; Gulliver, 1979; Bacharach and Lawler, 1980), while some (for example, French and Raven, 1959) have been criticized for adopting an individualistic or absolute approach to power. For the most part, however, even theorists and researchers who adopt a dependence approach have failed to recognize that a complete analysis of power requires separate consideration of absolute, total, and relative power.

Chamberlain argues that: "Bargaining power must always be expressed relative to another's bargaining power, that it has no meaning as applied to an individual. We can say that an increase in the number and quality of the alternatives open to an individual *tends* to increase his bargaining power in the relevant transactions. Whether his bargaining power has actually improved, however, depends on whether there have been simultaneous changes in the alternatives or aspirations . . . both for himself and for those with whom he seeks symbiotic relationships" (1955, pp. 126-127). It is clear that we are taking a different position from Chamberlain's with regard to the importance of relative power, as compared to total and absolute power. Chamberlain simply asserts that relative power is the factor of overriding importance, while our position is that the priority given to any one of these constructs must be an empirical question. If the parties are bargaining over the division of a fixed quantity of a single resource, then it may be appropriate to concentrate on relative power, but if the amount of resources to be committed in the bargain is either ambiguous or variable, or if the parties are bargaining over the exchange of qualitatively different resources, then concentrating on relative power will obscure issues that are at the heart of the bargaining process.

To illustrate the importance of distinguishing relative from total power, consider a situation in which a union (U) and management (M) are bargaining, and the ratio of M's power to U's power (that is, M's relative power) is 2 to 1. Assume further that the resource foundation of each party's power can vary from 0 to 20 on some hypothetical quantitative dimension. Power has to be based on some resource, and dependence theory posits that resources can be classified in terms of levels on dimensions of dependence. Now, given this conceptualization, the same relative power ratio would occur if M has eight units of power and U has four, if M has four and U has two, if M has ten and U has five, and so forth. While these situations encompass the same relative power, they differ in total power. Not only can total power vary within a given relative-power condition but relative power can differ within a given total-power context—for example, if total power is 10, relative power could be 8 to 2, 6 to 4, 4 to 6, and so forth. Relative power and total power are analytically distinct and can have quite different implications for bargaining interaction.

Zero-Sum Power and Variable-Sum Power. The distinction between relative and total power implies a contrast between zero-sum and variable-sum approaches to power. A zero-sum approach assumes, by definition, that an increase in one party's absolute power automatically produces a decrease in the other party's absolute power. If a union increases its own power, it has also decreased management's power. A zero-sum conception of power fosters a highly competitive image of power manipulations and suggests that there has to be a winner and a loser—at least with regard to how much parties improve or suffer declines in their respective power positions.

In contrast, a variable-sum approach treats the relationship between the parties' power (that is, absolute power) as an empirical question. A change that increases one party's power may decrease the other's power, but does not necessarily do so. In some contexts, both parties can increase their power or decrease their power, suggesting a change in total power but not necessarily relative power. In this sense, notions of absolute and total power are closely connected with a variable-sum approach to bargaining power. The individual power of parties is distinct, and the total resources, power, dependence, and the like are not constant or fixed. The major difference between zero-sum and variable-sum approaches is that a zero-sum approach assumes a fixed level of total power and a perfectly negative relationship between the power of each individual party, while a variable-sum approach assumes that the total power in the relationship can change (due to environmental changes, tactical action, and so forth) and that it is inappropriate to assume a priori a particular relationship between the power of each party. We adopt a variable-sum approach requiring that absolute, relative, and total power be treated as separate components of the analysis.

Prior analyses of dependence—in the abstract (for example, Emerson, 1972b) or in reference to bargaining power (for example, Chamberlain, 1951, 1955)—contain a number of theoretical problems or ambiguities: failing to distinguish individual, relative, and total power and failing to perceive or develop the variable or nonzero sum implications of the theory. Our approach to these problems represents one of the differences between the dependence theory of this volume and these earlier works and also makes dependence theory a better foundation for a general perspective on bargaining. However, there is a second problem with prior uses of dependence theory—failure to develop the tactical implications for bargaining. This requires treatment of the cognitive or subjective side of dependence covered in the remainder of this chapter.

Cognitive Dimension of Dependence Theory

A dependence theory of bargaining must treat the cognitive aspects of bargaining power and tactical action. The most general implication of a dependence perspective is that the dimensions of dependence (alternatives, commitment) are devices by which bargainers assess the nature of the power relationship. The dimensions of dependence can be construed as elements of the "schemata of interpretation" employed by bargainers to make sense of the environmental, historical, and structural underpinnings of bargaining. The dimensions of dependence capture the process by which bargainers translate the bargaining context into an image of the power relationship and tactical action at the bargaining table.

Two empirical questions are critical to initially judge the credibility of a dependence theory. The first question is whether bargainers who have information on the dimensions of dependence use it to estimate each other's power in accordance with the major propositions of dependence theory. The second question is whether bargainers use the dimensions of dependence as criteria for making preliminary, broad tactical decisions. Such decisions represent the first cognitive step in translating the conditions of dependence into tactical action. In terms of Hirschman's (1970) analysis of exit, voice, and loyalty, the issue is simply whether decisions to voice (that is, to attempt some kind of tactical action) are based on the dimensions of dependence. Let us now elaborate the implications of dependence theory for estimates of power capability and decisions to voice.

Subjective Power Capabilities. As noted earlier, any theory of objective power contains an implicit theory of subjective power. The most basic proposition of a dependence theory of power perception is a straightforward extension of proposition 1, presented earlier, that the perception of a party's bargaining power is determined by the opponent's dependence. However, our discussion of the zero-sum and variable-sum approaches suggests two alternative propositions. The zero-sum proposition assumes that bargainers perceive the power relationship in zero-sum terms (regardless of the objective situation). Specifically:

Proposition 2a. An increase in bargainer A's dependence on opponent B decreases the bargaining power attributed to A *and* increases the power attributed to B.

That is, any change in one of the four dimensions of dependence will have equal but opposite effects on the perceptions of the two parties' bargaining power. The zero-sum proposition leads to four hypotheses regarding the perception of power in labor-management bargaining:

Dependence Dimension	*Labor's Power*	*Management's Power*
Labor's alternatives	+	−
Labor's commitment	−	+
Management's alternatives	−	+
Management's commitment	+	−

The zero-sum foundation of these hypotheses is reflected in the opposite signs for each dimension of dependence, for example, an increase in the alternatives available to labor increases the perceived power of labor and decreases the perceived power of management. These hypotheses imply a perfect, negative relationship between perceptions of labor's power and perceptions of management's power.

If parties treat bargaining power in variable-sum terms, however, we obtain a somewhat different set of propositions. The variable-sum assumption generates the following general proposition:

Proposition 2b. An increase in a bargainer A's dependence on opponent B increases the perception of B's bargaining power, but does not affect the perception of A's power.

From this standpoint, the perception of labor's and management's power is based on different dimensions of dependence. A's dependence on B is used to estimate B's bargaining power, but does not affect either party's perception of A's power, while B's dependence on A is used to estimate A's bargaining power. The following four hypotheses govern the perceptions of labor's and management's power based on a variable-sum proposition:

Dependence Dimension	Labor's Power	Management's Power
Labor's alternatives		—
Labor's commitment		+
Management's alternatives	—	
Management's commitment	+	

There is very little empirical evidence on these zero-sum and variable-sum hypotheses. The behaviorist bias of exchange theory, in general, and power-dependence theory, in particular, has relegated such issues to a subordinate position. In previous work, we have examined the implications of dependence theory for power perceptions (see Bacharach and Lawler, 1976) by adopting a zero-sum approach to dependence theory. Our hypotheses, virtually identical to those in this chapter, were tested in a simulated employee-employer context. Subjects were presented with a description of a potential conflict between salespersons and a company over pay. They were asked to assume the role of a salesperson and were given a description of the situation that included information on the four dimensions of dependence. After reading the description, they estimated their own power and the power of the other.

The results of the study affirm the phenomenological importance of the dimensions of dependence. Subjects do indeed use the dimensions of dependence to estimate their own and the other's power. Furthermore, these estimates tend to correspond to our four zero-sum hypotheses, with one qualification. The size of the effect of dependence on power perception was unequal, though the signs did correspond to the zero-sum hypotheses. High alternatives for the employee increase the perceived power of the employee and decrease the perceived power of the employer, but these opposite effects are not equal in size and, strictly speaking, a zero-sum approach indicates equal and opposite effects for each dimension of dependence. Despite this qualification, our 1976 study provides preliminary evidence to suggest that parties may stress the zero-sum principle in evaluating power capabilities. This does not mean that the zero-sum principle will underlie the actual tactical decisions at the bargaining table, or that perceptions of power capabilities will always be cast in zero-sum terms. The primary importance of the Bacharach and Lawler (1976) study is its demonstration that parties in conflict will use information on the dependence relationship to estimate power capabilities.

The contrasting zero-sum and variable-sum hypotheses have some important implications for the tactical manipulation of power. Zero-sum and variable-sum concepts are essentially cognitive principles with which bargainers might integrate the dimensions of dependence and make tactical decisions. In this sense, our hypotheses not only predict how bargainers form impressions of power but also sensitize bargainers to how they might manipulate the other's perceptions of power. Each cognitive principle has different implications for the tactical manipulation of power. If a union adopts a variable-sum principle and wants to manipulate management's perception of the union's power, then it should direct its tactical effort at management's alternatives or commitment; specifically, the union should attempt to reduce management's perception of management's own alternatives or enhance management's felt commitment to resources controlled by the union. According to the variable-sum principle, such tactics, if successful, will affect only management's perception of the union's power, not management's perception of its own bargaining power. To affect the latter requires change in the other dimensions of dependence. In contrast, zero-sum imagery indicates that manipulation of any dimension of dependence increases the power attributed to one party and decreases the power attributed to the other. A final implication is that successful manipulations of power require that the manipulator have information on the cognitive principles used by the target, that is, whether the target adopts zero-sum or variable-sum imagery or some combination of both.

The cognitive processes underlying tactical action involve more than merely estimating power capabilities. By distinguishing power capability from tactical action, dependence theory implies that perceptions of power are not necessarily directly translated by bargainers into tactical action. For example, a bargainer may ground perceptions of power (and ideas for manipulating the other's perceptions) in a zero-sum principle but make other tactical decisions on the basis of a variable-sum principle. Thus, although there is a relationship between perceptions of bargaining power and tactical action, it is inappropriate to assume a one-to-one correspondence. As an initial step in the analysis of tactical action, we now examine the most basic and general tactical issue confronted by bargainers: whether to attempt influence. In Hirschman's (1970) analysis, this is essentially a decision regarding "voice."

Decisions to Voice. Given that bargaining itself can be construed as voice, decisions to bargain or not, to continue or cease bargaining, and so forth are decisions about voice. In the context of such broad decisions, bargainers confront other decision points that can also be construed in terms of voice. Specifically, bargainers must continually decide whether to attempt influence during the bargaining. Their first decision is whether or when to attempt some kind of influence, the second how to influence the other party (that is, decisions on specific tactics). The two decisions are not altogether distinct, however, and the theoretical principles for predicting decisions to voice should be valid for both types.

Hirschman (1970) identifies voice as one of three general options for parties in conflict; exit and loyalty are the other two. The exit option is leaving the relationship—for example, customers choosing to buy alternate products, workers leaving the organization, or the organization laying off workers. Exit does not involve an effort to influence the opponent, but rather is an escape from the relationship. Loyalty represents a decision to stay within the organization or relationship and to accept, more or less passively, the conditions that arouse conflict. As Hirschman suggests, some may stay and suffer in silence, while others may stay and attempt to influence policy through informal means. In either case they have chosen not to challenge the legitimacy of the other's authority in the area of conflict. Voice represents an explicit attempt to influence the other party—for example, customers protesting the quality of a product, workers objecting to working conditions. Rather than leave the relationship or accept the other party's resolution (or nonresolution) of the conflict, the actor attempts to change the situation or relationship.

Applying Hirschman's analysis to a bargaining relationship, we can delineate five options for workers in conflict with management.

1. Exit: Workers leave the organization and seek employment elsewhere. This option is likely to be available to a select number of workers, but is often unrealistic for a majority of workers in an organization. In an absolute sense, this is an option primarily for individual workers but not for a union. A union has little choice but to remain in its relationship with a given company, because the exit option implies that it

will withdraw the services of its members and find employment for them elsewhere. This choice may be conceivable in an expanding capitalist economy, but for labor issues that pertain to a sector of the economy in which corporations coordinate their efforts, the exit option is hardly viable for a union. However, a union (or workers) can develop a strategy that combines elements of exit with voice—a strike.

2. Strike: In a strike, the union-company relationship is normatively sustained but the union engages in a limited exit for tactical purposes. A strike meets Hirschman's definition of exit in that it is a withdrawal of services; but, unlike exit, a strike is a tactical strategy to enhance the union's strength at the bargaining table and maintain the union-company relationship. A strike combines exit and voice options—normatively, the labor-management relationship continues, but the worker-company relationship is temporarily suspended.

3. Explicit bargaining, the most general form of voicing in a labor-management context, implies relatively open lines of communication, a consensual definition of the relationship as a bargaining one, issues that allow intermediate solution points between the initially preferred positions of the opposing parties, and a willingness to consider compromise by exchanging offers and counteroffers (Bacharach and Lawler, 1980; Schelling, 1960). These conditions tend to underlie or define institutionalized union-company relations.

4. Tacit bargaining occurs when the bargaining relationship is not officially recognized or consensually defined by the parties. It takes the form of parties attempting to influence each other informally without necessarily being conscious that they are in a bargaining relationship. The conflict may be open and severe, but it often takes very subtle forms of mutual manipulation. This form of bargaining often connotes loyalty, since it presupposes a commitment to the organization and a willingness to avoid making explicit conflicts that can be left implicit. In this case, workers rely on informal influence and eschew the use of formal, explicit bargaining.

5. Submission—that is, suffering in silence—is the clearest form

of loyalty. Workers may decide that they have no means to influence management, that the available means are insufficient, or that the potential costs of raising an issue, even informally, exceed the potential benefits. In any case, they simply resign themselves to their current situation.

The foregoing options are not mutually exclusive, and various combinations emerge in actual situations. The issue of concern at this point is whether dependence theory enables us to predict decisions to voice—both decisions to bargain and those to attempt influence. In a labor-management context, these decisions occur not only at the bargaining table but also during the everyday interaction of workers, union, and management. These decisions are complicated because any influence attempt can have either of two opposite effects: overcome the resistance of the other and facilitate the actor's goal attainment, or antagonize the opponent and impede the actor's goal attainment. For this reason, decisions to voice are a major dilemma for conflicting actors.

An actor's evaluation of the option to voice or not voice is likely to be based on the anticipated consequences of each option. Some of these consequences may be negative and some positive. The most obvious theoretical construct for treating these consequences is *expected utility*. The notion of expected utility comes primarily from decision theory and game theory. The simplest and most generally accepted definition is the magnitude of outcomes expected to result from voice weighted by the expected probability that those outcomes will result, that is, magnitude X probability (Heath, 1976; Ofshe and Ofshe, 1970; Siegel, Siegel, and Andrews, 1964). Theorists have proposed a number of variants of this definition by incorporating additional aspects of expected utility. For example, Ofshe and Ofshe (1970) include equity as an aspect of utility; Siegel, Siegel, and Andrews (1964) add behavior variability (avoidance or boredom). The basic principle of decision theory, however, is that outcome magnitude and probability are the focus of an actor's utility judgments. Actors summarize their impressions and inferences regarding the bargaining context to estimate the magnitude and probability of the outcomes that will result from voicing. If the issue between labor and management is one concerning a pay raise, the expected utility of an influence attempt (voice) regarding the pay raise does not depend on the perceived magnitude of the expected pay raise alone but on the product of the anticipated magnitude and the anticipated probability of a pay raise. Therefore, one would expect that the greater the expected utility of voicing, the higher the probability that voicing will occur.

Hirschman (1970) indicates that decisions to voice are based on the potential influence or power that can be mobilized by those with grievances against an organization. When bargainers evaluate the expected utility of the voice option, they are essentially anticipating whether and how the power relationship will actually be transformed into outcomes at the bargaining table. In terms of our model, they are evaluating the link between potential bargaining power and bargaining outcomes. These evaluations lay the groundwork for tactical action designed to fulfill these expectations or to modify the power relationship. Overall, then, the expected utility of voice is grounded in a party's perceptions of its own and perhaps the other's power capabilities.

If we assume that the magnitude of expected outcomes from an influence attempt is dictated by what a party hopes to achieve, and if we focus on how it might estimate the probability that such an outcome might be obtained, dependence theory suggests the following two propositions:

Proposition 3a. An increase in the perceived dependence of B on A increases the perceived probability that an influence attempt by A will secure a given magnitude of outcomes and thus increases the subjective expected utility of A's voice option.

Proposition 3b. A decrease in the perceived dependence of A on B increases the perceived probability that an influence attempt by A will secure a given magnitude of outcomes and thus increases the subjective expected utility associated with A's voice option.

Note that proposition 3a discusses A's dependence on B, that is, A's absolute power in the relationship. Proposition 3b introduces the possibility that A also considers its own dependence—B's absolute power—implying that parties are sensitive to their relative power. We will return to this point in a moment, but first, note that these general propositions lead to four hypotheses, which we cast in labor-management terms:

Hypothesis 1. If management has few alternatives (high management dependence on labor), the union's expected probability of securing a given level of outcomes is greater than if management has many alternatives.

Hypothesis 2. If management has a high commitment to the outcomes at issue (high management dependence on labor), the union's expected probability of securing a given level of outcomes is greater than if management has a low commitment to the outcomes at issue.

Hypothesis 3. If labor has many alternatives (low labor dependence on management), the union's expected probability of securing a given level of outcomes is greater than if labor has few alternatives.

Hypothesis 4. If labor has a low commitment to the outcomes at issue (low labor dependence on management), the union's expected probability of securing a given level of outcomes is greater than if labor has a high commitment to the outcomes at issue.

These propositions and hypotheses represent the general implications of dependence theory for bargainers' evaluation of the voice option. They indicate that perceptions of power form the basis for evaluating whether tactical action will be fruitful and identify the general role of bargaining power in tactical decisions. The hypotheses are based totally on the power capabilities embedded in the dimensions of dependence. A complete analysis of tactical action, however, requires that we more thoroughly consider how bargainers use the dimensions in the bargaining process. The role of the commitment dimension could be particularly complex, as we noted earlier. On the one hand, bargainers may infer power capabilities from the commitment dimensions and use these inferences to guide their tactical behavior. Under these circumstances, tactical decisions should conform with the basic principles in hypotheses 2 and 4. On the other hand, bargainers can relate commitment to tactical effort, taking high commitment to imply greater tactical effort. A party with high commitment has less power capability but may overcome the implications of this power position through greater tactical effort—by pushing more strongly in the bargaining. If prospective effort is given the greatest weight in tactical decisions, then the relationship posited by hypotheses 2 and 4 would be reversed—high commitment to the outcomes by labor will increase the utility attached to labor's voicing, while high commitment by management will decrease the expected utility of labor's voice option.

Conclusions

We have used dependence theory to identify dimensions of bargaining power, and we conclude this chapter with some final comments on our conception of bargaining power. First, it is important to emphasize the significance of treating commitment as the *importance* of the outcomes at stake, rather than as some objective measure of outcome magnitude. Under some circumstances, one might expect the level of commitment and outcome magnitude to be directly related; for example, a bargainer would be more committed given higher outcome levels at issue. Under other circumstances, one might expect commitment and magnitude to be inversely related; a bargainer would become more committed to the outcomes, the lower those outcomes in an objective sense. The closest parallel to this concept in other bargaining theories is Hicks's (1963) suggestion that labor's resistance to making additional concessions increases as its aspirations decline. Our treatment of the commitment dimension stresses the importance of its subjective, manipulable nature.

Second, our approach offers a broader conception of

alternatives than that offered by sociologists, such as Blau (1964) and Emerson (1962, 1972a, 1972b), or economists, like Chamberlain (1955) and Pen (1959). We distinguish the alternative outcome sources of a group (for example, a union) from those of the group's members. This contrast, in conjunction with the emphasis on tactical and subjective aspects of bargaining power, enhances the applicability of the alternatives dimension to contexts where opposing groups are virtually stuck in the relationship. Overall, the alternative outcome sources of relevance to bargaining between groups include the exit options of its members, third parties who can exact concessions from the opponent, agreements with others that set precedents for current negotiations, and so forth. On a tactical level, there are innumerable ways to apply the alternatives dimension to specific contexts and innumerable ways for bargainers to manipulate each other's perceptions along this dimension. The alternatives dimension of bargaining power is not a highly restricted, unidimensional construct as often implied in prior work.

Dependence, as bargaining power, is not merely another variable or dimension of bargaining—it is the backbone of bargaining relationships. Dependence can both define the bargaining relationship and analyze the variation that occurs within bargaining relationships. It is a defining characteristic of bargaining in that some minimal degree of dependence is intrinsic to bargaining. Bargaining implies a conflict of interest, but more important, it implies a conflict of interest over goals that no party can achieve without taking the other into account. While some minimal dependence is essential for the establishment of a bargaining relationship, our critical task is to determine how different degrees of dependence beyond this minimal level relate to different aspects of bargaining.

3

Tactical
Concessions

▼▼

In this chapter, we apply the dependence framework, developed in the last chapter, to tactical concessions. The term *tactical concessions* connotes that concessions are tactical modes of action calculated to manipulate the behavior or cognition of the opponent. Concessions communicate intentions, aspirations, and the like to the opponent and can, in turn, alter the opponent's intentions, aspirations, or action. Concessions thus are methods of gaining advantage as much as they are means of giving something to the opponent. In this chapter, we relate tactical concessions to bargaining power, cast as dependence.

First we must distinguish two implicit perspectives on concession behavior in the bargaining field: the choice perspective and the information perspective. The choice perspective is implicit in the bargaining theories reviewed in Chapter One. Concession behavior is conceptualized by the choice between moving toward agreement and not moving toward agreement. The choices made throughout the bargaining process, or at critical points in it, are a function of the costs and benefits attached to those concessions. The costs and benefits—and thus the concessions—are determined by the environment, utility functions, strike costs, and so forth. Extreme versions of this approach fail to recognize or seriously examine the tactical element of concessions. Chamberlain (1951, 1955) and Pen (1959) adopt a moderate version of the choice perspective and suggest by implication that concessions are the *result* of tactical manipulation of the costs and benefits attached to a concession.

The choice perspective is associated with an emphasis on the nature of settlements and treatments of power as an outcome. The choice of whether to move toward agreement is typically transformed into a choice of whether to agree with the last proposal of the opponent. Concession decisions become agreement decisions. This is the manner in which the choice perspective is incorporated into the theories of Zeuthen (1930), Nash (1950), Hicks (1963), and others (see Chapter One). The ultimate concern of all these approaches is the nature of the settlement. In the terms of game theory, the extensive game consisting of the sequence of concessions and counterconcessions is transformed into a normalized game with one move: agree or do not agree. This concern with bargaining outcome is also manifested in treatments of bargaining power as an outcome (see, for example, Dunlop, 1950). Theories that do include power posit the nature of the settlement, that is, the relative concessions of bargainers, to be the empirical indicator of power. Bargaining power is essentially viewed as a theoretical construct for subsuming concession behavior. To summarize, the choice perspective treats concessions as a function of costs and benefits attached to different settlements, and concessions are viewed as the result ultimately of tactical action that manipulates the costs or benefits.

An information perspective on concession behavior is implicit in the work of Siegel and Fouraker (1960) and social psychologists (see Chertkoff and Esser, 1976; Hamner and Yukl, 1977; Magenau and Pruitt, 1979). This perspective does not reject the notion that concession behavior is choice, but it reconceptualizes concession behavior as the manipulation of information or management of impressions. Concessions are cues from which the opponent infers a party's aspirations, expectations, intentions, and the like. Concessions and counterconcessions constitute an exchange of information, and later concessions add to or modify the information embedded in earlier concessions. Concession behavior at any point in the bargaining, therefore, is a choice of how much and what information to communicate to the opponent.

From an information perspective, concessions are clearly tactical behavior. A party that transmits more of the right kind of information and less of the wrong kind of information will do better in the negotiations. This approach to concession behavior is illustrated by Siegel and Fouraker's (1960) theory that one party infers the other's aspirations by evaluating the other's concession behavior as tough or soft. If a party makes very small (or no) concessions, the opponent will attribute high aspirations and a tough image to the party, and the opponent will therefore reduce its aspirations and make greater concessions. Thus, a party's tough concession stance lowers its opponent's aspirations and thereby enables the party to exact more concessions from its opponent.

The information perspective is closely associated with a social psychological analysis of bargaining. Social psychologists have consistently emphasized impression management in bargaining (see, for example, Brown, 1977; Chertkoff and Esser, 1976; Deutsch, 1973; Hamner and Yukl, 1977; Magenau and Pruitt, 1979; Rubin and Brown, 1975). Two assumptions relevant to the information perspective are implicit in social psychological analyses of bargaining: An opponent's behavior is the basis upon which a party attributes aspirations, intentions, and orientations to the opponent; and the party's tactical action is based on these inferences and their implications for the opponent's future action. These assumptions indicate that a party's concession tactics are based on its opponent's concession tactics and make the level of aspiration a particularly suitable focus for social psychological work.

A number of social psychological experiments have tested the major prediction of level-of-aspiration theory, that is, that tougher concession tactics exact more concessions than softer ones. The research settings were a bilateral monopoly confronting bargainers with distributive issues and allowing them to exchange offers and counteroffers. The subjects were to bargain against a preprogramed opponent with a concession tactic that reflected some variant of the following: toughness (smaller concessions in response to a concession by the subject), matching (concessions of equal size), or softness (larger concessions than those made by the subject). Research in this tradition accords general support to the notion that it pays to be tough (see, for example, Chertkoff and Conley, 1967; Komorita and Barnes, 1969; Komorita and Brenner, 1968; Liebert and others, 1968; Yukl, 1974a, 1974b). Several studies, however, suggest qualifications of this notion. Some studies indicate that a reciprocal (matching) concession tactic is most effective (Esser and Komorita, 1975; Hamner, 1974; Komorita and Esser, 1975) and some demonstrate that extreme levels of toughness are counterproductive (Benton, Kelley, and Liebling, 1972; Lawler and MacMurray, 1980).

The role of power in the information perspective is variable. On the one hand, social psychologists tend to neglect bargaining power and thereby miss a potentially critical determinant of concession tactics. They emphasize the effectiveness of different concession tactics rather than the foundation of the tactics in the power relationship. As in the case of the choice perspective, the role of power is typically unspecified. Bargaining power is examined in a few studies (Komorita and Barnes, 1969; Michener and others, 1975), yet the focus remains on the conditions under which a tough concession tactic produces greater yielding than a softer one. The role of power is often included in analyses of matrix games (see Tedeschi, Schlenker, and Bonoma, 1973), but these studies do not allow parties to exchange offers and counteroffers and therefore do not fit our definition of bargaining.

There are thus three principal differences between the choice and information perspectives. First, they belong to different research traditions—the choice perspective to economics and industrial relations, the information perspective to social psychology. Second, these perspectives imply somewhat different approaches to power—power as an outcome and power as tactical action. Our discussion in Chapter Two reveals a number of defects in these approaches, for example, the former neglects tactics and the latter neglects the power relationship. Third, these perspectives suggest different emphases for the tactical analysis of bargaining. The choice perspective emphasizes the cost-benefit calculations that determine concession behavior, whereas the information perspective emphasizes the concession behavior itself. These differences are relatively subtle and suggest that the choice and information perspectives are as complementary as they are incompatible.

The complementarity of the choice and information perspectives allows for some integration, and we will take elements from both. Consistent with the information perspective, we conceptualize concession behavior as tactical choice and accept the basic assumptions of the information perspective. However, consistent with the choice perspective, we emphasize the determinants of concession behavior rather than its effects on the opponent. The most critical determinants of concessions for us are the dimensions of bargaining power (dependence) presented in Chapter Two. In contrast to both the choice and information perspectives, we place tactical concessions within a comprehensive theory of bargaining power.

Theoretical and Methodological Issues

Our task is to apply our framework on bargaining power (Chapter Two) to tactical concessions and to specifically address the question, How do the dimensions of bargaining power affect the adoption of tough or soft concession tactics? Two primary theoretical issues are suggested by our presentation of dependence theory in Chapter Two. An application of dependence theory to tactical concessions first must be related to zero-sum and variable-sum images of the power relationship. Our discussion of power perceptions in Chapter Two indicates that the type of image adopted by bargainers guides parties' efforts to estimate their own and the other's bargaining power. A zero-sum image indicates that bargainers treat power solely in relative terms, that is, judge one party's power only in relation to the other's, because an increase in one party's power necessarily involves a decrease in the other's. A nonzero- or variable-sum image indicates that parties treat each other's bargaining power as somewhat independent and that individual or total power modifies the effects of relative power. One of the critical tasks of this chapter is to develop the implication of these power images for tactical concessions.

The second theoretical issue is the role of the commitment dimension of bargaining power. Chapter Two poses two alternative interpretations. On the one hand, bargainers might emphasize the implications of A's commitment for B's power (that is, the higher A's commitment, the greater B's bargaining power) or for A's tactical effort (that is, the higher A's commitment, the greater A's tactical effort). In this chapter, we apply these contrasting ideas on commitment to tactical concessions.

To illustrate and focus our theoretical discussion, we present data from social psychology experiments. Although an experimental (laboratory) method is necessarily artificial, as Strauss (1979) indicates, there are few experimentally based hypotheses on bargaining that cannot be applied to ongoing labor-management relations. Our theory, as presented in Chapter Two, identifies the variables—for example, dimensions of dependence—included in our experiments and offers some basic propositions. However, we are not as concerned with testing these basic notions as we are with illustrating their potential merit and using the experimental data to facilitate our theorizing. Although experimentation is often portrayed solely as a theory-testing device of little use in the development of theories, the manner in which we use our experimental data reflects our partial disagreement with this classic methodological position. Furthermore, we do not consider the theory in Chapter Two to be fully developed, and we use the experimental data to simultaneously assess and further develop the implications of the theory. The experimental data can identify subtleties of bargaining overlooked by the theory and provide the basis for a preliminary resolution of certain theoretical issues, such as the role of commitment in tactical decisions.

The illustrative role of our data is exemplified by the fact that the data presented in this chapter are derived from experimental conditions whose number exceeds that required to strictly test the theory. Rather than focus on a few critical conditions, we incorporated all the dimensions of dependence in the experimental designs. Second, while we use statistical significance criteria, we are just as concerned with patterns or trends that have theoretical import or provide a foundation for additional ideas. Statistical significance is less critical to us than theoretical relevance or import. Third, we do not present all the findings of our data analysis; instead, we present only the data of greatest relevance to our theorizing.

Our overall position on the role of experimentation in the bargaining field is similar to that of Loasby (1976). He suggests that experimentation be construed as a "searchlight" rather than a "floodlight," that the experimentalist identify general theoretical principles that sacrifice descriptive power for explanatory power. Hypotheses from experimental contexts can and should be applied at an abstract or theoretical level, although the empirical indicators or referents are likely to be different from those found in real contexts. At issue is whether theoretical principles developed and tested in controlled laboratory contexts can systematize or organize some real-world empirical content or referents. An experimental (laboratory) context is best for testing or building theory, while empirical models, such as those offered by economists, can be used to expand and elaborate preliminary ideas developed by experimentation.

The data in this chapter and Chapters Five and Seven come from two experiments, both of which include the same general procedures. Both experiments utilized volunteer undergraduate students as subjects, manipulated conditions of dependence in a completely randomized factorial design (see Kirk, 1968), and adopted procedures like those found in social psychological experiments on bargaining (see, for example, Esser and Komorita, 1975; Komorita and Barnes, 1969).

Our theory calls for experimental procedures that allow two parties to exchange offers and counteroffers regarding some issue on which they have incomplete information on the payoffs attached to different agreement points. Beyond these general conditions:

1. The experiments placed each subject in a representative role or position. Many elements of the instructions to subjects were portrayed as guidelines from constituents. Since we are most concerned with situations in which bargainers are representatives, such as labor-management bargaining, we included constituent-representative relations in the setting but held this relationship constant across bargaining-power conditions.

2. The experimental situation was essentially context free. We did not tell subjects they were to play the role of labor negotiators, international negotiators, and the like, but only that they were negotiating for a group, labeled alpha or beta. The issue was not presented in specific terms (such as, wage rates) but as an abstract continuum with twenty-nine potential agreement points, labeled by whole numbers 1 to 29. We did not want subjects to act in terms of some image they had of particular issues in particular negotiating contexts. To have given them specific roles might have encouraged the subjects to act in terms of stereotypical images of bargaining.

3. Our theoretical focus is the relationship of the dimensions of bargaining power (dependence) to concession tactics, and we attempted to isolate these variables from all extraneous influences. For example, interpersonal cues or first impressions were removed by isolating bargainers from one another and concealing the identities of their opponent. Interpersonal cues are certainly important in real bargaining but such cues are likely to produce exaggerated effects in the laboratory, and our purpose was to examine the dimensions of dependence in as pure a setting as possible.

4. The instructions encouraged subjects to adopt a maximizing-gain orientation to the bargaining. The instructions indicated that their goal was to maximize the extent to which the

agreement was in their group's interest, and their pay for the experiment was based on the degree to which they achieved this goal. This maximizing-gain orientation is consistent with most prior theoretical and empirical work on bargaining (see Chapter One).

5. The information parameters assured that subjects were not aware of the opponent's profit at the various agreement levels. In addition, point values rather than monetary ones were attached to the subject's own profit schedule on the assumption that bargainers seldom have complete information even on their own profits. Our bargainers had more information about themselves than the other, but this information about themselves was still not complete.

The experiment of primary concern in this chapter manipulated each dimension of bargaining power: A's alternatives, A's commitment, B's alternatives, and B's commitment. The alternatives were manipulated by giving subjects a probability distribution showing the likelihood that they could get various agreements from an alternative group. Subjects would not really negotiate with another party if they chose the alternative. The alternative was designed to represent the fact that bargainers often have alternative outcome sources that they can pursue in the event of no agreement. In the experiment, agreement with the hypothetical alternative group was determined by a drawing in which the probabilities of different agreements corresponded to those in the probability distribution given to subjects. Furthermore, subjects could not quit bargaining before the last bargaining round and choose the alternative; the drawing occurred only in the event of no agreement at the end of the fifteenth and last round.

The commitment dimension was manipulated by varying the amount of money at stake in the bargaining. Under a low commitment, a bargainer had a maximum of $1.60 at stake, whereas the high-commitment condition called for a bargainer to have $6.40 at stake. To assure that all subjects could earn up to $8.00 for the experiment, we had a second bargaining session immediately following the first. Because of the second session, we did not have to deceive subjects about their potential pay, and we could still assure all an equal opportunity to earn \$8.00. Also, subjects were informed that they would bargain with a different person in the second session, so that they could not simply exchange good agreements across sessions.

The bargaining took place on a series of fifteen rounds. Each round consisted of one written offer by each subject in the pair. When it was a bargainer's turn to submit an offer, the bargainer had a minute or so to write an offer—any whole number between 1 and 29—on an offer sheet. The only restriction on the bargaining was that subjects could not withdraw or retract prior offers, that is, they had to engage in good faith bargaining. The offer sheets were carried back and forth between bargainers until they reached agreement or completed the fifteenth round.

Bargaining Power and Tactical Concessions

In Chapter Two, we argue that bargainers implicitly or explicitly adopt an image of the power relationship along the continuum of zero-sum to variable-sum principles. These images are often nonconscious, implicit principles within the schemata of interpretation that bargainers apply to their negotiations. The images do not have any necessary (or a priori) connection to the real power situation, but they are important to elucidate the logic underlying the cognitive and behavioral processes of bargaining. In Chapter Two, we demonstrate that the type of image determines the criteria bargainers use to make power judgments, that is, what dimensions of dependence form the basis for their power perceptions. In this chapter, we extend this analysis to tactical concessions. The basic question is whether (or to what extent) tactical concessions reflect a particular image of the power relationship. By making this the issue, we are arguing that an understanding of tactical action in relation to the power relationship requires an understanding of the implicit logic underlying tactical action. We cannot observe this logic or the zero-sum and variable-sum principles, but we can observe tactical action and determine which cognitive principles conform to it.

Our first step is to expand our earlier discussion of the

zero-sum and variable-sum principles. When scholars speak of power in zero-sum terms, they are treating only the relationship of each party's power, not tactical action. It is not tactical action that has a zero-sum or variable-sum quality but only the power of the parties. While this is true, it is also true that bargainers consciously or nonconsciously link tactical action to the power relationship and, therefore, also to the zero-sum and variable-sum imagery. Figure 3 shows the two images of the power relationship.

Figure 3. Zero-Sum and Variable-Sum Images of the Power Relationship

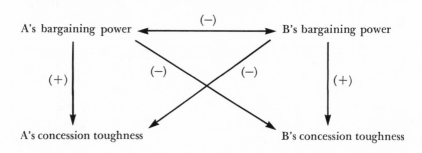

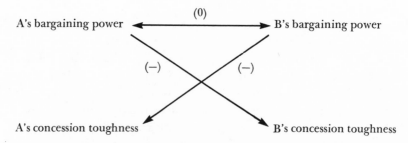

Zero-Sum Imagery. A zero-sum approach to the power relationship implies two assumptions: There is a perfect, inverse relationship between A's and B's bargaining power; and an increase in a party's bargaining power increases the toughness of that party's concession tactics. The first assumption is most critical for a zero-sum approach to power, while the second is a plausible addition required to relate the zero-sum principle to tactical action. As shown in Figure 3, these assumptions imply that each party's power is inversely related to the other's bargaining toughness. The relationship of A's power to B's toughness is mediated by B's power and, therefore, contingent on the validity of the first assumption. An increase in one party's power exerts a direct positive effect on its own toughness, a direct negative effect on the opponent's power, and an indirect (operating through the opponent's power) negative effect on the opponent's toughness. Thus, the basic proposition on tactical action derived from the zero-sum image is:

Proposition 1. An increase in a party's bargaining power increases that party's toughness while decreasing the opponent's toughness.

This proposition explicitly links the zero-sum imagery to a major dimension of tactical action: concession toughness. Given that we define bargaining power in terms of dependence, the zero-sum imagery leads to two additional propositions:

Proposition 2. An increase in A's dependence on B increases B's toughness and decreases A's toughness.

Proposition 3. An increase in B's dependence on A decreases B's toughness and increases A's toughness.

We can now see more clearly why such propositions are ultimately based on the zero-sum assumption of a perfect, negative relationship between each party's dependence on the other. We can also see why bargainers who adopt zero-sum imagery analyze the power relationship solely in relative terms. Constructs like total or absolute power should play no role in their tactical decisions because of the inverse relationship between each party's power. A party adjusts its exact level of toughness, therefore, to fit the ratio of its bargaining power to that of its opponent. In contrast variable-sum imagery fosters a looser conception of the power relationship in which absolute, relative, and total power are potentially relevant to tactical concessions.

Variable-Sum Imagery. The idea of variable-sum power is somewhat of a catch-all category including all that is not strictly subsumed by the zero-sum notion. The basic idea is that both parties can increase their own power without necessarily decreasing the opponent's power. Whereas zero-sum imagery implies that total power in the relationship is constant, variable-sum imagery implies that total power is not fixed or constant. Zero-sum and variable-sum images lie along a continuum, with a perfect negative relationship between parties' power at one end and no relationship at the other end. For purposes of illustration, we present the variable-sum imagery as the polar opposite of zero-sum imagery.

An extreme version of the variable-sum approach assumes that there is no necessary relationship between each party's bargaining power. Thus A's concessions are determined only by A's own power or only by B's power, and variable-sum imagery does not permit one to say which of the possibilities is more likely. However, dependence theory can be construed as favoring the latter over the former. A combination of the variable-sum postulate with dependence theory suggests the relationship depicted in Figure 3.

The zero relationship between parties' power is the basic assumption, while the other relationships are from dependence theory. Dependence theory suggests a variable-sum approach to power but not necessarily in the most extreme form, so the assumption should not be strictly interpreted as a position of dependence theory. The relationships between power and tactical action are suggested by the fact that dependence theory stipulates that the power of a party is based on the other's dependence. Assuming that bargainers can most easily interpret and manipulate their own dependence, one reasons that they base their tactical action more on their own dependence (that is, the opponent's power) than on the opponent's dependence (that is, their own power). Bargainers should feel they have greater control over and information on their own alternatives and commitment. Thus, the following propositions are suggested:

Proposition 1. An increase in a party's bargaining power decreases the opponent's toughness.

Proposition 2. An increase in A's dependence on B decreases A's toughness.

Proposition 3. An increase in B's dependence on A decreases B's toughness.

Thus, in terms of dependence, a party's concession behavior is a function of its own dependence on the other, not the other's dependence on it. Overall, the variable-sum approach of dependence theory illustrates the importance of absolute and total power.

The propositions, linking dependence to tactical concessions, are the most critical points of contrast between zero-sum and variable-sum principles. This contrast indicates that the image of power adopted by bargainers manifests itself in the observed relationships between the dimensions of dependence and concession behavior. If the dimensions of dependence have an equal and opposite effect on the toughness of the two bargainers, the implication is that they are using the zero-sum image; if a bargainer's own dependence, but not the other's dependence, determines the bargainer's toughness, then some version of the variable-sum image is plausible. In addition, bargainers who adopt a variable-sum image should respond to higher levels of total power with lower bargaining toughness. The variable-sum image does not preclude the relevance of relative power, but indicates that absolute and total power can modify the effects typically attributed to relative power. The variable-sum perspective implies that all three facets of power warrant some consideration by practitioners and scholars like. Traditional notions of power as relative power (see, for example, Chamberlain, 1955; Blau, 1964) implicitly or explicitly treat the variable-sum approach as implausible.

To consider the plausibility of the variable-sum approach, embedded in dependence theory, we present our experimental data. But first, a few comments about the analysis are in order. The experiment had a $2 \times 2 \times 2 \times 2 \times 2$ factorial design, manipulating the four dimensions of dependence (low or high) and treating subject (A or B) within each pair as a within-subjects factor (eight pairs per condition). The dependent variable most relevant to the above discussion is the overall yielding of each bargainer across the fifteen bargaining rounds. The data and analysis come from an overall analysis of variance with the four dimensions of dependence and subject as factors. Our discussion considers the data most relevant to the propositions just mentioned, that is, the yielding of each bargainer under each dimension of dependence.

Alternatives Dimension

The zero-sum and variable-sum assumptions yield different hypotheses regarding the effect of alternatives on tactical concessions. The zero-sum propositions indicate:

Hypothesis 1. An increase in A's alternatives decreases A's concessions and increases B's concessions.

Hypothesis 2. An increase in B's alternatives decreases B's concessions and increases A's concessions.

The variable-sum hypotheses, in contrast, are:

Hypothesis 1a. An increase in A's alternatives decreases A's concessions and has no effect on B's concessions.

Hypothesis 2a. An increase in B's alternatives decreases B's concessions and has no effect on A's concessions.

The major findings for the analysis of concession toughness are the interaction effects between subject (A or B) and each party's alternatives, shown in Table 1. High numbers represent greater yielding and lower bargaining toughness. The results

Table 1. Total Yielding by A's Alternatives and Subject
and by B's Alternatives and Subject

	A's Alternatives[a]	
	Low	High
Subject A	13.8	10.3
Subject B	10.6	11.9
	B's Alternatives[b]	
	Low	High
Subject A	11.6	12.5
Subject B	13.1	9.5

[a]ANOVA: A's Alternatives X Subject, $F(1,112) = 21.5, p < .001$.

[b]ANOVA: B's Alternatives X Subject, $F(1,112) = 18.8, p < .001$.

indicate separate interaction effects for each party's alternatives, also supported by Tukey's (Kirk, 1968) post hoc tests. In both cases, a party's own alternatives affect its own tactical concessions—for example, greater alternatives to A led to greater toughness (lower yielding) by A; however, the party's own alternatives do not affect the opponent's toughness. These data offer support to the variable-sum image.

The results do not suggest that bargainers at all times adopt variable-sum imagery. However, our results document, rather dramatically, the plausibility of the variable-sum approach to power and suggest that theoretical work on bargaining power must allow for this. A second point is that the results do not suggest that relative power is unimportant, but that bargainers also consider the absolute facet of power. They act as if their own bargaining power and the bargaining power of the other are not perfectly related. Thus an approach to bargaining power with variable-sum elements and related notions of absolute power is needed to account for how bargainers analyze the power relationship and use it to make tactical decisions.

The variable-sum perspective also poses some interesting practical implications. As an example, consider the implied advice on how best to extract concessions from the opponent. A zero-sum approach fails to distinguish the consequences of changing different dimensions of bargaining power. A change in any dimension can engender more yielding by the opponent. In contrast, the variable-sum approach of dependence theory advises bargainers to manipulate their own power, that is, increase the opponent's dependence on them. Decreasing the other's power by altering one's own dependence will not exact more concessions from the opponent. Given such implications, it appears important for both scholars and practitioners to understand the images of power that underlie divergent lines of tactical action at the bargaining table.

Commitment Dimension

The differences between zero-sum and variable-sum images of bargaining power are particularly important to an understanding of the relationship between alternatives dimension of dependence and concessions. With regard to commitment, the primary issue is whether bargainers act on the power implications of commitment or on the tactical-effort implications. The power implications are embedded in the previously stated propositions on dependence and tactical concessions. Specifically, the theory suggests two hypotheses about commitment dimension of dependence:

Hypothesis 1. An increase in A's commitment increases A's concessions.

Hypothesis 2. An increase in B's commitment increases B's concessions.

The assumption, of course, is that greater commitment makes one more dependent on the opponent and, thereby, gives the opponent more bargaining power.

Two other hypotheses are suggested by the assumption that high commitment may also motivate greater tactical effort. A party with high commitment to the outcomes at issue has every reason to push strongly in the negotiations, while a party with less commitment might be more inclined to yield to a party with greater commitment to the outcomes. This reasoning leads to the following alternative hypotheses:

Hypothesis 1a. An increase in A's commitment decreases A's concessions.

Hypothesis 2a. An increase in B's commitment decreases B's concessions.

If we translate commitment into power terms, these tactical-effort hypotheses have a rather provocative implication —a party with high power on the commitment dimension (meaning that the opponent is highly committed to the outcomes at issue) may have to yield more than otherwise during the negotiations. There are two basic motives for such yielding by the higher-power party: first, as a response to strong, unmitigated pressure by the lower-power opponent, who must overcome the power implications of high commitment by greater tactical effort; second, to convey an image of benevolence, reasonableness, or altruism, and thus improve the ongoing relationship of the parties and enable the higher-power party to exact concessions on other issues or have a good case to present to mediators or arbitrators in the event of an impasse. Note that these implications of the tactical-effort notion accentuate a basic tenet of our theory: The power relationship does not have a one-to-one correspondence to tactical action or to bargaining outcomes.

Table 2 presents preliminary data on the power and tactical-effort implications of commitment. As with the alternatives dimension, the interaction of each party's commitment by subject is most relevant to our purpose. The trend of our data offers some support for the tactical-effort notion. There is a weak pattern or tendency for greater commitment to the outcomes by a party to decrease the yielding of that party (and also increase the yielding by the opponent). These data should be approached cautiously, but clearly there is a general tendency for bargainers to act on the tactical-effort, rather than power, implications of commitment. This is consistent with our study

Table 2. Total Yielding by A's Commitment and Subject
and by B's Commitment and Subject

	A's Commitment[a]	
	Low	High
Subject A	12.5	11.7
Subject B	10.7	11.9
	B's Commitment[b]	
	Low	High
Subject A	11.8	12.4
Subject B	11.9	10.6

[a]ANOVA: A's Commitment X Subject, $F(1,112) = 3.98, p < .05$.
[b]ANOVA: B's Commitment X Subject, $F(1,112) = 3.41, p < .07$.

(Lawler and Bacharach, 1976) on the evaluation of a prospective influence attempt, in which we found that persons expect greater tactical success when they are highly committed to the outcomes at issue. Commitment can also simultaneously form the basis for power inferences (see Bacharach and Lawler, 1976). With regard to concessions in bargaining, commitment unleashes contradictory tendencies that may be resolved in the direction of tactical effort as parties adopt concession tactics.

The data in Table 2 do not distinguish situations in which both parties have the same level of commitment from those in which they have different levels of commitment. If A has high commitment, A's response should relate not just to that commitment but to the comparison between A's own commitment and the opponent's. Our tentative evidence shows that when both parties have equal levels of commitment (low-low or high-high), there is virtually no difference between the yielding of bargainer A and bargainer B—means of 11.9 for A and 11.3 for B, 11.7 for A and 11.3 for B, respectively. However, when one party has a low commitment to the outcomes and the other a high commitment, the differences are in the direction suggested by the tactical-effort notion. The party with high commitment concedes less and the party with low commitment concedes more—means of 10.0 compared to 13.0, and 11.6 compared to

12.6, respectively. Alone, these trends would have little meaning; but together with the other data, they add further weight to the tactical-effort interpretation of commitment.

The plausibility of the tactical-effort hypothesis indicates that alternatives and commitment may represent qualitatively different dimensions of bargaining power. Whereas high power on the alternatives dimension is a definite advantage, high power on the commitment dimension can be somewhat of a disadvantage. The commitment dimension engenders conflicting tactical tendencies and the comparability of effects for commitment and alternatives is contingent on how parties deal with this conflict. Our experiment suggests a general tendency for bargainers to treat commitment in a qualitatively different manner from alternatives. This tendency has theoretical and practical importance because it implies that bargainers are wise to convey a high commitment (or higher than that of the opponent) regardless of the negative effect this might have on the opponent's perception of the party's power. In the case of commitment, weakness may be a strength.

Total Power

Total power refers to the absolute amount of dependence *in the bargaining relationship*, that is, mutual dependence. Traditional approaches to bargaining, reviewed in Chapter One, treat mutual dependence as a constant or given, rather than as a variable, and thus imply that the amount of power in a relationship is finite and fixed—a basic tenet of a zero-sum approach—and that power should be defined solely in relative terms. Applied to tactical concessions, this principle means that bargainers who adopt variable-sum imagery of bargaining power should adjust their tactical decisions to account for the total power in the bargaining relationship. The basic proposition of our dependence theory is as follows:

Proposition 1. An increase in the total power (that is, the sum of A's dependence and B's dependence) within the bargaining relationship decreases the mutual toughness of the bargainers.

This proposition, in turn, leads to two hypotheses that are the focus of our discussion:

Hypothesis 1. A decrease in the total alternative outcome sources across bargainers decreases the mutual toughness of the bargainers.

Hypothesis 2. An increase in the total commitment across bargainers decreases the mutual toughness of the bargainers.

Our preceding analyses of alternatives and commitment suggest that these hypotheses are not equally credible. The first is quite compatible with our analysis of alternatives, which supported dependence theory, and extends that analysis by stipulating that bargainers also respond to the sum of each party's absolute power. The second hypothesis is another matter. The preceding analysis lends support to the tactical-effort hypothesis. An extension of the tactical-effort notion on commitment to the issue of total power suggests the opposite of hypothesis 2—namely, that total commitment is positively related to toughness.

Our preliminary data on total power consist of additional information from the experiment presented earlier in this chapter and a second experiment that is described in Chapter Five. The second experiment differs from the first in that it manipulated the total level of each party's alternatives and commitment while holding relative power constant and equal. With regard to the first experiment, the hypotheses predict an interaction between each bargainer's alternatives. The results for this interaction are presented in Table 3.

The results in Table 3 support the total-power hypothesis for the alternatives dimension of dependence. The most relevant comparison is the high mutual dependence cell (low-low alternatives) and the low mutual dependence cell (high-high alternatives). These data dovetail with those in the second experiment, which compared only the low-low and high-high cells. In that second experiment, the total yielding was 11.1 in the low-low cell (high mutual dependence) and 8.8 in the high-high cell

Table 3. Total Yielding by A's Alternatives and B's Alternatives

		A's Alternatives	
		Low	High
	Low	13.5	11.2
B's Alternatives			
	High	10.9	11.1

Note: ANOVA: A's Alternatives × B's Alternatives, $F(1,112) = 7.67, p <$ .01. The analysis is from an overall analysis of variance with the four dimensions of dependence and subject (A or B) as factors.

(low mutual dependence), and the difference was statistically significant. Together, these data indicate that total power in the relationship affects tactical concessions, independent of relative power or the absolute power of the individual party.

On the commitment dimension, there is no difference between high mutual dependence (high-high commitment) and low mutual dependence (low-low commitment) in the first experiment; and results from the second experiment are consistent with the first (means are 11.3 for low-low commitment and 11.6 for high-high commitment). The tactical-effort notion cannot be extended to the total power or total commitment in the relationship. The tactical-effort idea appears most relevant in accounting for tactical concessions when parties have different levels of commitment. This finding has implications for the role of commitment in conflict resolution, and we return to it in Chapter Seven.

Our theoretical and empirical analysis of total power provides additional support for the notion that alternatives and commitment are qualitatively different dimensions of bargaining power—at least, in the way they function tactically. The divergence regarding total power can be examined in terms of the relationship between total power and integrative bargaining. Integrative bargaining involves a redefinition of issues in a manner that enables parties to engage in cooperative effort rather than competitive give and take (see Pruitt and Lewis, 1977; Walton and McKersie, 1965). Total power, or mutual dependence, can be construed as the indicator of how much pressure the power relationship places on bargainers to engage in integrative bargaining. High levels of total power exert pressure on bargainers to redefine distributive issues, make trade-offs across issues, and establish a conciliatory tone for the negotiations. Viewed in this light, our analysis of total power suggests that the pressure toward integrative bargaining varies across different dimensions of bargaining power. Increasing total power on the alternatives dimension should increase the pressure toward integrative bargaining, while increasing total power on the commitment dimension could even have the opposite effect, that is, enhance pressure to bargain competitively. Overall, the concept of total power makes it apparent that the power relationship can have nondivisive, or even integrative, effects on the bargaining relationship.

In a previous work, we (Bacharach and Lawler, 1980) have offered a theory of power struggle that indicates further that total power is important to an understanding of tactics that manipulate the power relationship. If a party increases its opponent's dependence, and then the opponent reciprocates in kind, the result is an increase in mutual dependence (total power). However, if a party decreases its own dependence on its opponent, and the opponent responds in kind, the net result is a decrease in mutual dependence. Thus "the impact of a power struggle . . . is not necessarily disintegrative. Some countertactical patterns actually solidify . . . relationships by increasing mutual dependence" (1980, p. 173). Theories that lack a concept of total power overlook this positive side of bargaining power and tactical action.

To conclude, we have now elaborated the implications of a dependence theory of bargaining power for tactical concessions. Our most basic point is that the bargainers' image of the power relationship, along a zero-sum–variable-sum continuum, determines whether and how they use the dimensions of bargaining power to make tactical decisions. Our analysis offers three broad conclusions. First, parties use their own dependence on the opponent, but not the opponent's dependence on them, as a basis for deciding how tough or soft to be in negotiations. Second, different dimensions of bargaining power can have qualitatively different effects on concession tactics. With regard to alternatives, parties clearly use the power implications but, in the case of commitment, they emphasize the tactical-effort, rather than power, implications. Therefore, higher power on the commitment dimension may be counteracted by higher tactical effort by the opponent. Third, the total power in the bargaining relationship enhances tactical concessions and lays the groundwork for more cooperative or integrative bargaining. We emphasize the importance of including absolute and total power (in addition to relative power) in analyses of bargaining, and dependence theory implies such an emphasis by its variable-sum concept of power.

4

Theories of Deterrence and Conflict Spiral

▼▼

The "carrot-and-stick" image captures the prime modes through which actors use bargaining power. In fact, the bargaining process can be construed as a mixture of inducements (carrots) and sanctions (sticks). Inducements consist of provisional offers and counteroffers—tactical concessions—that reduce the difference between bargainers on an issue, while sanctions are grounded in punitive capabilities that permit bargainers to threaten and damage each other. Analytically, inducements and sanctions are complementary notions. An inducement implies a sanction because that which has been offered or given can be withdrawn—although there are often normative constraints that make bargainers reluctant to rescind earlier offers in an ongoing bargaining relationship. Sanctions, in turn, suggest inducements be-

104

cause the withholding of a sanction is a kind of inducement. The interrelatedness of inducements and sanctions, however, should not lead us to overlook the qualitative differences between tactical concessions and punitive tactics in bargaining.

Tactical concessions fall into a larger class of harmonizing tactics. Such tactics include actual concessions, redefinitions of prior offers or demands, and arguments about the quality or quantity of concessions made by each party. The defining characteristic of harmonizing tactics is that they involve real or perceived movement toward the position of the opponent. They lead parties to feel that the gap separating their positions on an issue is decreasing. Punitive tactics, in contrast, do not reduce the distance between the bargainers, but damage or threaten to damage resources controlled by the opponent. The resources attacked by punitive tactics are typically outside the bargaining in that they are not under negotiation at the bargaining table. The relationship of punitive tactics to the gap separating parties on issues is an empirical question. Punitive tactics may increase, decrease, or have no effect on this gap. Punitive tactics essentially attempt to force the opponent to make additional concessions beyond those that can be exacted by tactical concessions. There is no exchange of benefits implied in the use of punitive tactics, as there is with tactical concessions.

Because most theorists and researchers do not conceptualize bargaining as we do, we must develop a theory of punitive tactics and then relate it to the dependence theory of bargaining. We approach the first task by identifying perspectives on punitive tactics in the bargaining field, developing a theory of deterrence that treats the relationship of punitive capabilities to punitive tactics, and developing a theory of conflict spiral from which to analyze the escalatory processes that can result from punitive tactics. In the next chapter, we will relate these ideas to dependence theory and more thoroughly develop their implications for bargaining.

Perspectives on Punitive Tactics in Bargaining

As indicated in earlier chapters, bargaining inherently involves compromise and tactical manipulation. Punitive tactics are clearly manipulative but do not imply compromise or give and take, a characteristic that may explain why punitive tactics have an ambiguous role in many theories of bargaining (see Chapter One). Game-theoretical models include punitive capabilities in that they are considered part of the conflict payoffs. Punitive capabilities affect the outer limits of the contract zone by adding costs to the no-agreement option, but such game-theoretical and related economic models (see Young, 1975) do not fully explain the use of punitive tactics. Other theories, such as those which incorporate strike costs (see Hicks, 1963; Rabinovitch and Swary, 1976) or cognitive constructs (Chamberlain, 1955; Chamberlain and Kuhn, 1965; Pen, 1959), suggest that cognitive interpretations of punitive capabilities enter calculations at the deadline—in fact, some even indicate conditions under which punitive tactics, such as strikes, are likely to be used. Nevertheless, these theories do not present an analysis of punitive tactics in the course of bargaining. Punitive tactics are neglected as theorists attempt to develop some semblance of a determinate solution to the bargaining problem. Our approach clearly requires a more systematic and thorough analysis that conceptualizes punitive tactics as qualitatively different from tactical concessions. Let us now identify three perspectives on punitive tactics in bargaining: punitive tactics as antithetical to bargaining, punitive tactics as a last resort, and punitive tactics as an integral facet of bargaining.

Punitive Tactics as Antithetical to Bargaining. If one construes the bargaining relationship as implying a normative framework that undermines the legitimacy of punitive tactics, one may view such tactics as antithetical to bargaining. The normative framework stipulates that parties respect each other's interests, engage in action that fosters an environment of conciliation, and moderate their commitment to self-interest in accord with norms of fairness. This normative framework does not suggest that bargainers yield equal amounts or that they forego attempts to outmaneuver or bluff each other—only that their tactical manipulations remain within the boundaries implied by the normative framework that makes bargaining possible. The assumption of such a normative framework emphasizes inducements rather than sanctions. In this sense, punitive tactics strike at the very heart of bargaining relationships and essentially imply conflict without bargaining.

This view may appear extreme, but it remains implicit in a variety of literature on conflict and bargaining. Schelling's (1960, 1966) analysis of threats as commitment tactics is a prime example. Commitment tactics are means to maneuver the opponent into a position that produces acquiescence. They force the opponent to accept an outcome contrary to its interests and make concessions unnecessary by the party using the commitment tactics. Schelling is concerned primarily with tacit bargaining, as there is no explicit communication of offers and counteroffers, and parties do not necessarily define their transactions as bargaining. As suggested by Tedeschi and Bonoma (1972), Schelling's discussion essentially assumes that the conflict is not strictly a bargaining type. A similar point can be made about social psychological investigations of threat tactics, including those by Tedeschi (see Tedeschi, Schlenker, and Bonoma, 1973). These experiments are almost always conducted in matrix or trucking games that do not allow for the exchange of offers and counteroffers (see, for example, Deutsch and Krauss, 1962; Rubin and Brown, 1975; Tedeschi and Bonoma, 1972; Tedeschi, Schlenker, and Bonoma, 1973). Such games are typically represented as bargaining situations but are, strictly speaking, conflict or tacit bargaining relationships. Furthermore, while social psychological experiments on punitive tactics exclude bargaining, those explicitly on bargaining seldom give bargainers the capability of using punitive tactics (see reviews by Chertkoff and Esser, 1976; Hamner and Yukl, 1977). The general neglect of punitive tactics in the game-theoretical tradition (see Chapter One) can be construed in a similar manner. We infer from the literature that the antithetical perspective is a subtle, unstated assumption of some theoretical and research traditions.

Punitive Tactics as a Last Resort. If one views the normative framework as more flexible than the previous perspective, punitive tactics are unacceptable to the extent that the normative framework is manifest in the bargainer's behavior. Such tactics become legitimate only when the normative framework weakens or breaks down. Punitive tactics are antithetical to bargaining if overused, used too early in the bargaining, or used indiscriminately. Punitive tactics are to be adopted only when all else fails (Tedeschi and Bonoma, 1972), and the only justifications for punitive tactics are the failure of the opponent to support the normative framework and the depletion of other options for influencing the opponent.

The last-resort perspective, like the antithetical standpoint, assumes a fairly narrow normative framework, at least with regard to the legitimacy of punitive tactics. Neither of these perspectives allows for enough variation in the strength of the normative framework across or within bargaining relationships. The normative framework is viewed not only as inherent in bargaining but also as a reified entity that impresses itself on bargainers in virtually any context. Implicitly, both perspectives take the position that the transformation of a conflict relationship into a bargaining one involves a substantial transfusion of normative content into the relationship. Constraint on punitive tactics is one specific element of the normative framework. This somewhat narrow image of the normative framework suggests the need for the following perspective.

Punitive Tactics as Integral Facets of Bargaining Process. The following assumptions indicate that punitive tactics are best analyzed as integral parts of bargaining.

First, the normative framework underlying bargaining relationships is an emergent and fluid product of bargaining interaction. It does not impinge on bargainers from the outside but emerges from the bargaining; it is inherently ambiguous and subject to continual renegotiation by bargainers.

Second, the normative framework is embedded in the web of self-interest. Bargainers approach the normative framework in a pragmatic, utilitarian manner and tend to support those norms that are most consistent with their interests and reject those that counter their interests. Norms are used by bargainers to justify their self-interest and related tactical action, and the normative framework is a part of the tactical, manipulative processes of bargaining.

Third, the bargaining-power relationship establishes the parameters of self-interest from which parties consider the normative legitimacy of tactics. Like other elements of bargaining process, the normative framework reflects the power relationship. The normative framework underlying punitive tactics is based on bargaining power, and, therefore, normative constraints on punitive tactics develop from the power relationship; therefore, an emphasis on power is most appropriate for understanding punitive tactics.

These assumptions stipulate that punitive tactics are as central to bargaining as power itself. Few would deny that power is important (as mentioned in Chapter Two), but few treat power as central to bargaining. We posit power to be the essence of bargaining and thus punitive tactics to be integral facets of bargaining. After all, bargainers typically do have punitive capabilities affording them the option of punitive tactics. This point is implicit in the "normalized games" of game theorists and somewhat explicit in the work of Chamberlain (1955), Chamberlain and Kuhn (1965), Hicks (1963), and Pen (1959). Yet the implications of this point have not been developed or taken seriously. Theories that implicitly or explicitly adopt this perspective tend to neglect punitive tactics and fail to specify the links between punitive capabilities and punitive tactics or to make these a dominant concern. We must turn to political science and social psychology for ideas on punitive capabilities and punitive tactics. To this end, in the following sections, we develop theories of deterrence and conflict spiral, and in the next chapter we relate these theories to dependence.

Deterrence and Punitive Tactics

Most analyses of punitive tactics in conflict can be subsumed under or related in some way to deterrence theory. The term *deterrence* is not always used—in fact, social psychologists and collective-bargaining scholars have tended to avoid it—but the basic idea of deterrence is at least implicit in virtually all analyses of punitive tactics. Deterrence theory traditionally has been the province of political science. Its use as an analytical tool has been muddled by the politicization of the term *deter-rence* in public debates, particularly about the balance of power between the United States and Soviet Union. Conceptual diffi-culties lead one to question whether deterrence is an ad hoc construct for interpreting international events or whether it is a theoretic construct. Our purpose is to develop a theory of de-terrence useful for understanding punitive tactics in bargaining. It should be noted that, for the first time in this book, we are examining a theory from one institutional sphere (international relations) on the assumption that it is applicable to another in-stitutional sphere (labor-management relations).

The most thorough theoretical analyses of deterrence are found in the work of Morgan (1977) and of Schelling (1960, 1966). Morgan defines deterrence as follows: "Deterrence in-volves manipulating someone's behavior by threatening with harm. The behavior of concern to the deterrer is an attack; hence, deterrence involves the threat to use force in response as a way of preventing the first use of force by someone else" (1977, p. 9). Two points should be made about this definition. First, deterrence is grounded in the capacity to retaliate, that is, counterattack in response to an opponent's attack. Deterrence is not accomplished by a preemptive attack, and it is not truly de-fensive in nature as it does not involve the blockage of an at-tempted or ongoing attack by the opponent. Deterrence has a very specific purpose—to prevent or forestall the attempt itself. Strictly speaking, deterrence is not directed at concession mak-ing in bargaining. Its purpose is to keep the tactics of conflict within certain boundaries; namely, to preclude the opponent's use of punitive tactics. Second, while this definition is broad enough to apply to virtually any conflict, the application of de-terrence theory has been confined primarily to the analysis of military capabilities in international relations. We need to adapt deterrence theory to the study of punitive tactics in bargaining.

There are numerous theoretical, conceptual, and empiri-cal problems in the literature on deterrence. (See Morgan, 1977, for a detailed treatment of such problems.) We would like to stress three problems, which are neglected or not fully devel-oped by Morgan. First, analyses of deterrence suggest the existence of a subtle debate on whether deterrence is a single variable or a theory. Second, the unit of analysis for deterrence has typically been the individual rather than the dyad. Third, the exact nature of deterrence has been muddled by a failure to clearly and consistently distinguish various dimensions from which one must view deterrence. We now discuss each of these problems in turn.

Deterrence as a Variable or as a Theory. It is surprising, but there does not appear to be agreement on the theoretical status of deterrence. Is it simply a conceptual variable under which one subsumes the dependent variable *prevention of aggression*? Or is it a theory (however undeveloped) that specifies the relationships among a set of variables? Some simply treat deterrence as a dependent variable, while others conceptualize it as a theory. To Schelling (1960, 1966), deterrence is a general term applied to a dependent variable (prevention of attack) of relevance to international conflict. Schelling, of course, does detail the tactical mechanisms (for example, threats and variants thereof) for producing deterrence; however, deterrence is not a theory linking the punitive capabilities and tactics of the actors. In contrast, Morgan (1977) implicitly conceptualizes deterrence as a conflict process that relates actors' punitive capabilities and punitive tactics. Morgan's work lays the groundwork for a deterrence theory, while Schelling's work implicitly obviates the need or value of such a theory. We return to this difference between Schelling and Morgan later.

Although the distinction between deterrence as a single variable and as a theory is admittedly quite subtle, we consider it to have important implications for the further development of the deterrence notion. If one adopts the position that it is simply one among many variables relevant to conflict, then one's task is to develop a theory with which one can analyze the determinants of deterrence. But if one believes that deterrence is or should itself be a theory, one's primary task is to elaborate the way in which deterrence posits relationships between the capabilities and behavior of parties. We rather strongly believe that the latter position is most fruitful at this point and, therefore, follow Morgan more closely than Schelling.

Unit of Analysis. Few theorists or researchers would deny that the dyad is the appropriate unit of analysis, but most work on deterrence adopts as the unit the individual party, be it a collective (for example, a nation) or person (for example, the leader of a nation). Such work focuses on the conditions under which A can deter B rather than on the conditions under which A and B simultaneously deter each other. Schelling's (1960, 1966) analysis solely determines how one party can use threats to prevent aggression by the other party, neglecting the interactional or dyadic nature of deterrence. Any theory of deterrence, as opposed to treatments of deterrence as a single variable, must take the dyad as the unit of analysis.

We are not suggesting that to focus on the individual party is useless. One way to understand the dyad is to begin by separating its two components: A's ability to deter B and B's ability to deter A. Our basic point is that a theory of deterrence must integrate these two components by conceptualizing deterrence as a system that connects and interrelates components that are analytically and empirically separable. In addition, in some circumstances the prime obstacle to deterrence within a relationship resides in only one of these components—for example, in A's ability to deter B but not B's ability to deter A. An analysis of such circumstances should adopt a focus somewhat like that of Schelling but within an interactional theory of deterrence.

The Nature of Deterrence. Previous work on deterrence fails to distinguish clearly and consistently the dimensions relevant to deterrence. The major problem is the confusion of a threat with the punitive capabilities. Delineating the pertinent dimensions will not only resolve this problem but also clarify the prime focus of deterrence. We (Bacharach and Lawler, 1980) have discerned three elements or dimensions: punitive capability, threats, and punishment. Punitive capability, the maximum damage that one party can do to the other, is lodged in the power relationship of the conflicting parties and it consists of the sum total of resources that parties can use to damage the other's outcomes.

While punitive capabilities are structural in nature, the other two dimensions are behavioral or tactical in nature. A threat is an expression of intent to do harm (Deutsch and Krauss, 1962). More specifically, threats are verbal or nonverbal communications that specify the contingencies for actual punishment, that is, indicate that the punitive capability (or some portion of it) will be used under particular conditions. (See Bacharach and Lawler, 1980, and Tedeschi, Schlenker, and Bonoma, 1973, for more extensive discussion of the nature of threat communications.) Aside from being tactical behavior, threats differ from punitive capabilities in that they are typically directed at a specific situation, time period, and issue (or set of issues). Punitive capabilities are general in nature, and threats articulate the particular relation of these generalized capabilities to a specific context. The final dimension, punishment, is action by which an actor attacks or damages the opponent. Punishment, or actual damage, constitutes the major dependent variable of concern to the deterrence tradition.

Distinguishing punitive capability, threat, and punishment points to a basic ambiguity in writings on deterrence: Are punitive capabilities or threats the major predictors of deterrence theory? From Schelling's (1960, 1966) analysis, deterrence theory should predict the effectiveness of threats in preventing an opponent's attack. Schelling distinguishes two types of threats: deterrent threats and compellant threats. A deterrent threat is designed to get an opponent not to do something, while a compellant threat is designed to get the opponent to do something. In discussing deterrence, Schelling is solely concerned with deterrent threats. Morgan (1977), however, suggests that this form of deterrence is relatively rare because it assumes that the target of deterrence is seriously considering an impending attack and the deterrer attempts to utilize a threat to prevent the impending attack. Morgan argues that there is a more general form of deterrence that transcends the specific contexts of concern to Schelling. Morgan (1977, p. 28) states:

> Since in interstate relations there is a constant danger of harm, even if it is remote, analysts are attached to the view that threats are an intrinsic part of international politics, undergirding

peaceful as well as hostile, cooperative not just competitive, relationships. While this view can be carried too far, there is something to it. This leads me to suggest that there are really two kinds of deterrence. . . . Immediate deterrence concerns the relationship between opposing states where at least one side is seriously considering an attack while the other is mounting a threat of retaliation in order to prevent it. General deterrence relates to opponents who maintain armed forces to regulate their relationship even though neither is anywhere near mounting an attack.

The contrast of punitive capability and punitive tactics is embedded in Morgan's discussion of immediate and general deterrence, although he does not identify it as such. He fails to distinguish a situation that can be threatening to a party, such as facing an opponent who has substantial punitive capability, from the *use* of a threat tactic or communication. Our formulation emphasizes the need to distinguish the tactical and capability aspects of threats and limits the use of the term *threat* to the tactical level. From this standpoint, immediate deterrence applies only to threat tactics that are specifically directed at preventing aggression, a very small subcategory of threats. General deterrence, in comparison, refers to the bilateral punitive capabilities of conflicting actors. Our position is that general deterrence should be the prime concern to a theory of deterrence. Furthermore, a situation of immediate deterrence should occur only when general deterrence fails, that is, when the bilateral punitive capabilities are not enough to prevent an attack. The use of threats implies that general deterrence has already broken down, and successful deterrence implies that immediate deterrence is unnecessary. In this sense, general deterrence, and the concomitant emphasis on punitive capabilities, is the most crucial context for the development and application of deterrence theory.

The preceding three general criticisms of deterrence theory suggest that deterrence theory warrants more systematization and codification. In the following sections, we present a theory of deterrence designed to specify the major elements traditionally embedded in deterrence writings while taking account of the problems discussed herein.

The Scope of Deterrence Theory

The scope of a theory is the range of situations or contexts to which the theory can be applied. Scope is important because it communicates to researchers the appropriate context for testing the theory. Some theories have a very broad scope, whereas others have a narrow scope and are, thereby, applicable to only a small set of specific situations. Prior work on deterrence (see, for example, Morgan, 1977; Schelling, 1960, 1966), does not fully specify its scope but, implicitly, limits the scope to international contexts within which military aggression is the form of attack at issue. We believe deterrence theory can and should have a much broader scope than this. Four conditions define the scope of our theory of deterrence.

First, the situation is a conflict or bargaining situation that pits two adversaries against one another. This condition broadens the scope implied in prior work to include explicit bargaining. In effect, we are saying that the entrance of parties into a bargaining relationship does not remove coercion or punitive tactics from the relationship—a point implied in our earlier portrayal of punitive tactics. This first condition compels one to consider whether and how deterrence theory might analyze tactical action intrinsic to bargaining, especially tactical concessions.

Second, both parties have bilateral punitive capabilities; and, by implication, they possess the quite powerful tactical options of threat and punishment. Parties need not have equal levels of punitive capability, although there is some reason to contend that such a situation is the quintessential one. The critical point is that both parties have the capability of doing more than trivial damage to the other. This second condition helps to distinguish contexts to which the most basic propositions of the theory are applicable and those that must rely on auxiliary or modified propositions. Two examples illustrate this.

Criminology research focuses on the ability of the social system or legal system to deter individuals from committing crimes. The relationship between the individual and the system is of prime concern, a relationship that does not meet the condition of bilateral power, because the individual does not have more than trivial punitive capabilities. This does not mean that the individual has no power, but only that such power is not for the most part punitive in nature. Moreover, crime is not a punishment tactic used by the individual in a conflict with the system, but rather a matter of noncompliance with the laws of the system. The central focus of deterrence theory, preventing attacks, is not applicable, and thus a theory of deterrence for crime involves an auxiliary issue—the ability of a social system to induce the compliance of its citizenry.

A second example is the social psychological work of Tedeschi and his colleagues on the effectiveness of threats in conflict relationships (see Tedeschi and Bonoma, 1972; Tedeschi, Bonoma, and Schlenker, 1972; Tedeschi, Schlenker, and Bonoma, 1973). Although this work does not explicitly use deterrence theory, it is implied in the theoretical focus on subjective expected utility. The theory of subjective expected utility suggests that the effectiveness of a threat depends on the magnitude of the punitive capability underlying the threat weighted by the credibility of the threat, that is, the probability that the user will follow through with punishment. This idea is part of deterrence theory in the sense that deterrence is contingent on the magnitude of capability and perceived willingness of a party to use it. Analogous to work on deterrence in criminology, however, this research on threat tactics explores compliance to demands made by a threatener, rather than the prevention of punishment tactics by the opponent. The experimental procedures used by Tedeschi and his colleagues do not give the target of the threat the options of using threat and punishment tactics (see, for example, Horai and Tedeschi, 1969). Consequently, this line of research also falls outside of the scope of our theory of deterrence.

Our second condition defining scope also suggests that punitive capabilities encompass not only military capabilities in

international relations but any capability for damaging the outcomes of the opponent. This broadening of the notion of punitive capabilities is consistent with social psychological treatments
of coercive power (see French and Raven, 1959; Raven, 1974;
Raven and Kruglanski, 1970). Our first and second conditions
thus stipulate that punitive capabilities other than military ones
should be treated in applications to international relationships
and also that deterrence is important in virtually any conflict relationship involving punitive capabilities—for example, collective bargaining between union and management, bargaining between factions of a political party, or bargaining between
government and interest groups.

Our third condition is that parties be aware of each other's punitive capabilities. They need not have perfect or exact
information on the punitive capabilities, but they must be
aware that such capabilities exist and have a general idea about
how large or small they happen to be.

Fourth, both parties perceive each other as willing to use
the punitive capabilities. This information may come from prior
interactions with the party, observation of the opponent's behavior in other conflicts, or from inferences about the specific
situation. The less information parties have on the prior behavior of the other, the more likely they are to impute their own
inclinations or orientations to the other; that is, the more likely
they are to analyze the situation, develop plans of action, and
expect the other to engage in similar analyses and come to
somewhat similar conclusions.

Core Propositions

It is clear that work on deterrence has failed to clearly ex-
plicate or interrelate the basic ideas of the theory. One could
even argue that, at present, there is no theory of deterrence. If
we apply various principles of theory construction (see, for
example, Cohen, 1980; Gibbs, 1972; Hage, 1972; Stinchcombe,
1968) to deterrence, we are left with the feeling that the literature offers a number of disconnected theoretical fragments. At
best, deterrence is a theory only in the sense that it conforms to

the "spirit" of the principles of theory construction. Cohen (1980) suggests that well-developed theories consist of both core propositions and auxiliary propositions. Core propositions identify the most basic or central ideas of the theory, whereas auxiliary propositions supplement the core and involve extensions or applications to topics not encompassed by the core propositions. Our explication of the set of interrelated propositions that seem to characterize deterrence is organized by this distinction between core and auxiliary propositions. The core propositions of the theory, presented in Figure 4, are based on two assumptions.

Figure 4. A Theory of Deterrence

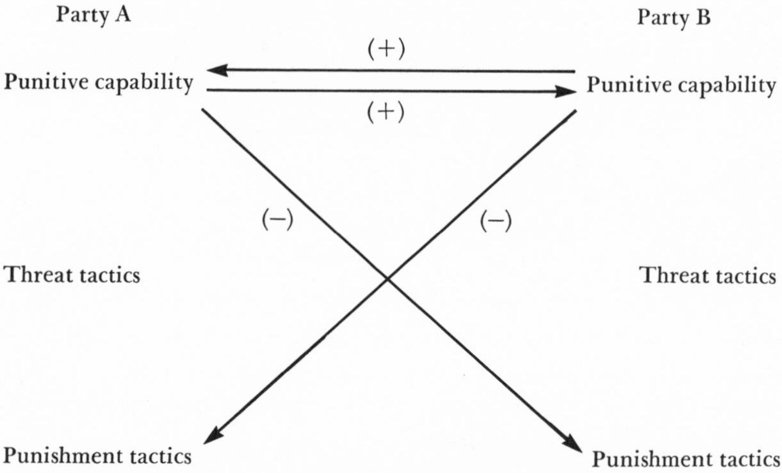

Party A   Party B

Punitive capability ←——————(+)——————→ Punitive capability
                          (+)

                    (−)   (−)

Threat tactics   Threat tactics

Punishment tactics   Punishment tactics

Assumption 1. An attempt by one party to increase its punitive capability will be followed by an attempt by the opponent to increase its punitive capability.

This first assumption indicates that changes in the punitive capabilities will be reciprocated, and it leads to two general propositions:

Proposition 1. An increase in A's punitive capability leads to an increase in B's punitive capability.

Proposition 2. An increase in B's punitive capability leads to an increase in A's punitive capability.

These propositions assume that both parties have the means to further develop their punitive capabilities and that they are successful in this endeavor.

Assumption 2. If a party increases its punitive capability, the opponent will view that party as more willing to use that capability in response to an attack.

The import of this postulate is that both parties fear the use of the other's punitive capability. This fear is ultimately based on the theory of subjective expected utility. The greater the magnitude of the other's punitive capability and the greater the perceived willingness of the other to use the capability, given an attack, the greater the fear of retaliation. This assumption and that of subjective expected utility lead to four additional propositions:

Proposition 3. An increase in A's punitive capability decreases the frequency of punishment tactics by B.

Proposition 4. An increase in B's punitive capability decreases the frequency of punishment tactics by A.

Proposition 5. An increase in the level of punitive capability within the relationship decreases the frequency of punishment tactics within the relationship.

Proposition 6. An increase in the inequality of punitive capability *in the relationship* increases the frequency of punishment tactics *in the relationship*.

Proposition 5 is a straightforward extension of propositions 3 and 4 to the relationship or dyad. It treats deterrence as a relational phenomenon, which we earlier argued was the most appropriate approach to deterrence. Proposition 6 is suggested by our first assumption on the reciprocal relationship of punitive capabilities. Our first assumption implies that deterrence is most effective when parties have equal or approximately equal punitive capabilities. A corollary is that if only one party is able or willing to enhance its punitive capability, it creates a situation of unequal punitive power. As a result, the advantaged party may be even more tempted to use punitive tactics, or the disadvantaged party may be tempted to initiate an attack, hoping to catch the other off guard. The overall implication of the reciprocity indicated by assumption 1 is that mutual deterrence is more stable and secure under circumstances of relatively equal punitive capabilities.

Auxiliary Elements of Deterrence Theory

Two implications of the theory presented in Figure 4 constitute extensions of the theory beyond its core notions. The first concerns the use of threat tactics. Figure 4 does not specify any links between punitive capability and threat tactics, thus omitting what Morgan (1977) calls "immediate deterrence" and also ignoring the critical role threats can play in conflict and bargaining. The social psychological literature posits that threats are effective only when they can be followed by actual punishment, that is, only when the threatener is able and willing to enforce the threat. Threats attain credibility only if the threatener is perceived as able and willing to follow through on the threat. From this notion of credibility, it follows that if conditions, such as punitive capabilities, make punishment tactics impractical or impossible, then threat tactics are less likely. In other words, if the punitive capabilities reduce the frequency of punishment tactics, they should concomitantly reduce the frequency of threat tactics. This argument suggests that we add the following assumption to the core assumptions:

Auxiliary assumption. Any condition that constrains the use of punishment tactics similarly constrains the use of threat tactics.

This auxiliary assumption in combination with the core assumptions leads to propositions similar to those for punishment tactics:

Proposition 7. An increase in A's punitive capability decreases the frequency of threat tactics by B.

Proposition 8. An increase in B's punitive capability decreases the frequency of threat tactics by A.

Proposition 9. An increase in the level of punitive capabilities within the relationship decreases the frequency of threat tactics in the relationship.

Proposition 10. An increase in the inequality of punitive capabilities within the relationship increases the use of threat tactics within the relationship.

It is particularly noteworthy that these auxiliary propositions indicate that threat usage is a function of the *other's* punitive capability, not of one's own punitive capability. These derivations from deterrence theory complement the traditional focus of social psychological research on punitive capability and threats. Researchers who discuss punitive magnitude primarily relate a party's magnitude to its own usage. Our formulation raises an issue that has received little attention in the social psychological literature (see Michener and Cohen, 1973, for an exception).

The second extension of the theory concerns its application to bargaining relationships. We have argued that deterrence can and should be broadened to include the process of making offers and counteroffers in bargaining. We are concerned here only with the most critical tactical option that conflicting parties acquire upon entering a bargaining relationship: tactical concessions. Although the concept of deterrence was not developed to explain or predict the toughness of concession making, any application to bargaining must consider this issue.

It is a common tenet that the use of threats and punishments impedes serious bargaining. Such tactics can distract the bargainers from the issues at hand, turning bargaining into a game in which projecting an image of strength becomes more critical to bargainers than resolving the conflict. If larger punitive capabilities reduce the frequency of threats and punishments, then larger punitive capabilities facilitate an environment more conducive to concession making. On this basis, we propose the following addition to the core of deterrence theory:

Auxiliary assumption. The use of threat tactics or punishment tactics increases the toughness of bargaining offers and counteroffers.

Proposition 11. An increase in A's punitive capability increases the magnitude of B's tactical concessions.

Proposition 12. An increase in B's punitive capability increases the magnitude of A's tactical concessions.

Proposition 13. An increase in punitive capabilities in the relationship increases mutual yielding in the bargaining.

To conclude, the most general implication of deterrence theory is that the size of the punitive capabilities in a bargaining relationship is negatively related to the level of aggression. Deterrence theory posits that bargainers tend to accumulate larger and larger punitive capabilities, take care to match an opponent's increases in punitive capabilities, and convey to the opponent a willingness to use the punitive capabilities. The result of these escalatory processes is to reduce the use of threat and punishment tactics and to enhance each party's tactical concessions. Large, bilateral, relatively equal punitive capabilities ostensibly have a positive effect on the relationship and on the willingness of the parties to confront the issue underlying the conflict—if for no other reason than to avoid the danger of mutual damage. In cases in which there is no current explicit bargaining relationship, the accumulation of punitive capabilities should facilitate the development of such a relationship. If parties have a bargaining relationship, large punitive capabilities should increase parties' willingness to compromise. Deterrence theory, therefore, offers a rather optimistic picture of the role punitive capabilities play in bargaining.

A Theory of Conflict Spiral

Social psychological work implies a more pessimistic image of punitive power than deterrence theory—specifically, that punitive capabilities give rise to threat-counterthreat and punishment-counterpunishment spirals. In this section, we use social psychological work to develop a theory of conflict spiral with which to compare deterrence theory. Our earlier conditions defining the scope of deterrence theory also apply to our conflict-spiral theory. Thus we will consider only research in which both parties have punitive capabilities (see, for example, Deutsch and Krauss, 1962; Deutsch and others, 1967; Hornstein, 1965; Michener and others, 1975) and exclude from consideration work on unilateral punitive capabilities and threats (for example, Tedeschi, Schlenker, and Bonoma, 1973). Let us briefly review the pertinent social psychological research.

Deutsch and Krauss (1962) based their research on two ideas: The mere availability of a punitive capability leads to its use, and the use of punitive capability by one party leads to counteruse by the opponent. These propositions suggest that the ultimate consequence of bilateral punitive capabilities is a damage-counterdamage spiral in which both parties lose. On the surface, these notions appear to directly contradict deterrence theory. Whereas deterrence theory indicates that the accumulation of punitive capabilities prevents aggression and minimizes conflict, the conflict-spiral notion suggests that disarmament or the removal of punitive capabilities is the way to minimize conflict. Whereas deterrence suggests that punitive capabilities, at least if sizable, prevent the use of threat and punishment tactics, the conflict-spiral notion suggests that the mere availability of punitive capabilities has the opposite effect. While deterrence theory posits reciprocal action only with regard to the accumulation of punitive capabilities, the conflict-spiral notion posits reciprocity at the tactical level as well. That is, bargainers not only reciprocate the development of punitive capabilities but also reciprocate threat and punishment tactics. Overall, the conflict-spiral notion seriously questions the practical advice offered to bargainers by deterrence theory.

A close examination of the conflict-spiral idea, however, indicates that while there is a basic contradiction between it and deterrence theory, there are also points of agreement and points of complementarity. To elucidate this, let us review some research. Deutsch and Krauss (1962) tested their ideas in the classic trucking game, an experimental setting that pits against one another two parties representing different trucking companies (Acme and Bolt). The goal of each party is to move produce from a starting point to a destination, with payoffs contingent on the time it takes to reach the destination. Each party can take one of two routes: a short route that is relatively straight or a winding road that takes much longer. The longer routes are separate for each party and enable them to avoid each other. There is only one short route for the two parties, and both cannot use the short route at the same time. If both try to use the short route simultaneously they will meet head-on and each will face a delicate tactical issue: yield to the other (that is, back up and let the other use the short route), or try to get the other to yield.

To offer the parties a threat capability, Deutsch and Krauss give one (unilateral) or both (bilateral) subjects a gate they can use to block the opponent's access to the destination through the short route. In order to test their hypotheses Deutsch and Krauss include three conditions: no threat (neither party has a gate), unilateral threat (only one party has a gate), and bilateral threat (both parties have a gate). For our purposes, only the comparison between the bilateral-threat and no-threat conditions is relevant. The results show frequent use of the gates in the bilateral condition as well as more and longer standoffs within the short route. The mere availability of a threat potential led to its use, and its use led to counteruse by the opponent, resulting in substantial joint losses over time. The combined payoffs of the parties were much greater in the no-threat as opposed to bilateral-threat condition. These results suggest that punitive capabilities accentuate conflict and undermine bargaining, a finding contradictory to deterrence theory.

However, several researchers identify theoretical and methodological problems in Deutsch and Krauss's experiment. Their major focus has been the conceptualization and operationalization of threats: In the experiment, the gates are punishment tactics as much as they are an expression of *intent* to do harm, threat tactics (see Shomer, Davis, and Kelley, 1966; Tedeschi, Bonoma, and Novinson, 1970). We have indicated that threats are communications that specify a contingency between the other's behavior and punishment (Bacharach and Lawler, 1980, chap. 9; Tedeschi, 1970), but the gates do not necessarily imply such a contingency. One major implication of this conceptual problem is that Deutsch and Krauss's results could represent a threat-counterthreat spiral or a punishment-counterpunishment spiral. Either is a reasonable interpretation or description of the results.

Other researchers attempt to distinguish between threat and punishment and, thereby, provide information on which (if not both) is encompassed in the conflict spiral. Both threat-counterthreat spirals and punishment-counterpunishment spirals have been observed, but there are enough exceptions that the generality of these patterns is open to question. For example, Shomer, Davis, and Kelley (1966) find that the spiral does not occur if the gates are transformed into warning systems that can be used for both cooperative and competitive purposes, while Tedeschi, Bonoma, and Novinson (1970) suggest that punishment-counterpunishment sequences may occur regardless of the purposes to which threat tactics are put. Nardin (1968) suggests that threat-counterthreat spirals occur primarily when actors perceive a competitive intent underlying the use of threats. Intent may indeed be a critical element. Punishment is clearly competitive in intent, whereas the intent underlying threats may depend on the context. If this is true, we would expect more consistent evidence for a punishment-counterpunishment spiral than for a threat-counterthreat spiral.

A more general problem with the conflict-spiral tradition, however, is that researchers make no attempt to take account of deterrence theory. Perhaps social psychologists implicitly accept the idea that deterrence is the exclusive province of international relations. However, the conflict-spiral notion applies to the same circumstances that underlie our formalization of deterrence theory, yet the broadest implication of the conflict-spiral notion contradicts deterrence theory. To make explicit the comparison of deterrence theory and the conflict-spiral notion, Figure 5 presents the core propositions of our conflict-spiral theory. A comparison of Figures 4 and 5 reveals one major

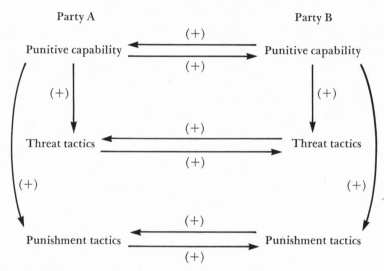

Figure 5. A Theory of Conflict Spiral

point of similarity, one major point of difference, and one major point of complementarity.

The major similarity is that the theory of conflict spiral also accepts assumption 1 and propositions 1 and 2 of deterrence theory. Recall these ideas indicate that each party attempts to match efforts by the opponent to accumulate more punitive capability and, therefore, an increase in one party's punitive capability produces an increase in the other's punitive capability. The major difference between the theories concerns the major determinant of threat and punishment tactics. Deterrence theory sees a party's use of threats and punishment as determined by the opponent's punitive capability, while conflict-spiral sees the use of threats and punishments as based on the party's own punitive capability. This difference, in turn, is based on divergent emphases on the fear of retaliation and the temptation implied in punitive capabilities. Deterrence theory indicates that actors attend closely to the prospective costs of retaliation by the opponent, and this fear reduces the tactical use of threats and punishments as punitive capabilities become larger. In contrast, conflict-spiral theory emphasizes the temptation of larger punitive capabilities. A party is tempted to use a punitive capability to bluff its opponent into yielding, and this temptation increases as the party's own punitive capability increases. As punitive capabilities in a relationship increase, someone will eventually succumb to temptation and resort to the use of punitive tactics. These contrasting hypotheses form the basic contrast between the theories: With the relationship as the unit of analysis, deterrence theory predicts greater punitive capabilities decrease the frequency of punitive tactics, while conflict-spiral theory predicts greater punitive capabilities increase the frequency of punitive tactics.

To summarize, assumption 1 and propositions 1 and 2 represent the points of similarity. In lieu of assumption 2 of deterrence theory, our theory of conflict spiral implies that both parties view their own magnitude of capability as an index of their opportunity to bluff or intimidate the other—the greater A's punitive capabilities, the greater A's temptation to use that capability. Thus the theory of conflict spiral substitutes the following propositions for propositions 3-5 and 7-9 of deterrence theory.

Proposition 1. An increase in A's punitive capability increases A's use of threat and punishment tactics.

Proposition 2. An increase in B's punitive capability increases B's use of threat and punishment tactics.

Proposition 3. An increase in the level of punitive capability *within the relationship* increases the level of threat and punishment tactics *within the relationship*.

The primary contrast of concern to us is between this proposition 3 and propositions 5 and 9 of deterrence theory.

Turning to the major point of complementarity, we note that the two theories can be construed as taking different but not incompatible positions on the role of reciprocity. Both theories indicate that parties reciprocate each other's efforts to accumulate punitive capabilities, but only the theory of conflict spiral extends this reciprocity principle to the tactical level. Specifically, conflict-spiral theory posits the following:

Proposition 4. The greater the use of threat tactics by one party, the greater the use of such tactics by the other.

Proposition 5. The greater the use of punishment tactics by one party, the greater the use of such tactics by the other.

These tactic-reciprocation propositions reflect the ways in which the use of punitive tactics involves behavior designed to "save face." Yielding in response to a punitive tactic ostensibly results in a loss of face, and parties will risk substantial costs in order to avert this. These propositions assume that parties in conflict are concerned with the image they project to others (and even to themselves) and that they go to great pains to avoid projecting an image of weakness. An image of weakness not only entails pragmatic or utilitarian consequences but also is, in the last analysis, socially demeaning. Yielding to a punitive tactic accords deference to the opponent and makes the party appear to be unwilling to defend and protect its rights, beliefs, or interests.

Social psychological research generally affirms the notion that parties are willing to "cut off their nose to save their face" and that saving face is often an obstacle to serious bargaining. However, there is relatively little understanding of the conditions under which threats do or do not arouse the face-saving responses (Brown, 1968, 1977; Rubin and Brown, 1975). We have suggested elsewhere (Bacharach and Lawler, 1980, chap. 8) that attribution theory can yield some insight into the conditions under which threats arouse face-saving responses, because this issue raises a question tantamount to the most basic one underlying attribution theory: When do persons attribute negative qualities to an actor? Weakness is the negative quality of concern in conflict relationships, and the basic implication of attribution theory is that weakness is attributed to a party that complies with a threat only when the compliance is ascribed to characteristics of the party (internal causality), not when it is ascribed to forces outside the party (external causality). From our approach, the party in question need not be an individual, as in attribution theory, but may be a group or organization. That is, internal causality does not refer solely to the psychological processes or personality characteristics of an individual, but also to the internal workings of a group in conflict with another group.

One of the most important implications of the attribution approach is that the relative power in conflict relationships qualifies the prominence or strength of face-saving behavior. If the target of a threat tactic is in a decidedly inferior power position, compliance to the threat may not entail a loss of face because the context, rather than the party, can be viewed as the prime determinant of compliance. However, the more equal the power of the conflicting parties, the more likely the use of punitive tactics is to arouse face-saving behavior. We have suggested that deterrence theory is of prime relevance to bilateral power settings in which all parties have substantial power, and in particular if the power is approximately equal. The attribution approach would argue that these are also the conditions in which the use of punitive tactics is least effective. Thus, the attribution approach (see Bacharach and Lawler, 1980) supports the tactic-reciprocation propositions of conflict-spiral theory.

These tactic-reciprocation propositions cannot be derived from deterrence theory, but neither do they clearly contradict that theory. First, these conflict-spiral propositions assume that one party has already used a punitive tactic. Thus in any specific context we could find support both for deterrence theory and for some propositions of conflict-spiral theory. Greater punitive capabilities could lead to less use of punitive tactics, but at the same time, when such tactics are used they could elicit reciprocal tactics, such as counterthreats. Second, one can argue that parties who practice deterrence are implicitly accepting the tactic-reciprocation hypotheses, that is, they expect each other to reciprocate punitive tactics. This is the essence of retaliation—the probability that the other will reciprocate aggression if a party initiates it. This point of complementarity is important because it affords a way to integrate the mutual concerns of the two theories and place the basic difference in context, as we illustrate in Chapter Five.

Summary

In this chapter, we developed a theory of deterrence and a theory of conflict spiral. These theories interrelate punitive capabilities, threat tactics, and punishment tactics in a somewhat different manner. Conflict-spiral theory indicates that the accumulation of punitive capabilities within a bargaining relationship increases the likelihood of punitive tactics and the degree to which parties reciprocate such tactics. In contrast, deterrence theory indicates that greater punitive capabilities enhance the fear of retaliation and, thereby, decrease the frequency of threat and punishment tactics. From the theory of conflict spiral, it is in the interest of both parties to avoid the reciprocal use of punitive tactics and to do so by reducing the punitive capabilities within the relationship. According to the theory of deterrence, the development of greater punitive capabilities is in the interest of both parties because this creates a significant obstacle to the use of punitive tactics in bargaining.

Our explication of these theories also identifies some similarities and complementarities between these theories. The major similarity is that both assume parties reciprocate each other's efforts to further develop punitive capabilities. The implication is that, all other things being equal, neither party is likely to acquire an advantage over the other by attempting to accumulate greater punitive capability—because the other will undertake reciprocal action. This reciprocal action maintains the relative punitive capability of parties as long as both are equal in their ability and willingness to develop additional punitive capability. The major complementarity is that conflict-spiral theory emphasizes reciprocity at a tactical level, an emphasis that is, at best, only implicit in deterrence theory. In the next chapter, we elaborate the similarities, complementarities, and differences within these theories, relate deterrence and conflict-spiral notions to our dependence framework, and illustrate these ideas with experimental data.

5

Punitive Tactics

▼▼▼

A comparison between deterrence and conflict-spiral theories raises two questions: Are there conditions under which punitive capabilities are negatively related to the use of punitive tactics (deterrence prediction), and other conditions under which punitive capabilities are positively related to the use of punitive tactics (conflict-spiral prediction)? Are the different behavioral patterns, specified by the theories, ever found simultaneously in the same context? In this chapter, we examine the similarities and differences between deterrence and conflict-spiral theories in the context of our dependence framework on bargaining. The neglect of the dependence or bargaining-power relationship represents a serious defect in the theoretical and empirical literature from which we developed deterrence and conflict-spiral theories. Most theorists and researchers implicitly assume that parties are dependent on one another, but no one has explicitly attempted to consider how variations in the underlying dependence relationship can affect deterrence or conflict-spiral processes. We attempt to fill this void by relating dependence the-

ory to punitive tactics and using some original experimental
data to examine empirical issues suggested by our contrast of
deterrence and conflict.

In this chapter, we stress circumstances in which punitive
capabilities are equal, but the total magnitude of these capabilities varies within the relationship; similarly, we focus on dependence relationships within which relative dependence is
equal but there is variation in total dependence. While these
conditions may appear to narrow our focus too greatly, precisely these conditions must be fully examined before we can
further extend our ideas about the relationship of deterrence to
dependence.

Dependence and Punitive Power

On an analytical level, there is little doubt that dependence and punitive notions of power are intertwined. Some
argue that power is ultimately coercive in nature (see Bierstedt,
1950), which obviously implies that punitive capability captures
the essence of power. Social exchange approaches imply a similar position by broadly conceptualizing power as the ability of
one party to levy costs on another (Emerson, 1962, 1972a,
1972b; Thibaut and Kelley, 1959). Within the exchange approach, the dependence notion of power can also be couched in
such cost terms—for example, the dependence of A on B can be
construed as B's ability to levy costs on A. We have shown elsewhere (Bacharach and Lawler, 1980) that the dependence of
one party on another is essentially identical to the other's punitive capability. However, the common foundation of dependence and punitive aspects of power does not obviate the need
to separate the implications of these forms of power, especially
in a tactical analysis, because these aspects are qualitatively different (Bacharach and Lawler, 1980), and their "costs" differ in
a way that is critical to a tactical analysis. Thus, while dependence and punitive power have a common, inseparable foundation, one must examine the different focuses embedded in these
notions of power.

Both notions of power assume that power is the ability to

impose costs, yet the costs of primary concern are different. Consider dependence theory first. Based on theories of social exchange, dependence theory tends to treat costs as the *outcome foregone,* that is, the benefits one forfeits by selecting between two mutually exclusive options. If one has two choices, and one chooses the first, then one's cost is the benefit attached to the second—the outcomes foregone. Consider a critical choice confronted by bargainers: agreement or nonagreement. In terms of outcomes foregone, the cost of agreement is the benefit that can be derived from the nonagreement option—for example, from alternative parties. This approach suggests that a party's power is proportional to its ability to induce an opponent to accept an agreement with smaller (rather than larger) differences between the outcomes from the agreement and those foregone. Dependence underlies this capability to impose outcome-foregone costs: The greater the dependence of A on B, the greater B's ability to induce A to accept an agreement in which the difference between the outcomes foregone and those obtained are small. The type of costs encompassed in outcomes foregone is essentially those that one incurs in order to maintain the bargaining relationship. In this sense, these costs are specific to the bargaining relationship. A party that leaves the relationship essentially removes itself from the situation in which such costs can or must be accepted.

In contrast, the costs emphasized in punitive concepts of power are not the outcomes foregone, but the punishment costs that bargainers might add to the outcomes foregone. These costs can be incurred at any point in the bargaining process, given the use of punishment tactics by one or both parties, and they can be incurred even if a party leaves the relationship. In fact, an opponent might levy the largest punishments in the event of such escape behavior by a party. For instance, the cost of leaving the relationship measured by the outcomes foregone is the benefit of staying in it; while the additional costs beyond these outcomes foregone, such as retaliation costs, are critical to the punitive approach. Thus, two types of cost are relevant to a party's power: outcomes foregone and punishment. The costs of agreement in bargaining should be conceptualized as equal to the sum of the outcomes foregone and punishment costs incurred during and after the bargaining that led to the agreement. The costs of nonagreement similarly include not only the outcomes foregone but also the punishments incurred by breaking off the relationship.

Given these different emphases regarding costs, we can ask whether and how the dependence and punitive dimensions of power may operate independently in actual social situations. Whether one distinguishes between dependence and punitive power is, in part, dependent on how finely one wants to draw certain conceptual distinctions, but it is also an empirical question. For our tactical analysis of conflict, the distinction appears to be critical. As noted earlier, tactical concessions and punitive tactics can be treated as very different strategies by bargainers. Attack, retaliation, and deterrence focus on punishment costs, while tactical concessions focus on manipulating the outcomes foregone. A tactical analysis that fails to take account of these differences blurs important empirical differences.

To further elucidate the contrast between dependence and punitive power, recall the theory and research on tactical concessions presented in Chapter Three. The theory did not explicitly refer to the punitive dimension of power, and the experimental procedures of the research did not give bargainers the ability to use punitive tactics (threats and punishment tactics). A punitive element of power was embedded in the dependence relationship, and the dimensions of dependence determined actors' capability of levying costs on each other. Nevertheless, bargainers were unable to directly manipulate each other's outcomes, that is, they had no punitive tactics. The explicit presence of punitive power gives bargainers tactical options that are not afforded by the dimensions of dependence. The dependence framework portrays the stakes each party has in the bargaining, but the dimensions of dependence do not provide the capacity for direct manipulation. In this sense, dependence relations can be construed as the context underlying punitive power and tactics.

To summarize, despite the common theoretical basis of dependence and punitive power, these dimensions of power imply different focuses, adopt different but complementary approaches to costs, and lay the groundwork for disparate forms of tactical behavior.

Empirical Issues

Six major empirical issues are posed by the theories of deterrence and conflict spiral. These empirical issues are ones that bargainers themselves must confront, but also ones that investigators must consider when applying the theories to particular contexts. Let us elucidate these issues and examine whether and how an integrative treatment of dependence and punitive capability facilitates more understanding than a sole concern with punitive capability.

The first issue is the most obvious and also most critical, because it concerns the primary point of contrast between deterrence and conflict-spiral theories: What effect do punitive capabilities have on the use of punitive tactics? The theories make directly opposite predictions: Deterrence posits a negative relationship, while conflict spiral posits a positive one. One of the most important questions is whether the level of mutual dependence in the relationship specifies or qualifies the predictions of these theories. This question is a major focus of our later theoretical discussion.

The second issue, closely related to the first, is whether the theories apply equally well to threat and punishment tactics. We noted in the last chapter that deterrence theory implies a sharper distinction between these tactics than conflict-spiral theory. Deterrence theory essentially sees threats as last-resort mechanisms for preserving deterrence and punishment tactics as symptomatic of the total breakdown in deterrence. Conflict-spiral theory offers a rationale for grouping threat and punishment tactics under a single rubric, but research in this tradition also hints that the spiral may occur more frequently for punishment than for threat tactics. The applicability of these theories to both threat and punishment tactics is an important empirical question for both deterrence and conflict-spiral theory.

The third issue, also related to the first, is whether the relationship between punitive capability and punitive tactics has a linear or nonlinear form. Previous research does not provide the answer because studies that manipulate punitive capability with bilateral power do not include enough punitive-capability conditions to examine the form of the relationship. By omission, deterrence and conflict-spiral theories imply linear relationships, but intuitively one can see some reason for curvilinear patterns. For example, the deterrence pattern may occur only with relatively high levels of punitive capabilities, meaning that a minimal threshold of punitive power is necessary before there is a reduction in punitive tactics. Or a conflict spiral might occur between very low and moderate levels of punitive capability, while deterrence is supported beyond moderate levels. These questions can be answered only through research that includes a full range of punitive capabilities, from very low to very high. This issue has obvious importance to scholars and practitioners alike, and our data allow a preliminary investigation.

The fourth issue is raised by the primary point of complementarity between the two theories: What is the relationship between the use of punitive tactics by one party and the use of such tactics by the other? Is the correlation between each party's use of threat and punishment tactics positive and, if so, how large or small are these relationships, and do they vary for threats and punishments? A low relationship would suggest that one of the principal grounds for maintaining deterrence, the fear of retaliation, is not strong and also that one of the core propositions of conflict-spiral theory is unwarranted or inapplicable to particular contexts. A high relationship not only would support a foundation for deterrence but would also support the idea of tactic-reciprocation in conflict-spiral theory. This issue is important because one of the tactical issues bargainers confront concerns the strength of the tactic-reciprocation for threats and punishments.

The fifth issue concerns the role of time. In a bargaining relationship in which parties have punitive capabilities, does the use of punitive tactics tend to increase or decrease over time? The conflict-spiral notion implies an increase because the temptation to punish leads parties to use punitive tactics early in the bargaining. The result is an upward spiral of use and counteruse without any specified endpoint. The spiral continues until the parties deplete their punitive resources, or they reach some accord, or a third party steps in to ameliorate the conflict, or they simply destroy each other. In contrast, the deterrence notion posits that the early use of such tactics is likely to make parties more aware of their respective punitive capabilities and, while there may be an immediate, brief spiral, the experience of retaliation tends to reduce the level of use over time in a bargaining relationship. Information on the use of punitive tactics at different times will indicate the greatest points of danger in a bargaining relationship. Such information could assist participants and third parties in their efforts to minimize damage.

The sixth, and last, issue is of unique relevance to explicit bargaining—the effect of punitive capabilities and the use of punitive tactics on tactical concessions. In Chapter Four, we developed an auxiliary component of deterrence theory predicting that greater punitive capabilities increase tactical concessions. Implicit in this notion is the corollary: The use of punitive tactics decreases tactical concessions. Indeed, the latter proposition is essentially the rationale for the former one. Conflict-spiral theory would accept the latter implication of deterrence theory but reject the former. Both theories would posit that the use of punitive tactics reduces tactical concessions and generally obstructs conflict resolution in explicit bargaining. But, given different analyses of punitive capabilities, deterrence theory hypothesizes a positive relationship between punitive capabilities and tactical concessons, whereas conflict-spiral theory suggests a negative relationship. In both cases, these hypotheses are auxiliary to the central propositions of the theories, so refutations do not bear on the credibility of the core propositions.

In the following theoretical discussion and presentation of illustrative experimental data, our major purpose is to indicate how the dependence relationship might relate to the deterrence and conflict-spiral theories. Dependence theory is most relevant to the first three issues and to the last issue. Thus, our concerns are actually twofold: to illustrate and apply deterrence and conflict-spiral theory and to show the relevance of dependence theory to the concerns of these theories.

Methodology

A few methodological comments about our data are warranted. First, the experimental procedures were virtually identical to those described in Chapter Three, with the following exceptions:

1. Each party's dependence on the other was equal across all experimental conditions. Total dependence was manipulated as low or high along both the alternatives and commitment dimensions.
2. Each party had a punitive capability, operationally defined as the maximum percentage of the other's winnings it could destroy. There were five punitive capability conditions: 10 percent, 30 percent, 50 percent, 70 percent, and 90 percent. Within each of these conditions, both parties had an equal punitive capability—both could destroy up to 10 percent of the other's winnings, up to 30 percent, and so forth. As noted earlier, to hold the punitive capabilities equal and the relative dependence equal is most consistent with the conditions of greatest concern to deterrence and conflict-spiral theories.
3. On each of fifteen bargaining rounds, bargainers could, in addition to submitting an offer, administer a warning or fine—the warning was a threat to fine if the other did not yield more, and the fine was the actual administration of the punishment. These threats were tailored to a bargaining situation in that they were directed at the other's concession behavior.
4. A bargainer could not administer a threat and a punishment on the same bargaining round. This restriction is realistic because these are theoretically exclusive forms of behavior—a threat is a threat only in the absence of a simultaneous punishment. Threats typically precede punishment tactics and, at given points in time, are an alternative way of using punitive tactics. A bargainer did not have to administer a threat before a fine, a rule unlike that of some studies (see, for example, Michener and Cohen, 1973).

5. There was no limit on the number of threats, except that no
   more than one per round was possible. In the case of fines,
   we set a maximum of five in order to make the maximum
   number of fines constant across punitive capability conditions. In the absence of this control, one could argue that
   high punitive capability conditions allow for more punishments because it can take longer to reach the maximum level
   of damage. In this context, support for the conflict-spiral
   theory—higher use of punishment in higher punitive-capability conditions—could be construed as an artifact of the experimental manipulations. To eliminate this problem, we set
   the maximum at five and each fine reduced the opponent's
   winnings by one fifth of the maximum allowed by the punitive capability condition: 2 percent, 6 percent, and so on.
   Thus bargainers could decide whether, when, and how often
   to punish, but could not establish the magnitude for each
   punishment. This slight reduction in the bargainer's discre-
   tion was necessary to provide a clear contrast for deterrence
   and conflict-spiral theories.

Within these rules, the research design manipulated the
total dependence on the commitment dimension (low or high),
the total dependence on the alternatives dimension (low or
high), and the five mutual punitive capabilities in a 2 X 2 X 5
factorial design. Ten pairs (half male and half female) were ran-
domly assigned to each of the twenty experimental conditions.
Our analysis treated subject within the pair as a within-subjects
factor and, therefore, any role or subject effects are removed
from our treatment of the experimental manipulations. Our
analysis focused on three primary dependent variables: proportion of rounds on which punishment administered, proportion
of rounds on which threat administered, and the average size of
concession. To measure these variables, we used the ratios of
punishments to rounds and threats to the number of rounds because the number of rounds varied somewhat, given that bargainers could reach agreement before the last (fifteenth) round. The
measure of tactical concessions is the average concession per
round because the control for round makes this more com-

parable to the measures of punitive tactics. With these methodological comments as a backdrop, we now turn to the six empirical issues detailed earlier in this chapter.

Interaction of Dependence and Punitive Capability

The dependence relationship can be construed as the context within which punitive capabilities can have either deterrence or conflict-spiral effects. The dependence relationship em-
bodies the stakes bargainers have in the conflict, and consequently, bargainers' strength or weakness on the two dimensions
of dependence determines their stakes. A pair of bargainers have
a high mutual stake in the conflict to the extent that both are
highly committed to the outcomes and both have relatively
poor alternatives from which they can get the same or substitutable outcomes. Although these dimensions are qualitatively
different in some respects, both are indicators of bargaining
power. Our purpose here is to determine whether these dimensions of bargaining power are equally important in qualifying or
specifying deterrence and conflict-spiral effects of punitive
capabilities. Our earlier discussion leads us to expect the alternatives dimension to be of greater importance.

The basic question is: Does mutual dependence (on either
or both commitment and alternatives dimensions) specify conditions under which we find support for deterrence or conflict-
spiral predictions? One approach to this question is to simply
stress the commonality of tactical concessions and punitive tactics. One could argue that punitive tactics, like small concessions, are means to convey toughness in bargaining, and one
would simply extend the ideas on the relation of total dependence and tactical concessions to punitive tactics. This extension leads to the proposition: Greater mutual dependence induces parties to act in accord with deterrence rather than conflict-spiral theory. Although this proposition is certainly reasonable, the approach is faulty because it neglects the qualitative
differences between tactical concessions and punitive tactics, in
particular, the differential orientation or intent underlying these
tactics. Therefore, we must adopt a somewhat broader approach,

one which considers the intent or orientation motivating the use of or failure to use punitive tactics.

In conflict and bargaining research, three primary orientations receive the greatest attention: individualistic, competitive, and cooperative (Rubin and Brown, 1975). A party with an individualistic orientation attempts to maximize its own individual gain without regard for the gains or losses of the other party. A party with a competitive orientation focuses on outdoing the other—that is, maximizing the difference between itself and its opponent. A party with a cooperative orientation attempts to maximize joint or mutual gain. Parties are likely to adopt all three orientations at different times or on different issues in bargaining relationships, but the individualistic orientation is implicitly or explicitly held to be the most dominant in conflict and bargaining.

A similar assumption underlies our theory and research, as we have indicated earlier. It is worth noting that orientations such as individualistic ones are global categories. In some cases, these orientations assume the connotations of a personality characteristic and, for example, the individualistic orientation becomes a generalized tendency to adopt certain patterns of behavior across conflict issues, tactics, time, and specific situations (Rubin and Brown, 1975). While this global approach has merit, a tactical analysis of bargaining leads one to consider subcategories of this general orientation. If we define *gain* as net gain, an individualistic orientation can imply maximizing gain or minimizing losses.

This distinction between gains and losses seems particularly important to an analysis of punitive capabilities and punitive tactics. Consider the temptation that is critical to conflict-spiral theory and the fear of retaliation that is so important to deterrence theory. The construct *temptation* implies that parties are likely to "go for broke," that is, concentrate on anticipated gains from the use of punitive tactics. The fear of retaliation, in contrast, implies a primary concern with the losses anticipated from using punitive tactics. Thus two variants of the individualistic orientation underlie the predictions of deterrence and conflict-spiral theories. Deterrence implies an emphasis on minimizing losses, while conflict-spiral theory implies an emphasis on maximizing gain. The traditional equation of individualistic and maximizing-gain orientations is inappropriate—an individualistic orientation can lead to a focus on maximizing gain or minimizing losses.

The contrast between maximizing gain and minimizing loss is also important to the relationship of dependence and deterrence. The consequences of a maximizing-gain or minimizing-loss orientation should vary with the stakes in the bargaining, and dependence theory integrates the stakes in the analysis. Given that the conflict spiral implies a focus on maximizing gain, one might argue that the conflict spiral is most likely to occur when parties have much to gain—that is, when both have poor alternatives or both have high commitment to the outcomes. Yet these are precisely the conditions under which parties might have the greatest fear of retaliation and be most concerned with minimizing losses. If minimizing losses is the dominant concern, then one should find support for the deterrence predictions under high stakes. These considerations suggest that the nature of the interaction between the dependence relationship and punitive capability is contingent on the type of individualistic orientation adopted by the parties. Specifically, one can justify two contradictory propositions:

Proposition 1. The deterrence prediction (that is, negative relationship of punitive capability and use of punitive tactics) occurs when stakes are high, and the conflict-spiral prediction (that is, positive relationship of punitive capability and use of punitive tactics) occurs when stakes are low.

Proposition 2. The deterrence prediction occurs when stakes are low, and the conflict-spiral prediction occurs when stakes are high.

The first proposition assumes that bargainers focus on the problem of minimizing losses. Given high stakes, such as high dependence on the alternative dimensions, bargainers are especially concerned about risking a conflict spiral and act in accord with deterrence theory. However, low stakes imply that they have less to lose by using punitive tactics. Temptation would probably override fear of retaliation, and consequently, bargainers would act in accord with conflict-spiral theory. The second proposition is based on the assumption that bargainers focus on the problem of maximizing gain. With this orientation, high stakes tempt both parties to "go for broke" by using punitive tactics to intimidate the other. The result, of course, is a higher rate of punitive tactics under higher levels of punitive capability, that is, the conflict spiral. With low stakes, bargainers with a maximizing-gain orientation simply see less to win by "going for broke." The potential costs are less, but the temptation underlying the conflict spiral is also lower. Under these circumstances, bargainers attempt to protect their current situation and respond to different levels of punitive capability in a manner consistent with deterrence theory. In sum, our reformulation of individualistic orientations leads to two contradictory, but equally plausible, propositions. Let us examine some preliminary data on these issues.

Two basic analyses are necessary to fully examine these propositions: first, an analysis of variance relating punitive capability and the dimensions of bargaining power (dependence) to the use of threat and punishment tactics and, second, a trend analysis for the five conditions of punitive capability in our data. As we turn to the findings, the commitment dimension has no main or interaction effects, so our discussion will focus on the interaction of the alternative dimensions and punitive capability.

The major finding for punishment tactics is an interaction of mutual or total dependence (on the alternatives dimension) and punitive capability. These data (and pertinent significance tests) are presented in Table 4. The pattern of means and trend analysis suggests greater support for proposition 2, based on the maximizing-gain orientation. Specifically, a linear trend for punitive capability under low mutual dependence reveals a deterrence pattern in support of the second proposition. Under high mutual dependence, the conflict-spiral prediction of proposition 2 is not fully supported, although there is a trend toward

Table 4. Frequency of Punishment Tactics and Threat Tactics by
Punitive Capability and Mutual Dependence on Alternatives

Level of Mutual Dependence	Type of Tactic	Punitive Capability, in Percentages				
		10	30	50	70	90
Low	Punishment	.23	.17	.17	.18	.13
	Threat	.31	.28	.26	.26	.16
High	Punishment	.15	.24	.13	.09	.14
	Threat	.21	.24	.20	.26	.22

Note: The numerical values in the table refer to the proportion of rounds on which one of the parties used a punishment tactic or threat tactic. The behavior of both subjects is combined in the table, consistent with the dyad level of analysis. (No role or by-subject interactions specify these data.)

ANOVA results for Punishment: Mutual Dependence, $F(1, 180) = 2.42$, NS; Punitive Capability, $F(1, 180) = 2.37$, $p < .05$; Mutual Dependence $\times$ Punitive Capability, $F(4, 180) = 2.91$, $p < .02$.

Trend Analysis for Punishment: within low mutual dependence: Linear $F = 4.15$, $p < .04$; Quadratic $F < 1$; Cubic $F = 1.92$, NS; within high mutual dependence: Linear $F = 3.30$, $p < .07$; Quadratic $F < 1$; Cubic $F = 12.18$, $p < .001$.

ANOVA results for Threat Tactics: Mutual Dependence, $F(1,180) = 2.15$, NS; Punitive Capability, $F(1, 180) = 1.61$, NS; Mutual Dependence $\times$ Punitive Capability, $F(4, 180) = 1.62$, NS.

Trend Analysis for Threat Tactics: within low mutual dependence: Linear $F = 8.01$, $p < .005$; Quadratic $F < 1$; Cubic $F < 1$; within high mutual dependence: All F's < 2.

a conflict spiral at the lowest and highest levels of punitive capability. (This overall cubic trend is judged significant by the trend analysis—see Table 4.) Overall, our preliminary data on the interaction of punitive and dependence dimensions of power imply somewhat greater support for proposition 2.

The pattern for threat tactics within the low mutual dependence condition dovetails with that for punishment tactics (see Table 4)—although the data for threat tactics are weaker than for punishment tactics, because the mutual dependence-punitive capability interaction is not significant. The trend analysis, once again, indicates a significant linear trend in support of the deterrence prediction (and proposition 2). In the case of high mutual dependence, there are no significant trends, indicating that the cubic trend for punishment tactics does not generalize to threats. Overall, the absence of completely consistent results for punishment and threat tactics affirms the importance of considering the differences, as well as the similarities, of threat and punishment tactics.

These data on threat and punishment tactics must be viewed as tentative. We consider the data as illustrative or suggestive and use them as much to generate ideas as to test ideas. With this caveat, we present a number of broad implications. First, deterrence is most likely to occur when mutual dependence is low. This is interesting because it suggests that it is not that parties have "everything to lose" that underlies deterrence but that they simply have "less to win." It appears that deterrence is based, in part, on a desire of parties not to endanger their current situation, as any costs suffered, in a conflict spiral, are incurred regardless of whether they reach agreement or opt for the alternative. Given good alternatives, the most prudent approach is to "sit tight" and conclude the current bargaining encounter with a minimum of losses from the opponent's punitive capability. Deterrence, in this context, can be construed as a means for parties to keep their distance and not interfere with other relationships or outcome sources that are available to them. Thus, the development of mutual deterrence may be contingent not just on high punitive capabilities but also on the ability of bargainers to develop and maintain alternatives that minimize their dependence on each other.

It is interesting that conditions of high mutual dependence show little evidence of deterrence. As noted earlier, if one classifies tactical concessions and punitive tactics under the toughness rubric, our analysis of total power (dependence) and tactical concessions (see Chapter Three) indicates that high mutual dependence adds to the total power (sum of dependence power and punitive power) such that deterrence is even more likely under high mutual dependence. The failure of this idea implies, once again, the importance of viewing tactical concessions and punitive tactics as qualitatively different modes of tactical action and the importance of distinguishing the foundation of these tactics: dependence and punitive capability, respectively.

Another reason for expecting deterrence under high mutual dependence is expressed in the rationale for proposition 1. The combination of high mutual dependence and high punitive capability should accentuate the fear of retaliation and make the minimizing-loss orientation dominate the maximizing-gain one. The failure of deterrence under these conditions strongly implies the importance of considering the temptation component of conflict-spiral theory in establishing and fostering a deterrence relationship. Even though a conflict-spiral pattern was not observed consistently under high mutual dependence, the failure of deterrence, itself, implies difficulties for bargainers who assume that accumulating punitive capabilities is a pathway to security and defense.

Overall, the support for proposition 2 has implications for comparing bargaining relationships in different institutional spheres. Consider bargaining in international and labor-management relationships. Within each of these spheres, the level of mutual dependence can and does vary substantially. Nevertheless, if one conceptualizes mutual dependence as a continuum, one can argue that international relationships are more likely to have lower levels of mutual dependence than labor-management relationships. The institutionalization of collective bargaining between unions and corporations tends to limit the lower threshold of mutual dependence at a level above the theoretical minimum. Extrapolating from our data, we hypothesize that deterrence is more likely in international than in labor-management bargaining, because the former relationships are more likely to involve lower levels of mutual dependence. Therefore, participants in international and labor-management relationships should have different approaches to punitive capabilities and tactics. In international contexts, participants should emphasize the deterrent capabilities of punitive power, while labor or management bargainers should be more concerned with the conflict-spiral effects of punitive power. We speculate that accumulating punitive capabilities is a more fruitful strategy in international relations, while the mutual reduction of such capabilities is more central to collective bargaining between labor and management. These speculations are, of course, contingent on many of the specific circumstances of international and labor-management bargaining. Clearly, both deterrence and conflict-spiral theories are relevant to both settings, but there may be some difference in the relative emphasis practioners should place on deterrence and conflict-spiral analyses of punitive tactics in their bargaining.

Beyond these interpretive comments, a qualification of the deterrence effect warrants mention. The pattern of means indicates that the primary difference is between the lowest and highest levels of punitive capability. Thus, even under conditions of low mutual dependence, deterrence seems to succeed at very high levels of punitive capability and fails at very low levels. The practical import of this pattern is that further accumulation of punitive capabilities inhibits punitive action only when parties start at a very low level or move from a situation of relatively high to very high levels of punitive capability.

Punitive Tactics over Time

Do punitive tactics escalate, deescalate, or reveal a curvilinear pattern across time in a bargaining relationship? This question is primarily the province of conflict-spiral theory, but one can also draw implications from deterrence theory. Conflict-spiral theory suggests that the use of punitive tactics begins early in the bargaining and generally increases with time. Strict deterrence theory predicts little or no use of punitive tactics early and even later in the bargaining. However, in the event that these tactics are used, deterrence theory implies a curvilinear pattern. Early use begets counteruse and a small spiral. Yet, as bargainers cognitively process their experience of retaliation and counterretaliation, the use of punitive tactics decreases during later phases of bargaining. Deterrence theory predicts an initial increase followed by a decrease in the use of punitive tactics, a pattern that should be particularly evident at high levels of punitive capability.

To explore this issue, we divided the fifteen rounds of the bargaining into three blocks of five rounds each (excluding those pairs that concluded before the fifteenth round). These blocks roughly represent the early, middle, and late phases of the bargaining. We then added bargaining phase as a factor, creating a $2 \times 2 \times 5 \times 3$ design, and did an analysis of variance with frequency of threats or punishments as the dependent variables. The results for threat and punishment tactics are presented in Figure 6. The major findings are effects for bargaining

Figure 6. Threat and Punishment Tactics over Three Phases of Bargaining

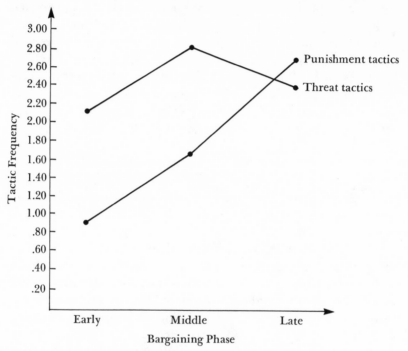

Note: Phase main effect, for punishment tactics, $F = 247.95$,
       $p < .001$; phase main effect on threat tactics, $F = 35.19$,
       $p < .001$.

phase on both threat and punishment tactics. Only one other effect occurs—for punishment tactics, the interaction of punitive capability and mutual dependence on alternatives (discussed earlier).

Figure 6 clearly shows that punishment tactics escalate over time in a bargaining relationship. This fact provides rather strong support for the conflict-spiral hypothesis and refutes our derivation from deterrence theory. This finding is important because, given the support for deterrence in the last section, it illustrates that elements of both deterrence and conflict spiral can occur simultaneously. The overall rate of punitive tactics, across conditions of punitive capability, reveals a deterrence pattern, while, at the same time, the actual use of punishment leads to an escalation over time. A low use of punishment tactics under high levels of punitive capability may conceal a tendency toward escalation within the context of that low overall rate. Simultaneous patterns of deterrence and conflict spiral, of course, are possible only if deterrence is not perfect; that is, if punitive capabilities do not completely eradicate the use of punitive tactics. There has to be some minimal level of tactic use, within the context of the negative relationship to punitive capability, in order for both patterns to be evident in an actual setting. In this sense, the escalation of punishment tactics over time, regardless of the absolute usage level, is symptomatic of the absence of perfect deterrence. Given the potential copresence of deterrence and conflict-spiral tendencies, an overall deterrence effect should not mislead bargainers into believing that periodic use of punitive tactics does not have deleterious effects on the bargaining relationship.

For threat tactics, Figure 6 reveals a curvilinear pattern. Threat tactics increase from early to middle phases of the bargaining and then decrease in the late bargaining phase. This pattern is consistent with the prediction derived from deterrence theory. However, the curvilinear notion from deterrence applies only to punishment tactics, not to threats. Deterrence assumes that the experience of retaliation evinces to bargainers the "error of their ways" and prompts them to lower use later in the bargaining. Because threats do not provide the direct experience of retaliation or damage, it is not appropriate to interpret the curvilinear pattern for threats as support for deterrence.

Instead, the pattern for threats should be viewed in relation to punishment tactics. There are more threats than punishments in the early and middle phases of the bargaining, which seems to suggest more bluffing at these points. If threats are used as a bluff tactic, then one would expect an excess of threats over punishment because bluffing implies that the threats will not always be enacted. With this interpretation, the escalation of threats from the early to the middle phases of bargaining can be construed as an attempt to induce concessions from the other without having to resort to punishment. Once the escalatory processes for both threats and punishments is well established, however, such bluffing becomes futile, and the conflict spiral turns primarily into a punishment-counterpunishment spiral. This explains the dip in threat tactics and continued increase in punishment tactics in the late phase of the bargaining. Overall, this interpretation of Figure 6 suggests that punishment tactics are the most critical elements of the spiral, while threats are best conceived as tactical devices for avoiding a mutually damaging spiral but which inadvertently contribute to it at the same time. Bargainers appear to escalate their use of threats and punishment tactics when bluffing with threats, but they reduce their bluffing once the escalatory processes are fully established.

Tactic Reciprocation

The escalatory processes in the use of threat and punishment tactics suggest that parties reciprocate. How strong is this general pattern of tactical reciprocity? Is it comparable across threat and punishment tactics? Let us recall that this is the primary point of complementarity between deterrence and conflict-spiral theories—conflict spiral explicitly assumes tactical reciprocity while deterrence implies it by focusing on the fear of retaliation. Table 5 presents our correlational data on the reciprocity of threat and punishment tactics.

The data show a general tendency toward reciprocity across tactics, but it is stronger for punishment tactics. This finding adds further credence to our earlier contention that punishment tactics are most critical to the escalatory processes underlying a conflict spiral. On a practical level, this finding also suggests that threat tactics have a less damaging effect on an overall pattern of deterrence. Another implication is that the tendency toward tactic reciprocity is not determined by the level of punitive capability in the relationship. Tactic reciprocity

Table 5. Tactic Reciprocity by Punitive Capability

	Punitive Capability, in Percentages				
	10	30	50	70	90
Threat reciprocity	.62	.53	.55	.57	.46
Punishment reciprocity	.88	.88	.83	.83	.96

Note: Threat reciprocity refers to the correlation between the frequency of bargainer A's threats and bargainer B's threats; punishment reciprocity is the correlation of each bargainer's frequency of punishment tactics.

is a general pattern, and high or low punitive capabilities do not insulate bargainers from the consequences of these tactical patterns. Thus we see once again that an existing condition of deterrence does not safeguard against a conflict spiral in the event of tactic use.

The correlations suggest that the more one party uses a tactic, especially a punishment tactic, the more the other will use that same tactic. This pattern is only one form of reciprocity, which we label *general reciprocity*. Another form, *specific reciprocity*, involves actual "tit for tat" use of punitive tactics. Specific reciprocity implies that the immediate response to a punishment tactic is a punishment tactic. General reciprocity, in contrast, suggests that a punishment by one party tends to be followed *at some point* by counterpunishment but not necessarily immediately. Obviously, correlational data can illustrate only the general form of reciprocity.

For some preliminary information on specific reciprocity, we did a contingent probability analysis of threat and punishment tactics. The data indicate that there was about one chance in three (.35) that a party would immediately respond to a threat with a threat, and there was about one chance in two (.48) that a punishment tactic would be followed immediately by a punishment tactic. Consistent with the correlational data, punishment tactics are more likely to be reciprocated than threat tactics. However, these probabilities are in an absolute sense smaller than one might expect. Bargainers appear to act in terms of general reciprocity more than specific reciprocity, which suggests that a bargainer who uses a punishment tactic might be misled by the lack of immediate retaliation—retaliation is not necessarily immediate.

Punitive Tactics and Tactical Concessions

Deterrence and conflict-spiral theories have convergent and divergent implications for concession behavior. They converge in that both theories implicitly posit a negative relationship between punitive tactics and concession making, but the theories differ in their explanation of this relationship. Conflict-spiral theory links this proposition to the face-saving consequences of punitive tactics and suggests that a bargainer can lose face by making concessions in response to an opponent's threat. Deterrence theory argues that the fear of retaliation in a bargaining context is based partly on the possibility that punitive tactics heighten the level of mutual antagonism and create an impasse. For different reasons, then, the theories imply that punitive tactics inhibit concession behavior. Combining this convergence with different ways of treating punitive capabilities, the theories make different predictions regarding the effect of punitive capabilities on concession behavior. Since high capability reduces the use of punitive tactics, according to deterrence theory, greater capability should also facilitate greater concessions. In contrast, since high capability increases the use of punitive tactics, according to conflict-spiral theory, greater capability should reduce concessions.

Our analysis of variance does not reveal any effects for punitive capability on concession behavior. In conjunction with the information in Chapter Three, this finding indicates that the dependence aspect of power is more critical to an understanding of tactical concessions than punitive capability. This comparison again emphasizes the need to distinguish dependence from punitive aspects of power in an analysis of bargaining. Earlier in this chapter, we argued that the relevance of this distinction is partly an empirical question. These and other data in this chapter repeatedly affirm the importance of the distinction.

Although punitive capability has no effect on concession behavior, punitive tactics could be related to concession behavior. As noted earlier, both theories imply a negative relationship. Table 6 shows the zero-order correlations between a given

Table 6. Relationship of Concession Behavior to
Opponent's Punitive Tactics

	Punitive Capability, in Percentages				
	10	30	50	70	90
B's threats and A's concessions	−.33	−.13	−.18	.04	−.18
A's threats and B's concessions	−.32	.13	.07	.09	−.01
B's punishments and A's concessions	−.01	−.26	−.25	−.45	−.21
A's punishments and B's concessions	.05	−.24	−.28	−.24	−.29

Note: These data are zero-order correlations between A's punitive tactics and B's concessions and B's punitive tactics and A's concessions.

bargainer's punitive tactics and the opponent's concession behavior for each punitive-capability condition. With very low punitive capability, threats have a negative relationship to concession behavior, but at higher levels of punitive capability such tactics are unrelated to concession behavior. The negative relationship under very low punitive capability may represent the fact that threats with little capability backing them up seem insulting to the opponent. The party using such threats may project an impression of being petty or stupid, or attempting to exploit every possible advantage. Beyond very low levels of punitive capability, those using threats might be taken more seriously as the prospective level of damage increases. In this sense, punitive capabilities can be construed as the context within which parties attach meaning to the threat and attribute intentions to the threatener.

In the case of punishment tactics, the results are the reverse of those for threat tactics. There is a negative relationship to concessions only when the punitive capability is beyond the minimal level (that is, 30 percent or above). Punishment tactics are evaluated on the basis of the damage, probably because damage is actually realized. Beyond some minimal threshold, the damage of such tactics is sufficient to engender the negative relationship to concession behavior. Overall, in deciding how to respond to punishment tactics, bargainers appear to pay greatest attention to the actual damage, while their response to threats may be determined by the symbolic import of threats because threats themselves do not produce damage.

The most interesting implication of the data in Table 6 is that our experiments produced no evidence that threat or punishment tactics facilitate an opponent's concessions. There are a few positive correlations, but these are very small and do not show a consistent pattern. While these data are correlational, they call into question the usefulness of employing punitive tactics in a bargaining relationship—at least, when parties' stakes are relatively equal. In fact, these tactics can be counterproductive. Threats, as bluffs, are useful to convey a willingness to use punitive capabilities or make the opponent aware of these capabilities (see Bacharach and Lawler, 1980, chap. 8, for a detailed discussion of threat communications); however, if the bluff is called and the threatener follows through with punishment, the result may be a reduction in the opponent's concession making. This general conclusion is somewhat similar to ones reached by theorists concerned with strikes and other forms of punitive action in labor-management settings. It is ostensibly the threat of a strike or potential damage implied in the threat that induces concessions near the deadline (see, for example, Hicks, 1963). Threats and punishments before the final phases of bargaining are as likely to engender resistance as compliance.

However, we must make an important qualification to this general conclusion on the relationship of punitive tactics to concession making. The qualification is based on a distinction between the resources a bargainer wishes to obtain from the opponent and the resources the bargainer must give in exchange for those desired from the opponent. This distinction is applicable not only to the bargaining relationship in progress but also to alternative ones. Bargainers evaluate what they might get from alternatives and what they might have to give in return, and compare these resources to those at issue in their current bargaining. The critical point is that the resources (to be obtained or to be given) are likely to be qualitatively different, especially when bargaining involves multiple issues. Traditional approaches to bargaining attempt to reduce these qualitatively different resources to some unidimensional construct like utility and conclude that punishment tactics are counter to the user's interests because such action depletes the resources that the opponent is able to exchange in the final settlement.

The dependence framework, however, allows qualitative differences to be considered in analyses of punitive tactics. Our separation of dependence and punitive aspects of power implies the need to consider qualitatively different resources controlled by bargainers. Only some of these resources are likely to be under direct negotiation; that is, some fall outside current bargaining, while others are intrinsic to the particular issues under negotiation. It follows that the most effective punishment tactics are those that deprive the opponent of resources that the user neither wants nor expects the opponent to surrender in the bargaining. With such tactics, the target of punishment suffers some loss, but a loss is not necessarily incurred by the user of the tactic—a point neglected by most bargaining theories. Thus, we offer the following proposition:

Proposition 3. Other things being equal, punitive tactics that are directed at resources not a part of the bargaining have a positive effect on the concession behavior, while those directed at resources directly involved in the bargaining have a negative effect on the opponent's concessions.

To conclude, let us emphasize four points. First, on both a theoretical and empirical level, scholars and practitioners must distinguish punitive and dependence facets of power. This distinction is particularly important to tactical decisions on punitive action. Second, these separate facets of power are related in bargaining contexts: Lower stakes or low mutual dependence create conditions favorable to deterrence, while high stakes or high mutual dependence create conditions favorable to the spiral of punitive action. Third, certain elements from deterrence and conflict-spiral theories can be integrated in an analysis of punitive tactics in bargaining. Specifically, greater punitive capabilities can reduce punitive tactics, consistent with deterrence theory, while actual use can prompt counteruse and an upward spiral of punitive action over time. Finally, the effectiveness of punitive tactics depends, in part, on the resources attacked by the tactics.

6

Issues, Bluffs,
and Arguments

▼▼▼

Arguments are the justifications, explanations, rationalizations, or legitimizations that parties give for the positions they take in bargaining. Arguments are an instance of tactical dramaturgy, directed at recasting the opponent's definition of the bargaining situation. The objective validity of any redefinition is irrelevant as long as the opponent accepts its validity. Our basic premise in this chapter is that modes of argumentation reflect the bargainers' image of the power relationship. Whereas we earlier analyzed the effect of bargaining power on tactical concessions and punitive tactics, we now examine the role of bargaining power in the arguments bargainers use to buttress their offers or demands.

The literature offers surprisingly few theoretical or empirical analyses of argumentation in bargaining settings. Work under rubrics such as debate, argumentation, or interaction process analyze some aspects of the verbal interchanges in bargaining, but this work does not explicitly examine the tactics of argumentation, and it lacks an analytic framework that emphasizes the tactical aspects of argumentation (see, for example, Hopmann and Walcott, 1977; Landsberger,1955; McGrath and Julian, 1963; Morley and Stephanson, 1977; Walcott, Hopmann, and King, 1977). A tactical approach to argumentation implies a focus on argumentation as a means of negotiating the definition of issues, argumentation as a means of justifying offers and counteroffers, and argumentation as a means of establishing or changing the opponent's perception of the power relationship. These are the three topics of primary concern in this chapter.

First, we identify some basic dimensions along which bargainers define bargaining issues and examine the role of consensual and nonconsensual definitions in bargaining. Second, we use the dependence framework to identify major types of power arguments, and we analyze bluffing as a special case of argumentation. Finally, we classify normative arguments and suggest that these arguments be traced to the power relationship.

Definition of Issues

The definition of bargaining issues is neither a simple nor an unimportant task in bargaining. If bargainers adopt divergent definitions of an issue, they often have difficulty in agreeing on the specifics of a settlement. However, divergent definitions sometimes produce redefinitions that actually facilitate the task of constructing an agreement. The nature of each party's definition and its consequences for the bargaining outcome should be a major concern for both scholars and practitioners. To this end, we identify and discuss three dimensions of issue definition: scope of the issue, isolation or interrelation of issues, and relationship between the issue and the outcomes of the parties.

At the bargaining table, some issues are relatively specific and have well-defined implications for both parties, while other issues are broader and affect a wider range of interactions. This difference in specificity or breadth is a difference in scope. Objectively, for example, wage appears to be a relatively specific issue, and workers' rights or union security appear broader in scope. The objective nature of the scope can be misleading, however, because different bargainers might view the same issue in different ways. For example, a union representative may choose to cast a workers' rights issue in the broadest possible terms in order to encompass as many subissues as possible. Or management might attempt to delineate and focus on the particular rights of concern to the workers. Some of the early jockeying at the bargaining table, in fact, involves debate about the scope of issues. Defining an issue in broad or specific terms can be a calculated tactical decision on the part of the bargainers. Such decisions should affect arguments about a given issue —that is, the type of argumentation depends, in part, on whether bargainers hold similar or different definitions of the issue's scope.

The following list posits the consequences of divergent or convergent definitions concerning the scope of issues:

		Union Definition of Issues	
		Specific	Broad
Management Definition of Issues	Specific	Focused argumentation	Conflictual argumentation
	Broad	Conflictual argumentation	Diffuse argumentation

First, let us consider the cases in which both parties adopt a similar definition of the issue—that is, consensual definition of scope. If both define the issue in specific terms, the argumentation is focused; if both adopt a broad conception of the issue, the argumentation is diffuse. Focused argumentation implies a detailed pragmatic and utilitarian consideration of the specific elements embedded in the issue. Diffuse argumentation, in contrast, is likely to be infused with larger principles. When parties engage in such debate, they often become bogged down in matters of principle or in the ambiguous connections between the specifics of an issue and larger principles. With all other things equal, focused argumentation should be more likely than diffuse argumentation to lead directly to some conclusion, whether an impasse or an agreement. This guideline is consistent with the commonly articulated notion that negotiations involving matters of principle are more difficult to resolve. However, there are some ways in which diffuse argumentation may actually facilitate a settlement. Bargaining proposals that address specific changes may not capture the general concerns motivating a party to place an issue on the table. Arguments that justify specific proposals in more general terms often indicate possible areas of settlement better than specific proposals.

Focused and diffuse argumentation occur when there is consensus about the scope of the issue being negotiated. Conflictual argumentation occurs when there is not a consensus, when one party treats the issue in specific terms and the other party treats it in broad terms. Conflictual argumentation is most likely to occur in the earlier stages of bargaining, when parties have not yet agreed on precisely what is to be negotiated. Bargaining may break down because of the conflict over the scope of an issue, but such conflict early in the bargaining can also lay the foundation for an agreement. For example, conflictual argumentation may reveal that various issues are comprised by what was initially defined as a single issue. If parties have a stake in qualitatively different outcomes, conflictual argumentation may transform single issues into multiple ones that make trade-offs possible.

In addition to scope, the relationship among different issues is also a principal dimension of issue definitions. With regard to any given issue, bargainers can adopt a single-issue or multiple-issue approach. A single-issue approach treats an issue in isolation from other issues, whereas a multiple-issue approach stresses the packaging or grouping of issues. Bargainers are likely to view this choice between single and multiple approaches in the context of the power relationship. For example, an employer might believe that its relative bargaining power is enhanced with multiple-issue bargaining if this facilitates trade-offs that reduce the cost of the overall settlement. But a union might feel its relative power will be increased by minimizing the flexibility of the employer to push for certain trade-offs or by casting the bargaining in zero-sum terms, that is, by single-issue bargaining. Thus bargainers relate single- and multiple-issue strategies to their bargaining power and select that approach from which they expect the greatest power advantage. The particular approach taken by the bargainers also has consequences for the types of argumentation:

		Union Definition of Issues	
		Single Issue	*Multiple-Issue*
Management	*Single*	Concentrated	Issue-linkage
Definition		argumentation	argumentation
of Issues	*Multiple-Issue*	Issue-linkage	Trade-off
		argumentation	argumentation

We distinguish between consensual and nonconsensual. If bargainers consensually define the relationship as a single issue, argumentation will be concentrated; if both use multiple-issue definitions, trade-off argumentation ensues. Concentrated argumentation implies that the task of parties is to evaluate how much they and their opponents are willing to concede on that particular issue. In such argumentation, bargainers tend to emphasize the zero-sum aspects of the issue and to be more obstinate than if both adopt a multiple-issue stance. If bargainers are strictly concerned only with wage rates rather than being concerned with wage rates, supervision, and work conditions, they do not have the opportunity to exchange gains and losses in wage rates with gains and losses in supervision and work conditions. Their arguments will concentrate strictly on wages, ignore the broader context of nonwage issues, and treat wages in zero-sum terms. However, if both bargainers adopt a multiple-issue approach, their trade-off argumentation is likely to stress the relation of qualitatively different issues. The translation of one issue into terms that make it comparable to another issue is a complex matter, and comparing the "value" of a concession on

one issue to a concession on a separate issue is even more difficult—for example, How much shift in the wage offer is equal to
a given shift in holidays, overtime, union security, and so forth?
The difficulty of such comparisons changes with the nature of
the issues. If both issues have quantitative dimensions, the debate should be less intense than if bargainers are relating a quantitative to a qualitative issue.

In nonconsensual cases, the argumentation focuses on
whether to link issues, with one party arguing for linkage and the
other arguing for separate, isolated treatment of a particular issue.
A union might prefer to bargain over wages without reference to
other issues on the table, whereas management might choose to
raise other issues (such as insurance, work roles, and so forth) and
treat them all in a package. Issue-linkage arguments differ from
trade-off arguments. In trade-off argumentation, the issues are already linked, and the debate is not whether to draw linkages
among issues but how to do so. In issue-linkage argumentation,
the debate is over whether or not to package issues together.

The third characteristic of issue definitions is the prospective payoffs or outcomes associated with the issue. Each party expects to receive some benefits from an issue, and each attempts to
evaluate the relationship of its own outcomes to the opponent's.
Issue outcomes might be cast in terms of Walton and McKersie's
(1965) distinction between distributive and integrative bargaining, although this is not specifically a categorization of issue outcomes. Bargainers might define an issue as distributive in nature—
involving a distribution of finite resources—or they might define
an issue in integrative terms—as providing a basis for mutually
beneficial action. As with other aspects of issue definitions, parties may have consensual or nonconsensual definitions of issue
outcomes.

		Union's Definition of Issue Outcomes	
		Distributive	Integrative
Management's Definition of Issue Out- comes	Distributive	Competitive argumentation	Cooptative argumentation
	Integrative	Cooptative argumentation	Cooperative argumentation

If both parties define the outcomes attached to an issue as distributive, the argumentation over that issue is likely to have a distinctly competitive flavor; if both define the issue as integrative in nature, the argumentation is more cooperative. This contrast should be reflected in the extent to which bargainers aggressively attack the opponent's arguments and vociferously defend their own arguments. Competitive argumentation implies that bargainers do not accept the legitimacy or validity of the other's bargaining stance or supporting arguments. Cooperative argumentation assumes mutual acceptance of each other's most basic arguments, as the focus of such argumentation is on the synthesis or compatibility of their positions on the issues. Competitive argumentation is likely to overlook areas of commonality and emphasize the differences separating bargainers, whereas cooperative argumentation is likely to overlook basic differences between arguments or attempt to smooth over them. Interestingly, both cooperative and competitive argumentation may lay the foundation for contractual agreements that are somewhat inconsistent with the objective characteristics of the parties' relationship. Cooperative argumentation, to the extent that it is effective, may lead to agreements that imply more grounds for cooperation than in fact exist, while competitive argumentation may imply more conflict than suggested by the actual relationship.

The nonconsensual definition of issue outcomes, when one party treats the issue in distributive terms while the other treats it in integrative terms, is likely to result in cooptative argumentation. The party with the integrative definition is likely to use arguments that emphasize their mutual interests and to urge the opponent to redefine the issue in more integrative terms. A cooptative argument essentially smooths over the differences between parties and tries to bring the opponent into the fold. Successful cooptative arguments move the mode of argumentation into the cooperative category.

To summarize, parties' definition of issues along each of the three dimensions is related to general modes of argumentation. The contrast of consensual and nonconsensual definitions helps to specify the relationship between issue definitions and argumentation. Because the importance of consensual definition transcends the particular dimensions of concern, we now consider the consensual or nonconsensual nature of issue definitions in a more general way.

Consensual Definitions

When consensual definitions of an issue exist, argumentation is likely to focus on the substantive proposals and demands of the parties. In this sense, consensual definitions allow bargainers to devote exclusive attention to the resolution of specific issues. In contrast, nonconsensual issue definitions make the actual nature of the issue the focus of argumentation. Nonconsensual definitions mean that bargainers are not yet ready to focus on the substance of each other's proposals, and attempts to do so are likely to bring to the surface their divergent definitions and sidetrack serious bargaining. In other words, nonconsensual issue definitions imply that bargainers cannot even agree on how to approach their specific proposals.

Researchers and theorists devote remarkably little attention to the fact that parties might not agree on how to define the issues of bargaining. As noted in Chapter One, most theories of the bargaining cast labor-management negotiations in terms of a single issue—wages. In addition, bargaining theories typically assume that parties observe a common set of rules that prescribe what behavior is rational. Even within this limited framework, of course, there are a number of different theories, each with its own set of rules, and each with different predictions about the nature of bargaining settlements. That observation, alone, suggests that there is substantial room for parties to disagree about the definition of the issues, and that parties have some incentive to disagree. For the most part, comparisons of different bargaining theories are treated as debates over which set of rules and related assumptions is more realistic. Such debates imply that consensual definitions are important to scholars but do not pose practical problems for bargainers themselves.

Walton and McKersie's (1965) discussion of the difference between distributive and integrative bargaining poses a different kind of problem. Although they illustrate the tactical implications of treating issues in distributive or integrative terms, they too tend to side-step the question of issue definition when they suggest that the bargainers' approach is dictated by objective properties of the particular issues. With occasional lapses, they assume that bargaining over economic issues involves the division of a fixed sum of resources and, therefore, calls for the competitive tactics they associate with distributive bargaining, whereas bargaining over mutual rights and obligations involves problems that the two parties share in common and, thus, calls for more cooperative, integrative behavior. This distinction precludes Walton and McKersie from explaining the fact that qualitative issues, like union security and management rights, often generate the most intense conflict, provoke the most heated debates, and result in the least "civilized" strikes, while issues such as wages are often included in package deals that give the appearance of something for everyone.

One explanation for such observations is that qualitative issues provide fewer compromise positions for the parties to choose among than quantitative issues, but a better explanation is that parties are less willing to compromise or trade-off on issues defined as matters of principle. Just as important, a party yielding on quantitative issues often refuses to treat such issues as subjects for isolated bargains, but insists on making concessions in such areas contingent on acceptable settlements in other areas. However, wage issues can also become issues of principle if they are perceived as breaking a pattern set by some other contract, while issues such as union security can be subject to a variety of compromises that are consistent with the principles held by parties. The quantitative-qualitative distinction, therefore, is ultimately a matter of perception and definition, and not one that is dictated by objective properties of the bargaining issue itself. Bargaining theory needs to explain how the parties choose to define an issue and whose definition is likely to prevail if they are inclined to make different choices.

Walton and McKersie (1965) come closest to answering this question when they address what they call *attitudinal structuring,* defined as the maintenance and restructuring of attitudes participants have toward each other. Developing this concept in terms of the parties' attitudes toward their relationship, rather than in terms of their attitudes toward particular issues, is useful because so doing suggests that issues are not defined in isolation or without reference to the context. Walton and McKersie, however, characterize attitudinal structuring in a way that limits its usefulness. Their discussion focuses on how one party convinces the other to reduce the level of conflict in their relationship. The process of attitudinal structuring does not involve parties' choosing between distributive and integrative issue definitions, but their attempts to overcome the tendency to treat issues in distributive, rather than integrative, terms. The weakness in Walton and McKersie's approach lies in their association of integrative bargaining with problem solving; this association implies that problem solving does not involve a different approach to resource allocation but a way of overcoming the competitive aspects of allocation. Had Walton and McKersie treated integrative bargaining as a different approach to resource allocation, they would have been compelled to address the following question: Given that parties have different interests in how issues are defined, how might bargaining power affect the ability of a party to have its definition accepted by its opponent?

Our dependence framework provides a way of addressing this question. Rather than associating power exclusively with the concept of force, we cast power as dependence within an exchange relationship in which each party has some resource that the other needs. In a strict sense, conceptualizing bargaining as exchange is more closely associated with integrative bargaining than with distributive bargaining, to use Walton and McKersie's terms. The distributive notion of competition for the same resource is relevant primarily when one considers the costs to a party of surrendering resources the other is seeking. The following propositions about issue definition incorporate the costs of meeting the other's demands.

Proposition 1. The more costs a party associates with meeting the other party's demands, the greater the likelihood that it will define bargaining in single-issue, distributive terms; the fewer costs a party associates with meeting the other party's demands, the greater the likelihood that it will define bargaining in multiple-issue, integrative terms.

Proposition 2. The more congruent parties' perceptions of the costs associated with meeting each other's demands, the greater the likelihood that they will reach a consensual definition of bargaining issues; the less congruent parties' perceptions of the costs associated with meeting each other's demands, the greater the likelihood that they will have nonconsensual definitions of bargaining issues.

These propositions indicate how individual bargainers are likely to define issues and when their definitions are likely to be consensual or nonconsensual. These propositions alone, however, do not provide a basis for predicting which definition will prevail in the event of a conflict. The outcome of such a conflict should be a function of the parties' relative bargaining power as defined by the parties. That is, the more importance a party ascribes to the resources from the opponent, and the poorer its alternative opportunities for securing such resources, the more leverage the opponent has to dictate the conditions (for example, issue definition) under which it will consider surrendering some of its resources. This reasoning leads to the following proposition:

Proposition 3. The greater a party's relative power, the greater the likelihood that its definition of bargaining issues will prevail.

Taken together, these three propositions suggest that the nature of the arguments, particularly in the earlier stages of bargaining, plays a much more critical role in shaping the eventual bargaining outcomes than other theorists acknowledge. If perceptions of bargaining power determine individual and collective issue definitions, then one focus of the parties' argumentation is the cognitive manipulation of each other's bargaining power. To extend our analysis, therefore, let us consider how different types of arguments might be related to different dimensions of bargaining power (dependence).

Power Arguments

On the broadest level, bargainers can ground power arguments in resources, dependence, or sanctions. The resources are those commodities being negotiated or exchanged at the bargaining table. The dependence dimensions reflect the overall control over resources with regard to a particular issue or the whole range of issues under negotiation. Sanctions represent the probability that the resources available will be used in a punitive manner. Given our emphasis on a dependence approach, our primary task is to illustrate how dependence theory can classify arguments in terms of bargaining power and predict the choice of specific power arguments.

Power arguments attempt to manipulate the other's perception of the power relationship. The four dimensions of the dependence relationship imply four general modes of argumentation: arguments that manipulate the other's commitment, arguments that manipulate the opponent's perception of its alternatives, arguments that manipulate the opponent's perception of one's own commitment, and arguments that manipulate the opponent's perception of one's own alternatives. The dependence framework implies that parties code bargaining power in terms of dependence and use the dimensions of dependence to specify points of vulnerability upon which they develop argumentation tactics.

Within the four modes of argumentation suggested by the dependence framework, there are many variants that bargainers might develop in specific situations. Our classification of modes emphasizes the point that the dimensions of bargaining power are manifested in the argumentation tactics of the parties. Parties may shroud these power arguments in other terms or use them in very subtle ways, but many of the arguments at the bargaining table belong to one of these modes. When a union stresses the importance of some issues over others, it is manipulating management's perception of the commitment dimension of bargaining power; when a union directly or indirectly refers to alternative outcome sources when pushing a particular proposal, it is using the alternatives dimension of bargaining power in its argumentation, and so forth. Argumentation at the bargaining table often concerns the nature of the power relationship and such arguments can be related to the four modes of power argumentation.

To illustrate some uses of these arguments, consider the following examples.

1. Coalition arguments. An employee may attempt to convey its capacity to form coalitions with others outside the immediate relationship. Such labor coalitions could alter the dependence relationship by limiting the alternative outcome sources for management. Similarly, management may raise the possibility of joint action with other units in the same sector to counter the demands of a union.
2. Threat-to-leave arguments. A union may argue based on a threat to leave, while management may argue based on its ability to replace employees or take action that increases unemployment. These arguments could raise the possibility of a party's leaving the *bargaining* relationship—lockout or strike—or leaving the relationship altogether—seeking new employees or employers.
3. Self-enhancement arguments. A party argues to the other that its contributions to the relationship are high enough to warrant a better agreement. For example, management can argue that it already does so much for the employees that the employees should modify their demands. Likewise, employees can argue that their performance within the organization already suggests management should modify its demands.
4. Priority arguments. These arguments manipulate the opponent's impressions of a party's priorities and, thereby, communicate the party's commitment to different issues in the bargaining.

Each of these arguments is based on or directed at different aspects of the bargaining-power or dependence relationship. The two arguments grounded in an actor's own alternatives and commitment—threat-to-leave and priority arguments—are essentially defensive tactics. The other two arguments—self-enhancement and coalitions—are directed at or attack the opponent's alternatives or commitment, and constitute offensive arguments. Defensive arguments are designed to change the opponent's perception of a party's dependence—that is, improve a party's own dependence situation. In contrast, offensive arguments attempt to manipulate the opponent's impression of its own dependence—that is, attack the opponent's situation.

The dependence framework can specify general relationships between bargaining power and the choice of argumentation tactic. The logic of these relationships is similar to that used in our (Bacharach and Lawler, 1980, chap. 7) discussion of power struggle and bargaining tactics. Specifically, one assumes that parties select arguments that have the maximum probability of success and that they use the dimensions of bargaining power to anticipate the success of different argumentation tactics. The dimensions of bargaining power essentially identify the points of strength and weakness in each party's dependence situation. Given that parties use these points of strength or weakness to judge the probable success of different arguments, we suggest the following proposition:

Proposition 4. The dimension of bargaining power that a tactical argument is intended to manipulate is the primary criterion for decisions about when and how often to use that mode of argumentation.

To conclude, the dependence framework offers a basic classification of power arguments. It implicitly contends that the dimensions of bargaining power are intrinsic, often very subtle, elements of the verbal interchanges at the bargaining table. Arguments, in the last analysis, are attempts to emphasize or maintain points of strength and deemphasize or improve points of weakness. Dependence theory allows us to analyze the points of strength and weakness, and thus it provides a starting point for more systematic analyses of argumentation tactics.

Bluffing

The dependence framework on power arguments is applicable to both bluff and nonbluff argumentation. A bluff argument is an attempt to persuade the opponent to act in terms of an illusory conception of the power relationship, while a nonbluff argument is an attempt to convince the opponent of the actual power relationship as perceived by the party using the argument. Stevens (1963) indicates that a party is engaged in a bluff when asserting or implying that it will do what it does not intended to do at the time it makes some assertion. Stevens' notion of bluff is based on an actor's intention—saying one will do something that one does not intend to do. Our conceptualization of bluff is based on an actor's power potential, the actor's capacity to carry out certain actions rather than an intention to act. That is, a bluff is an attempt to exaggerate one's own power.

In Chapter Two, we suggested that bargainers attempt to convince the opponent of their own control of resources, of the opponent's need for the resources, and of their own ability to use the controlled resources in a sanctioning manner. A bluff argument is an effort to convince the other along these dimensions. Three modes of bluffing parallel these tasks: resource bluff—a party attempts to convince the opponent that its resources exceed what can be objectively verified; dependence bluff—a party attempts to convince the opponent that the opponent is highly dependent upon the resources controlled by the party; sanction bluff—a party attempts to convince the opponent that it will apply sanctions against the opponent when, in fact, the party is not able or willing to do so. These bluff tactics can be construed as cumulative. The sanction bluff presupposes that the opponent already accepts its dependence on the party and the party's control of certain resources. A dependence bluff presupposes that the party doing the bluffing controls resources. Thus, when a party uses bluffing tactics it must consider how convincing it has been on other dimensions.

The effectiveness of a bluff must be judged in terms of its durability over bargaining rounds, that is, to what degree the bluff is continuously accepted by the opponent. Clearly, a bluff argument that is preceded by or intertwined with a nonbluff argument is more potent and durable. If a sanctioning bluff is based on a nonbluff in regard to dependence (that is, the dependence is verifiable) and a nonbluff regarding resources (verifiable resource control), then the sanctioning bluff should be more effective and durable than one based on additional bluffing regarding dependence and resources. To predict the effectiveness of bluffing tactics, therefore, requires one to consider the extent to which the particular bluff is, in turn, grounded in bluff or nonbluff arguments on the resource, dependence, or sanction dimensions.

In addition, one must consider two other questions: How does the amount of information bargainers have about each other affect the risk of bluffing? and, What aspect of the power relationship constitutes the basis of bluffing? The most common assumption about information and bluffing is that bluffing by A is determined by the amount of information that B has about A (see Liebert and others, 1968; Siegel and Fouraker, 1960). Most analyses of information and bluffing neglect the role of A's information about B. One must consider both A's information about B and B's information about A as determinants of A's bluffing. The relative amount of information parties have about each other is a critical determinant of a party's tendency to bluff.

When evaluating information available to parties, one can become trapped in an infinite spiral. A party has infinite bits and pieces of information about itself and about its opponent. One could consider information about oneself to include the information the other has about oneself, and information about the other to include information that the other has about the information one has about oneself. Bargainers must take into account the endless cycle of "what he knows that I know that he knows." Although bluff tactics can be determined by such bits of information, we are concerned here with the overall level of information parties have about the other. Since the relative amount of information parties have is the major determinant of the risk of bluffing, let us consider four examples of relative levels.

If both union and management have low information on each other, the risk of bluffing is high, because bluffing may give the opponent information. Bluffing that does occur may simply involve "feelers" that prompt the opponent to reveal something about its situation. For example, a union representative may use a bluff as bait to elicit more information; yet, there is danger that management will see the bait for what it is and conclude that the union representative, indeed, has low information about management's situation. Such a perception could strengthen management's position at the bargaining table. The danger of making visible one's lack of knowledge increases the risk of bluffing when both parties have low information about the other. If both parties have high information on each other, the situation changes substantially. High information about the opponent enables a party to pinpoint the areas of greatest vulnerability and adjust bluffing tactics accordingly. However, since the opponent also has high information, the risk of bluffing diminishes only for those tactics that are not transparent.

The cases in which parties have differential amounts of information are the least ambiguous. If management has high information about the union, while the union has only low information about management, management is more aware of the union's strengths and weaknesses than the union is of management's strengths and weaknesses. In this situation, the risk of bluffing is low for management and high for the union. These inferences about the risk of bluffing are decidedly general and concern only the most basic tendencies implied by gross categorization of information into high and low levels. A more complete analysis of information requires greater attention to the specific types of information available to each party.

The treatment of information can be applied to resource, dependence, or sanction bluffs. However, our earlier discussion of power arguments suggests other types of bluffing should also be considered. We divided power arguments into offensive and defensive categories, and we can apply these same categories to bluffing tactics. The distinction implied here is between bluffing about the opponent's situation and bluffing about one's own situation. The former is an offensive bluff, which conveys a particular image of the opponent's situation and indicates a party's willingness to act on that image. A defensive bluff implies action on a particular image of one's own situation. Thus the dominant modes of bluffing fall into three categories: (1) a combination of offensive and defensive bluffing in which parties bluff about their own and the other's situation; (2) offensive bluffing, in which parties bluff only with regard to the other's resources, dependence, or sanctions; (3) defensive bluffing, in which parties bluff only with regard to their own resources, dependence, or sanctions.

By observing the frequency of these types of bluffing tactics, one can infer the information conditions that bargainers are acting on and, by implication, what information they think they and their opponent have about each other. Defensive bluffing is most likely when parties are particularly concerned about their vulnerability to each other. A union may choose to convince management that it controls more resources than management suspects; management may choose to convince a union that it is less dependent on the union's resources than believed by the union. In contrast, offensive bluffing attempts to persuade the other of its own vulnerabilities. A union may exaggerate management's dependence on the union, while management may attempt to exaggerate the union's dependence on it. Offensive bluffing is most likely when a party's own situation is relatively secure.

Normative Arguments

Thus far, we have focused on arguments that make more or less explicit reference to bargaining power. Normative arguments, which justify or explain bargaining behavior in terms of commonly recognized standards of behavior, also play an important role in bargaining. Both power and normative arguments involve the application of general rules. In the case of power arguments, these rules are utilitarian. When a union argues that certain concessions by management are in the interests of management, it is applying a utilitarian rule and making a power argument. The union is essentially saying that the power relationship is such that management should make concessions on grounds of their utilitarian value. In contrast, when a union argues that certain concessions by management are fair, it is making reference to a normative rule. Normative rules refer to external, nonutilitarian standards that ostensibly should be upheld by both parties.

Three types of normative arguments are generally relevant to bargaining: equality appeals, equity appeals, and responsibility appeals. An equality norm provides a basis for arguing in favor of equal outcomes or payoffs. It implies that a concession should be evaluated in terms of whether it represents a commitment to equally split the payoffs at issue. Such appeals provide a justification for arguing that the power relationship should not be the criterion for constructing a fair agreement (we elaborate this point in Chapter Seven). An equality rule posits that a party's contributions to or sacrifices in a relationship should not dictate its proceeds or yield from that relationship; that is, inputs should not have a bearing on outputs. In contrast, an equity rule implies a concern with both inputs and outputs. An equity norm leads bargainers to compare the ratio of inputs to outputs implied in the proposals of each party (Adams, 1965) and to argue that the inputs of parties to the relationship should determine the distribution of outputs. Use of the equity principle often creates conflict over the appropriate normative principles—parties argue over their respective inputs, the relation of inputs to outputs, and whether specific proposals equalize the bargainers' input-output ratios. Finally, a responsibility norm implies that need should serve as the criterion for evaluating bargaining proposals (Berkowitz, 1970). It simply states that those in need warrant assistance. When a union argues on the basis of workers' needs, it is appealing to a norm of responsibility.

Equality, equity, and responsibility arguments imply different ways of distributing payoffs, and parties select those normative arguments that serve their interests. That interests determine the selection of norms is a basic principle of Komorita and Chertkoff's (1973) bargaining theory of coalitions. They indicate that those with lower resources in a prospective coalition argue for equality and those with higher resources argue for equity, because such arguments are most consistent with their respective interests. This assertion implies a much closer relationship between bargaining power and normative arguments than that indicated by the explicit nature of such arguments. Extending this assertion, the following propositions relate bargaining power and normative argumentation:

Proposition 1. The greater the difference in bargaining power, the greater the tendency of the higher-power party to use equity appeals and the greater the tendency of the lower-power party to use equality or responsibility appeals.

Proposition 2. If the difference in bargaining power is very large, the lower-power party will use responsibility appeals; if the power difference is not large, the lower-power party will use equality appeals.

Proposition 3. If the total bargaining power in the relationship is very high, both parties will use equality appeals.

These propositions assume that bargainers select normative arguments in concert with their interests. Parties with higher power, insofar as they use normative arguments at all, tend to favor equity norms because their superior power might allow them to demand and normatively justify greater concessions from the opponent—as long as bargaining power is treated as an input in the equity ratio. The only real constraint on the tendency of higher-power parties to use equity appeals is the total power in the relationship. Extremely high total power makes the costs of an impasse so severe for the higher-power party that equality is a more acceptable tactic of argumentation.

Parties with lower bargaining power have a choice between arguments based on equality norms and those based on responsibility norms. Our propositions posit that lower-power parties use equality appeals, alone or in conjunction with responsibility appeals, except when they are in an extremely disadvantageous power position. Responsibility norms are the only hope for bargainers in a highly disadvantaged position because equality norms require more concessions from the opponent than a very weak party can reasonably expect. The only way for a lower-power party to receive more concessions than implied by equity (which would involve very low payoffs in an absolute sense) is to appeal to the opponent's responsibility for its plight. Social psychological research on helping behavior indicates that responsibility norms are activated when the needy party is highly dependent on the helper (see Macaulay and Berkowitz, 1970). In a bargaining relationship, responsibility appeals cast the opponent in the role of helper and portray the needy party as unfortunate and desperately needing more concessions from the opponent. In addition, such arguments may invoke norms of responsibility to a larger collectivity of which both parties are members. The disadvantaged party essentially argues that the opponent has normative responsibilities that transcend the opponent's particular interests.

The success of normative arguments is likely to be affected by the parties' definitions of the issues. The persuasiveness of normative appeals is greatest to bargainers when the issues are couched in broad terms, when trade-offs are of prime concern, and when bargainers are prepared to exaggerate the cooperative elements of their relationship. Normative principles are less persuasive when issues are treated singly, in specific terms, and appear distributive to bargainers.

Normative arguments are likely to serve different functions when the parties are inclined to reject the moral implications of each other's arguments. The most important function normative arguments serve under such circumstances is informational. Because a party is likely to select the normative argument that best serves its interests, the opponent can learn a good deal from the party's choice of arguments; for example, how that party perceives the absolute, relative, and total power in the relationship, what types of concessions the party expects to receive, the conditions under which it will make concessions, and so forth. Whether the opponent accepts the party's normative position is less important than whether it believes the party really accepts that position.

This informational aspect of normative arguments acquires special significance in light of our earlier discussion of tactical concessions and punitive tactics. Normative arguments afford parties the opportunity to sound out one another without committing themselves to specific concessions or resorting to punitive tactics that might lead to a conflict spiral. Concessions need not be interpreted as a sign of weakness if presented in a normative argument that implies that additional concessions will not be forthcoming unless the opponent satisfies the conditions implicit in the normative argument. By the same token, a party can reveal its punitive capabilities or use threat tactics by embedding such tactics in normative principles regarding the nature of a fair bargaining outcome. Normative arguments, therefore, provide an indirect means of making implicit power arguments that if explicitly stated in power terms would make a party appear too vulnerable or too belligerent.

7

Convergence
of Power and
Bargaining Outcome

▼▼

The bargainers' power relationship and related tactical action culminate in their choosing to either accept an agreement that reflects the equalities or inequalities embedded in the bargaining-power relationship and tactical success of bargainers, or refuse an agreement that manifests these equalities or inequalities. Bargaining tactics are designed to manipulate equalities or inequalities in power and thereby produce an agreement favorable to one's own interests. How bargainers respond to these equalities or inequalities at the point of agreement is a crucial issue. Given that bargaining implies bilateral power, mutual consent to bargain, and so forth, those in a disadvantageous power position may not be inclined to accept an agreement that reflects differential power, while those in the advantageous position may be reluctant to accept an agreement that does not reflect the power differences. The role of equal or convergent power in agreements is a central theme of this chapter.

The bargaining outcome or agreement differs from the tactical behavior discussed in earlier chapters in that it is a collective act. While bargainers have their own tactics—for example, tactical concessions—agreement is a uniquely collective phenomenon. Furthermore, while tactical behavior occurs throughout the bargaining process, agreement constitutes an endpoint or outcome that emerges from the bargaining process. Thus the properties of a bargaining outcome differ from those of tactical action. While tactics are designed to gain some measure of submission from the other and to feign or give a measure of submission to the other, agreement implies a collective willingness not only to resolve the issues but also to cease further tactical action (at least, temporarily or until other issues emerge for negotiation). Specifically, agreement connotes that bargainers mutually or collectively consent to a particular settlement and accept collective responsibility for the nature of the agreement.

We distinguish two issues in discussing this collective phenomenon. First, not all bargaining relationships facilitate agreement, so we must ask how the bargaining-power relationship affects the *likelihood* of agreement. We believe that dependence theory provides a better foundation for understanding the likelihood of agreement than other approaches to bargaining. Second, the exact *nature* of realized agreements varies substantially. Some agreements favor the party with greater power or tactical success, while others reflect a normative commitment to equality. One of the questions raised by dependence theory is whether or when the dependence relationship fosters departures from the agreement points predicted by an equality or split-the-difference principle. In this chapter, we elaborate the approach of dependence theory to the likelihood and nature of agreement.

A Dependence Framework on Agreement

Our two issues, the *likelihood* of agreement and the *nature* of agreement, are given unequal attention in bargaining theory. As indicated in Chapter One, the primary focus of bargaining theory is the nature of agreement. Zeuthen (1930) initially established this emphasis, and it has generally been maintained, especially by scholars developing economic and game-theoretical models (see Young, 1975). One reason is that economists are concerned primarily with only one bargaining issue, wage outcomes, and bargainers usually reach some kind of agreement on this issue. Game theorists and others posit a finite bargaining range or contract zone that gives bargainers greater payoff than that attached to the nonagreement option. Under these circumstances, only incompetent, stupid, or irrational bargainers fail to reach an agreement. Thus, these approaches lead to an exclusive concern with the nature of the agreement, that is, the point of settlement.

By equating bargaining outcome with the point of settlement, bargaining theories neglect important empirical questions and limit their applicability, as illustrated by the implicit assumptions of most bargaining theories. First, and most important, bargaining theories typically assume that some agreement will, indeed, be reached by bargainers. The importance and extremeness of this assumption varies in different approaches, with game-theory and economic models incorporating the most extreme versions of this assumption (see Young, 1975). Regardless of such variation, however, this assumption informs most, if not all, of the major approaches to bargaining (see Chapter One). The major problem with this assumption is that it makes questionable empirical claims about bargaining. Specifically, it implies that reaching agreement is not problematic to bargainers—agreement is basically inevitable and the only real variation occurs in the process through which it is reached or the actual nature of the agreement; tactical action, therefore, is directed toward reaching agreement or designed to manipulate the nature of agreement rather than to evaluate whether an agreement is possible or worthwhile. Virtually all theorists, with the possible exception of Pen (1959), assume parties evaluate offers at any given point as if they were on the verge of settling. Overall, these empirical claims indicate that bargainers themselves take agreement for granted and adapt their tactical action accordingly.

We reject all the empirical claims embedded in the foregoing assumption on both empirical and theoretical grounds. Reaching an agreement is more problematic than admitted by most formal theories of bargaining. The likelihood of agreement varies along with the difficulty, which suggests that we conceptualize both agreement and its nature as problematic not only to bargainers but also to our theories. On theoretical grounds, we question the value of making such restrictive assumptions as a matter of convenience or practicality or to enhance the purity of theories. There is always some tension between the determinateness, elegance, purity, and substance of a theory, and it appears to us that the substantive value of bargaining theory is severely limited by stringent assumptions of the type discussed here. Strictly speaking, theories that assume agreement can be applied only to settings in which an agreement is indeed inevitable and both parties accept this inevitability. Such cases appear to represent a relatively small subset of bargaining relationships.

The second assumption of theories emphasizing the nature of agreement is a bilateral monopoly. Recall from Chapter One that a bilateral monopoly assumes that parties completely control each other's access to resources or outcomes of value. In dependence terms, a bilateral monopoly assumes extremely high, and probably unrealistic, levels of mutual dependence in the relationship—neither party has any alternative outcome sources and both are highly committed to the outcomes at issue. A bilateral monopoly essentially identifies the conditions under which an assumption of agreement is reasonable. However, theories based on bilateral-monopoly conditions treat as constants those variables that make reaching an agreement problematic. The confluence of assuming agreement and a bilateral monopoly relegates the likelihood of agreement to an inferior, if not irrelevant, position in a theory.

Social psychological research provides some information on the likelihood of agreement, though the topic remains a secondary concern. Data on agreement from social psychological experiments are typically weakened by the use of a bilateral monopoly with the concomitant pressure to reach agreement—thus the overall rate of agreement tends to be quite high. Also, such experiments typically use confederates to manipulate tactical concessions, which violates the assumption that agreement is a collective product between two or more bargainers. Thus although social psychological work gives some attention to the problem of reaching agreement and, implicitly, to the contrast of *likelihood* and *nature* issues, the value of this work is limited by its assumption of a bilateral-monopoly condition.

Our critique of traditional bargaining theory's approach to agreement suggests the need for a broader theory of bargaining. Such a theory should treat the *likelihood* and *nature* of agreement as analytically distinct and empirically interrelated, and it should treat the constants of the bilateral monopoly as variables that affect not only the likelihood of agreement but also the nature of any agreement. A dependence framework provides such an approach. First, it implies that reaching agreement is problematic—agreement varies with the alternatives and commitment of the parties to the outcome at issue. The constants of the bilateral monopoly, therefore, are the principal dimensions of bargaining power that predict the likelihood of agreement. Second, a dependence approach treats bargaining power as a condition that modifies the nature of any agreement reached by the parties. It specifically implies that power equalities and inequalities are basic to the nature of agreement, and, in this sense, it can recast and further specify the concerns central to game-theory approaches. In the following sections, we elaborate the implications of dependence theory for the likelihood and nature of bargaining agreements.

Likelihood of Agreement

The most extensive review of work related to the likelihood of agreement is offered by Rubin and Brown (1975). Focusing on social psychological work, Rubin and Brown find some support for the following propositions:

Power-Convergence proposition. Equal power produces more effective bargaining than unequal power.

Total-Power proposition. The lower the total power in the relationship, the greater the bargaining effectiveness.

However, Rubin and Brown's concept of bargaining effectiveness is somewhat ambiguous in that it appears to imply an amalgam of elements, for example, low threat use, satisfaction with the agreement, likelihood of resolution, and the overall adequacy of any resolution. Moreover, the research underlying these propositions frequently did not include data on agreement per se. Much of the research was conducted in settings, such as matrix games, that did not allow offers and counteroffers or explicit agreements and nonagreements. At best, these games exemplify tacit bargaining. Finally, most of the supporting research focuses on punitive rather than dependence dimensions of power. The experiments create and hold constant very high mutual dependence, essentially creating a bilateral monopoly. These qualifications indicate that the propositions offered by Rubin and Brown may be incorrect or inadequate.

Approaching Rubin and Brown's propositions from dependence theory, we note several additional points. With regard to the proposition on power convergence, dependence theory indicates not just that alternatives and commitment are dimensions of bargaining power but also that these dimensions can have very different implications. Specifically, our reformulation of dependence theory indicates that this power-convergence proposition may apply to the alternatives dimension but not to the commitment dimension of bargaining power. Equal alternatives may facilitate agreement, while equal commitment may actually prevent agreement. In addition, our reformulation of dependence theory suggests a proposition opposite to the total-power proposition—namely, that greater total bargaining power (cast as dependence) increases the likelihood of agreement. Given our earlier analysis, this proposition may also apply more to alternatives than to commitment. Overall, a dependence analysis of Rubin and Brown's propositions clearly suggests that further specification and elaboration is warranted. Let us consider the power-convergence and total-power ideas, in turn.

Power Convergence. An analysis of power convergence

from dependence theory leads to two contradictory propositions:

Proposition 1. The likelihood of agreement is greatest when the bargainers' power positions are equal on *both* the alternatives and commitment dimensions.

Proposition 2. The likelihood of agreement is greatest when the bargainers' power positions on alternatives are equal and when their positions on the commitment dimension are unequal.

The first proposition indicates that equal alternatives, whether poor (low) or good (high), facilitate agreement, and the same holds true for equal commitment. This first proposition is the stricter derivation from dependence theory and is closely linked to the traditional approaches to dependence by Emerson (1962, 1972a, 1972b) and Blau (1964). The second proposition takes account of our reconceptualization of the commitment dimension and our discussion in Chapter Three. It suggests that Rubin and Brown's general notion applies only to the alternatives dimension of dependence.

Consider the rationale for these dependence propositions. The first proposition is grounded in the broad notion that equalities or similarities between bargainers make it easier for them to reach a mutually satisfactory agreement. Applied to the power relationship, equal bargaining power suggests an equal division of the outcomes, that is, an equal level of concession making by both parties on the issues at hand. (Or, more accurately, equal power does nothing to contradict an equal division.) A splitting-the-difference rule is often cited by both bargainers and third parties to arrive at the "best" possible solution. Equal power should make this rule more salient, defensible, and persuasive to the bargainers. Under equal power, a splitting-the-difference rule may appear to both bargainers as a normatively justifiable way to resolve a conflict.

With unequal power, however, the equality rule is likely to hinder an agreement as much as it might facilitate it under equal power. Unequal power raises the question, for both bargainers, of whether and how the power relationship should be manifested in the actual agreement. One can defensibly argue that those with greater power have a special responsibility to those with less, or even that the power relationship should not have much effect on the agreement because "might does not make right." The relationship between power and the appropriate norms is inherently ambiguous under unequal power, and bargainers are likely to take positions on this matter that reflect their interests. The result is that bargainers work at cross-purposes and become bogged down in normative issues. The advantaged party is likely to act as if greater power implied an agreement more favorable to its interests, while the disadvantaged acts as if normative rules, such as equality, should guide the construction of an agreement. Along these lines, Rubin and Brown (1975) suggest that under unequal power, an advantaged party acts in an exploitive manner, while the disadvantaged acts in a submissive manner. The behavior of the advantaged may, indeed, be construed as exploitive, but we are suggesting that the submissive behavior of the low-power party is a matter of degree. Submission in a bargaining relationship is likely to occur only after substantial resistance. This resistance in combination with the high-power party's intransigence may obstruct agreement and even prevent the final submission of the low-power party. Overall, unequal power simply creates more obstacles for bargainers to overcome before they can reach agreement.

In regard to the second dependence proposition, the underlying assumption is that certain inequalities in the power relationship create complementarities that make agreement easier. This is the case with commitment, but not with the alternatives dimension of bargaining power. The alternatives dimension raises the same issues noted in our contrast of equal and unequal power. With regard to commitment, however, recall that it can have two contradictory implications for the bargainers: on the one hand, high commitment suggests lower power; on the other hand, it implies more tactical effort. If we emphasize the implications of commitment for power capability, we arrive at the same proposition as for alternatives. If we emphasize the tactical-effort implications of commitment, then inequalities should be more likely to produce agreement than equalities. Unequal commitment suggests that the party with high commitment will push strongly in the bargaining, whereas the party with low commitment will feel less need to do so. The party with lower commitment has more potential power, but is less likely to use it. The respective commitments in the unequal case are complementary, such that one party is motivated to "go all out" while the other does not have much to lose by acquiescing to the highly committed party. This analysis leads to the proposition that a combination of power convergence on alternatives and nonconvergence on commitments produces the greatest likelihood of agreement.

We can derive some preliminary data on this issue from the experiment described in Chapter Three. This experiment contains the conditions for separating convergence and nonconvergence on the alternatives and commitment dimensions. To discuss the convergence issue, we reclassify the sixteen conditions of dependence into four categories: convergence on both alternatives and commitment, nonconvergence on both alternatives and commitment, convergence on alternatives with nonconvergence on commitment, and convergence on commitment with nonconvergence on alternatives. The percentages of pairs ($N = 32$ for each condition) reaching agreement within these four conditions are as follows:

1. Convergence on alternatives and commitment: 44 percent.
2. Nonconvergence on alternatives and commitment: 28 percent.
3. Convergence on alternatives and nonconvergence on commitment: 69 percent.
4. Convergence on commitment and nonconvergence on alternatives: 38 percent.

The first dependence proposition predicts the greatest likelihood of agreement in the convergence-convergence condition, while the second dependence proposition predicts the greatest agreement in the convergent alternatives–nonconvergent commitment condition. Our data are not dramatic but clearly favor the second proposition over the first. Thus Rubin and Brown's convergence proposition applies to the alternatives dimension of dependence, while the commitment dimension operates in the opposite manner. Our data indicate, once again, the difference between the two dimensions of dependence and imply that a bargaining-power relationship may embody complementarities or inequalities that facilitate agreement. The commitment dimension of dependence is one such element.

Let us note that the data on convergence were collected under the following conditions: only a single issue was being negotiated, and there was no possibility of a trade-off across issues or bargaining sessions. These are stringent conditions that should depress the effect of nonconvergent commitments compared to actual labor-management settings in which multiple issues are negotiated and trade-offs are possible. Our experimental effect for nonconvergent commitments implies that the high-commitment party pushes more strongly in the bargaining and the low-commitment party is less reluctant to resist, such that agreement becomes possible. We would expect a similar pattern in labor-management contexts but with an additional element: yielding by the low-commitment party on a given issue is likely to imply an expectation that the opponent will act similarly on other issues to which the party is more committed. The possibility of trade-offs or exchange across issues should increase the strength of the effects for nonconvergent commitments well beyond those observed in our experiment. Since our experimental procedures should work against the nonconvergence effects, it is even more impressive that this pattern is evident in our data.

Total Power. From the standpoint of dependence theory, total bargaining power refers to the degree of mutual dependence in the bargaining relationship. On the alternatives dimension, high total power means that both bargainers have low or poor alternatives, while, on the commitment dimension, high mutual commitment indicates high total power. The position of dependence theory on the role of total power contradicts Rubin and Brown (1975). Rubin and Brown's total-power proposition posits a negative relationship between total power and bargaining effectiveness, while dependence theory proposes a positive relationship. According to dependence theory, mutual dependence or total power fosters cohesion in the relationship (Emerson, 1972b), and greater cohesion, in turn, suggests greater chances of agreement. The difference between these predictions reflects a difference in emphasis on punitive and dependence aspects of the power relationship. Rubin and Brown stress punitive power and essentially espouse a key proposition of conflict-spiral theory—that greater punitive capabilities are likely to unleash a conflict spiral. The contrasting proposition for agreement adds further weight to the importance of distinguishing dependence and punitive aspects of power.

Our reconceptualization of *value* as commitment suggests that the effects of total power depend on the dimension of bargaining power. Specifically, total power on the alternatives dimension should reveal the positive relationship to agreement espoused by dependence theory, but total power on the commitment dimension should reveal little or no relationship to the likelihood of agreement. Thus, our reformulation of dependence theory takes issue with the implication of traditional approaches to power dependence (see, for example, Emerson, 1972b) as well as with Rubin and Brown's proposition on total power. Our theory clearly predicts a positive relationship for alternatives and agreement, but implies that high total power on the commitment dimension produces conflicting tendencies that generate little or no relationship. On the one hand, high mutual commitment leads both parties to push strongly to overcome each other's resistance. This situation could lead to very tough bargaining, frequent impasses, and conflict spirals that would afford support to Rubin and Brown's hypothesis. On the other hand, high mutual commitment also encourages parties to arrive at some settlement, as they both have a substantial amount of their resources at stake. The desire to reach some agreement should counterbalance the former tendency, and the precise relationship of mutual commitment to the likelihood of agreement is contingent on the strength of these cross-pressures felt by the bargainers. All other things being equal, the safest prediction is simply that high total power on the commitment dimension has no relationship to the likelihood of agreement;

however, contexts that alter the relative strength of the cross-pressures could produce either a positive or negative relationship. To summarize, the following proposition, suggested by our theory, is an alternative to Rubin and Brown's prediction:

Proposition 3. An increase in the mutual dependence on alternatives increases the likelihood of agreement, while mutual dependence on the commitment dimension has no effect on the likelihood of agreement.

This total-power proposition can be evaluated in two ways. First, we should ask whether and how total power affects the likelihood of agreement, given a situation of power convergence. Second, we should ask whether and how the total-power hypothesis can be integrated with our power-convergence proposition. To consider the effects of total power independent of power convergence, we examine data from two experiments that held power convergence constant across conditions—the one described in Chapter Five and another experiment that had the same manipulation of mutual dependence. We can also examine those particular cells (four of the sixteen) from the first experiment discussed in Chapter Three that are comparable to the conditions of these two experiments.

The information in Table 7 provides consistent support for the total-power proposition (proposition 3) from our re-

Table 7. Likelihood of Agreement by Total Dependence on Alternatives and Total Dependence on Commitment, in Percentages

	Both Low Commitment		Both High Commitment	
	Both Low Alternatives	Both High Alternatives	Both Low Alternatives	Both High Alternatives
Experiment 1				
($N = 8$/cell)	75	25	75	0
Experiment 2				
($N = 50$/cell)	48	16	56	22
Experiment 3				
($N = 40$/cell)	30	10	45	5

Note: Experiment 3 is not reported elsewhere in this volume, but the procedures and manipulations of dependence are virtually identical to those for Experiment 2 (described in Chapter Five).

formulation of dependence theory. In all three experiments, greater total power on alternatives dimensions increases the likelihood of agreement, while total power on the commitment dimension does not reveal any strong or consistent results. The tactical implication is that bargainers who work to cut or limit each other's alternatives enhance the cohesion within the relationship and facilitate agreement. Manipulating each other's commitment does not have the same consequences, although this may still be effective in gaining some advantage in the bargaining. The power-convergence proposition suggests that a bargainer who reduces the opponent's commitment to the outcomes may get a better agreement. A complete consideration of this case must await our analysis of the nature of agreement.

The next issue is whether the total-power proposition implies any modifications in the power-convergence proposition. Clearly, it does not for the commitment dimension of dependence because of the conflicting processes produced by convergence on the commitment dimension. In the case of the alternatives dimension, however, the total-power proposition suggests that certain forms of convergence are more important than others. An integration of the total-power and power-convergence propositions indicates that convergence of poor or low alternatives facilitates agreement more than convergence of good or high alternatives. If so, we should find evidence that agreements are particularly likely when both parties have low or poor alternatives. This requires us to break down the sixteen conditions of experiment 1 into low-low, low-high, high-low, and high-high alternatives; $N = 32$ for each condition. Our data on the likelihood of agreement are:

1. Low alternatives for A and B: 81 percent.
2. High alternatives for A and B: 31 percent.
3. Low alternatives for A and high alternatives for B: 28 percent.
4. High alternatives for A and low alternatives for B: 38 percent.

These results suggest further specification of the power-convergence proposition to take account of total power along the alternatives dimension. Agreements seem most likely under conditions of high mutual dependence (low-low alternatives). Clearly convergence on low or poor alternatives facilitates agreement more than convergence on high or good alternatives.

To conclude, our two propositions from dependence theory, one based on power convergence and the other on total power, indicate that the likelihood of agreement is greatest under the following conditions: (1) Parties are equal in bargaining power on the alternatives dimension; (2) Total bargaining power along the alternatives dimension is high; and (3) Parties have unequal bargaining power on the commitment dimension. Dependence theory indicates that the role of equal power and total power in producing agreement is contingent on the particular dimension of bargaining power. These are general implications that represent avenues for further modification and elaboration of the basic propositions of Rubin and Brown (1975). These implications transcend the specific content of dependence theory. Regardless of one's particular approach to power, one must identify the multiple dimensions of bargaining power and determine whether different dimensions of bargaining power have divergent effects on agreement in bargaining.

The Nature of Agreement

The terms of the contract constructed by bargainers define the nature of their agreement. Information on the likelihood of agreement does not tell us much about the nature of an agreement, and information on the nature of an agreement does not necessarily tell us much about the likelihood of agreement. These two issues are analytically distinct and warrant separate attention, as noted earlier. This distinction does not imply that there is no empirical relationship between the likelihood and nature of agreements. Some agreements are easier to make than others, and conditions that foster these types of agreement should also enhance the likelihood of agreement, as we imply in our analysis of unequal power. Unequal power obstructs agreements by making certain easily justifiable agreements—for example, those based on an equality principle—more difficult to achieve. Such relationships between likelihood and nature do not obviate the importance of separate attention to both. To develop theoretical themes that reveal the differences and the similarities between the likelihood and nature issues, we maintain our focus on power convergence. We primarily concern ourselves with the following question: To what extent does unequal bargaining power produce departures from agreements based on equality? Our answer illustrates how dependence theory might supplement and extend the approach of game-theoretical models to the nature of agreement.

It is evident that our dependence theory of bargaining falls outside the game-theory tradition, which is a progressive search for determinate solutions to the bargaining problem. Our theory of dependence posits that the nature of agreement contains an inherently indeterminate quality and that a determinate solution to bargaining is a contradiction in terms. The image of bargaining fostered by our dependence theory stresses the manipulative, tactical, and cognitive nature of bargaining interaction and implies that the outcome of bargaining is an emergent product of the bargaining process. To conceptualize outcome as an emergent product is not to characterize it as chaotic, unpredictable, or nondeterministic in a philosophical sense; any such characterizations would undermine a scientific analysis of agreement. We do hold, however, that attempts to identify a priori determinate solutions, based on the bargaining context or utility functions, are doomed to failure.

Game-theoretical models, however, are not worthless. Although the assumptions of the models are very stringent, artificial, and unrealistic, the theoretical issues embodied in these assumptions are quite important. We argued in Chapter One that theories of bargaining should consider the assumptions of game-theoretical approaches as variables, treat these variables as problems confronted by bargainers, and use the predictions generated by these assumptions as reference points for examining the effect of the power relationship on the nature of agreement. In the case of dependence theory, then, we need to examine whether and how the variable dimensions of our theory relate to the assumptions of game theory and also whether variation in these dimensions creates departures from the reference points suggested by game theory.

We use Nash's (1950) model to illustrate the relationship of dependence theory to game theory. We select Nash's model because it is the most basic model and most other game-theoretical models are developed from it. Furthermore, Nash's model yields predictions that are surprisingly similar to those of apparently very different models (for example, see our discussion of Zeuthen in Chapter One). Nash's model is optimal for illustrating points of contrast and similarity between dependence theory and game theory.

Nash's basic assumptions are a bilateral monopoly with the following conditions: (1) Both parties are rational; (2) Both parties have complete and perfect information on each other's preferences and payoffs; (3) Both parties adopt an individualistic motivation, that is, attempt to maximize their own gain regardless of what the other gets; (4) Neither party will settle for an agreement that is not Pareto-optimal; (5) Linear transformation of the utilities or payoffs does not change the solution; and (6) To restrict the settlement to a subset of outcomes does not change the solution, as long as the solution that would be reached in the absence of such restrictions is still available.

Comparing Nash's model with dependence theory, we find that dependence theory treats as variables two dimensions of bargaining power—commitment and alternatives—held constant by Nash. Our commitment (or value) variable should have, according to Nash, no effect on the solution, because of his linear-transformation assumption. In our experiments, the manipulation of commitment involved a change in the amount of payoff at stake in the bargaining. Nash's model predicts that the nature of the agreement remains constant across the commitment levels: that the commitment variable does not affect the solution. Our alternatives dimension of dependence is, strictly speaking, outside the domain of Nash's model because it violates the assumption of a bilateral monopoly.

In the case of the alternatives dimension, however, one can integrate the dependence relationship into Nash's model, as we illustrate using the experiment described in Chapter Three.

Recall that alternatives were manipulated by giving subjects a probability distribution specifying the likelihood of various types of agreements from an alternative group. This experimental condition implies more uncertainty than allowed by Nash, but the game-theory notion of expected utility can incorporate this uncertainty into Nash's theory. The *expected utility* of a group of outcomes (that is, all those possible under a given experimental condition) can be calculated by multiplying the probability of each bargaining outcome by the magnitude of the midpoint of that agreement category and then summing these products. This calculation appears justified because there is a linear relationship between the twenty-nine agreement levels and the expected levels of payoff.

These expected utilities essentially specify the "points of origin" for the utility functions of bargainers within the four alternative conditions. To apply Nash's theory, therefore, we need only assume that the point of origin is no longer 0—where 0 represents no payoff—for nonagreement, but rather the expected utility of the alternative. This assumption seems quite reasonable given that virtually any numerical value can constitute the point of origin without substantially changing Nash's model. In fact, this assumption is implied by Nash's incorporation of "threat" into a later model. The inclusion of threat merely involves a change in the point of origin so that it reflects the relative costs to bargainers of not reaching an agreement. Incorporating alternatives into Nash's model simply requires a change in the point of origin to reflect the relative gains expected from the alternative. Just as inclusion of threats led Nash to incorporate unequal punitive capability in the solution, so the inclusion of alternatives begins to feature unequal dependence relationships.

Given these points of origin, Nash's model applies a split-the-difference rule; that is, bargainers agree at the midpoint between the expected utility of their alternatives. For example, if A has high alternatives and B has low alternatives, and the expected value for A is an agreement of 17 (from the alternative) and the expected value for B is 21—the midpoint is 19. Given an agreement under this condition of unequal alternatives, our adaptation of Nash's model predicts an agreement at 19. In technical terms, this split-the-difference rule engenders an agreement on the Pareto-optimal line at a forty-five degree angle to the point of origin (see Chapter One). In the case of high alternatives for both, no agreement is predicted because the point of origin is above the Pareto-optimal line, and consequently, there is no contract zone.

Our application of Nash's model has implications for the role of the equality principle in bargaining. Extrapolating from Nash, we find that the equality principle is contingent on and constrained by the power relationship. Equality is not an absolute principle adhered to regardless of the power relationship but a way for bargainers to translate the power relationship into a particular agreement. Given unequal power, the division of payoff stipulated in the actual agreement will likewise be unequal, because the equality principle essentially dictates that the outcome should match or reflect the inequality of bargaining power. In one sense, the equality principle is transformed into an equity norm with relative power being the input. More accurately, it is best to view this form of the equality principle as contingent, because its normative quality is more ambiguous than that usually attached to equity. Contingent equality implies that bargainers tailor their use of the principle to the specific context and, thereby, use or apply equality in a contingent manner.

This contingent use of equality, implied in Nash's model, differs from our treatment of the equality principle. In analyzing the likelihood of agreement, we stress the normative, absolute character of equality and posit that bargainers adopt a noncontingent approach to equality and use it as a reference point for excluding or limiting the effect of the power relationship on the bargaining outcome. Recall the suggestion that power convergence makes it easier for parties to come to agreement because this absolute, noncontingent norm is less troublesome to apply. Applied to the nature of agreement, a noncontingent-equality rule indicates that bargainers view the midpoint of the issue continuum—range of solutions regardless of utilities—as equality. Since this midpoint is different from the midpoint of expected utilities, these two versions of the equality principle point to somewhat different settlements. Such contrasting reference points might not only account for the difficulty of reaching agreement under unequal power conditions but also explain the nature of any agreement reached.

The distinction between contingent and noncontingent equality indicates that there are two ways for bargainers to use the equality principle. On the one hand, if they emphasize the absolute, normative character of equality, they are likely to use the principle in a noncontingent manner, and treat the issue continuum, unmodified by utilitarian or power considerations, as the foundation for equality. Thus in our experiment, bargainers would identify an agreement level of 15—the midpoint of the abstract issue continuum, which ranged from 1 to 29—as the appropriate midpoint, regardless of the dependence conditions. That is, when agreements do occur, they should be at the midpoint of 15. On the other hand, if bargainers emphasize the utilitarian aspects of equality, they are likely to treat the equality principle in a contingent manner. Bargainers will thus modify their judgments of equality to fit the power relationship. The midpoint, therefore, is relative to the power conditions, and 15 would be the predicted agreement only for equal power conditions. Under unequal power, the midpoint depends on the differences in bargaining power—specifically, the expected utility of the alternative. In sum, these two versions of equality identify different reference points for examining the effects of bargaining power on the nature of agreement.

Our prime concern is whether the dimensions of bargaining power in dependence theory create departures from the agreement points predicted by contingent and noncontingent versions of equality. We are concerned with questions such as: Is equality, by whichever reference point, most likely under conditions of power convergence? Do both the commitment and alternatives dimensions of power account for departures from equality? These questions are critical to an understanding of the role power convergence plays in the development of agreements. If we find that the dimensions of dependence account for departures then we must suggest that these equality standpoints are insufficient to predict or analyze the nature of agreements in bargaining.

The most general assumption of our discussion of agreement likelihood is that power convergence facilitates agreement more than nonconvergent power. This general idea leads to two contrasting hypotheses for the nature of agreement. First, given that nonconvergent power hinders agreement by making the meaning of equality ambiguous to bargainers, we may reason that any agreement that does occur presupposes that bargainers overcome this problem—that is, any agreement under nonconvergent power should reflect the equality principle. By the same reasoning, any departures from equality should not be a function of power. In contrast, a second approach suggests that the ambiguity associated with nonconvergent power is manifested in the nature of the agreement as well. Specifically, ambiguity about the equality principle results in bargainers' adopting ad hoc principles tailored to specific characteristics of the situation. From this standpoint, bargaining power is likely to create departures from equality. Thus, two conflicting propositions are indicated:

Proposition 1: Whether power is convergent or nonconvergent it has no effect on the nature of the agreement.

Proposition 2: Convergent power produces a smaller departure from equality than nonconvergent power.

Let us examine the absolute departure from contingent and noncontingent equality in four conditions: convergence on both alternatives and commitment, nonconvergence on both, convergence on alternatives and nonconvergence on commitments, convergence on commitments and nonconvergence on alternatives. Of necessity, our analysis is restricted to the fifty-seven pairs that reached agreement in our first experiment. For each pair, two departure scores were constructed, one for noncontingent equality and one for contingent equality. For noncontingent equality, we took the absolute difference between the actual agreement and the midpoint of 15. For contingent equality, we took the absolute difference between the actual agreement and the midpoint of bargainers' expected utility for the alternative, as suggested by our adaptation of Nash's model. With regard to the condition for which Nash would not predict an agreement (high alternatives for both bargainers), we used the same reference point as for the other power-convergence condition (low alternatives for both bargainers). This procedure seems reasonable because any agreement that does occur in the high conditions should reflect equality in the same manner as the other equal-power condition.

Table 8 presents the relevant information, including the analysis of variance results for the departure scores. The results

Table 8. Departure from Noncontingent and Contingent Equality by Convergence on Commitment and Alternatives

Alternatives		Commitment	
		Convergent	Nonconvergent
Convergent	Noncontingent equality	1.0	3.0
		(N = 14)	(N = 22)
	Contingent equality	1.1	3.2
		(N = 14)	(N = 22)
Nonconvergent	Noncontingent equality	3.8	2.9
		(N = 12)	(N = 9)
	Contingent equality	2.4	4.7
		(N = 12)	(N = 9)

Note: ANOVA results for Noncontingent Equality: Commitment, $F(1,56) = 1.37$, $p < .25$; Alternatives, $F(1,56) = 3.02$, $p < .09$; Commitment × Alternatives, $F(1,56) = 3.49$, $p < .07$.

ANOVA results for Contingent Equality: Commitment, $F(1,56) = 12.24$, $p < .001$; Alternatives, $F(1,56) = 4.92$, $p < .03$; Commitment × Alternatives, $F(1,56) < 1$.

for both forms of equality indicate that agreements under non-convergent power depart from the equality principle. This finding applies to both the commitment and alternatives dimensions of bargaining power, although the nature of the departure varies somewhat for the two forms of equality. With regard to non-contingent equality, nonconvergence on a given dimension of power creates the greatest departure from equality when bargainers converge on the other power dimension. The combination of convergence on one dimension of power and nonconvergence on the other dimension creates the greatest problem of application for the noncontingent-equality principle. Turning to contingent equality (which is sometimes called *equity*), we find somewhat different but stronger results for power convergence. Both dimensions of bargaining power have independent and additive effects on departures from Nash's equality point, regardless of bargainers' relationships on the other power dimension. Given the importance of Nash's model in the bargaining literature and the fact that we adapted it to incorporate one of the power dimensions, these departures from Nash's model point to the importance of the dependence relationship to the nature of agreement. Overall, these data, especially for Nash's model, suggest that the second proposition is quite plausible. Clearly, the power relationship must be considered in explaining or predicting the nature of agreement. A reliance on normative or utilitarian principles to identify a priori agreement points is inadequate because such predictions neglect the tactical aspects of bargaining power and the concomitant processes of bargaining interaction.

We argue throughout this book that power is as much a subjective as it is an objective phenomenon; it is as much a part of the bargaining process as it is a part of the bargaining context; it is independent of, yet constrained by, utilitarian and normative considerations. To state our view in its extreme form: Power is not simply a part of bargaining, it is the essence of it. This image of bargaining power implies that principles, such as equality, are valuable reference points for examining the effects of power or tactical action but are not a reasonable foundation for serious predictions of the actual agreement. Our dependence theory does not permit us to predict the agreement point from the power relationship but to understand when and why agreements frequently depart from points that are likely to be salient to bargainers. The points that are salient to bargainers are identified by economic or game-theoretical models, while dependence theory can treat departures from these points. Overall, the data in this section illustrate how a power analysis can and should complement and extend the formal models of economists and game theorists (see Young, 1975). The basic implication is that nonconvergent power not only reduces the likelihood of agreement but also engenders greater departure from equality when agreements do occur.

The effect of convergent power on both the likelihood and nature of agreement suggests a qualification of the old adage: It is best to bargain from strength. If bargaining from strength implies only that a bargainer has, in an absolute sense, sufficient power to avoid domination from the other, there is no problem. However, this adage is often interpreted to mean, It is best to bargain from *relative* strength, that is, with more power than the other. This interpretation suggests a situation of nonconvergent power, which reduces the likelihood of agreement and increases the likelihood that any agreement will depart from split-the-difference principles. The more an agreement departs from such principles, the more difficult it is for the higher-power party to justify or the lower-power party to live with the agreement over time. To develop greater objective or subjective power than the other may enable one to extract more tactical concessions from the opponent but, at the same time, one reduces the chances of agreement or one produces an agreement less stable or satisfactory over time.

Termination of Bargaining

The mode of terminating bargaining can affect the nature and level of future conflict as well as the ability of parties to control it. Some forms of termination do not merely terminate bargaining on a particular issue or set of issues but actually destroy the bargaining relationship. Some forms exacerbate future conflict, while others tend to limit it. Specifically, there appear to be four basic ways that bargainers terminate their bargaining: mutual withdrawal, open conflict, consensual resolution, and managed resolution. The first two types assume nonagreement, whereas the latter two assume agreement. The first two further imply a destruction of the bargaining relationship, while the latter two imply its continuation.

Mutual withdrawal indicates that parties essentially leave the bargaining relationship. Their interdependence will probably continue, and the conflict of interest that originally led to bargaining will pose problems in the future. In response to such problems, we would expect the parties to adopt conflict-avoidance tactics to limit their interference with each other and segregate their continuing interdependence from their relationship with others. Avoidance of conflict, however, is a short-term strategy designed to give both parties time to gradually reduce their mutual dependence. The dual tactics of immediate conflict avoidance and reductions in dependence on the other compose one way of responding to nonagreement.

Open conflict is a second response to nonagreement. The immediate strategy in this case is confrontation rather than conflict avoidance, and the parties simply transfer the conflict to a nonbargaining arena. Their ensuing tactical effort is directed at overwhelming the opposition and winning in the purest sense of the term. With this mode of termination, each party attempts to increase the other's dependence on it, and the long-term effect is an increase in mutual dependence or total power in the relationship. In this sense, the combined strategy of confrontation and increasing the other's dependence may lay the groundwork for the reestablishment of bargaining as parties become more aware of their inability to avoid or ignore each other. The breakdown in the bargaining relationship, therefore, is likely to be temporary in the case of open conflict.

Turning to agreements, we distinguish consensual and managed resolution. The literature on bargaining generally treats conflict resolution as a global construct subsuming any process or outcome that leads to or reflects agreement. The contrast of consensual and managed resolutions assumes that the process through which bargainers resolve their differences has important, long-term consequences. Consensual resolution refers to an agreement created by the parties themselves, a self-generated, emergent product of the bargaining process. Consensual resolution implies that both parties freely consent to make the particular agreement and that both parties feel substantial responsibility for the nature of the agreement. This form of conflict resolution generates a high level of subsequent support from the parties and affirms or solidifies the bargaining relationship.

Managed resolution, in contrast, results from manipulated or forced consent. The consent may develop from force or manipulation exercised by an outside party, for example, through compulsory arbitration, or even from one bargainer's coercing the other into an agreement. With this form of conflict resolution, one or both bargainers are likely to feel less responsibility for the agreement, have less commitment to it, and view it as a less satisfactory resolution of the issues. Consequently, the agreement is likely to be perceived as temporary, and future conflict over the same issues is probable. While consensual resolution is freely created by both parties, managed resolution alienates one or both bargainers. While consensual resolution usually strengthens the bargaining relationship, managed resolution essentially maintains the existing relationship.

As presented, these forms of conflict resolution are archetypes rather than descriptions of alternate empirical realities. The major importance of this typology is that it identifies two principal dimensions of the bargaining process that bear on the effectiveness of conflict resolution: mutual consent and felt responsibility. The importance of these dimensions varies with given bargaining relationships and different types of third-party intervention—for example, compulsory arbitration, mediation, and fact finding. Our general contention is that conflict resolution is effective to the degree that bargainers view themselves as freely consenting to the agreement and feel a high degree of responsibility for the nature of the agreement. Higher levels of mutual consent and felt responsibility make parties more committed to the agreement and more satisfied with it in the aftermath of bargaining.

8

Theory of Power
in Bargaining

▼▼▼

The theoretical value of our dependence approach to bargaining power is both conceptual and propositional. Our conceptual contribution is a general framework that offers scholars and practitioners an integrative approach to the major facets of bargaining: bargaining power, concession behavior, punitive tactics, argumentation, and bargaining settlements. Our propositional contribution comprises a number of testable hypotheses that elucidate the more specific implications of the general framework. With these propositions, we begin to relate bargaining power (context), tactical action (process), and bargaining settlements (outcome). In this final chapter, we summarize the implications of our conceptual framework and systematize the core propositions of the dependence approach.

The most general implication of our approach is that we need not and should not resign ourselves to having separate theories for separate facets or processes of bargaining; we can and should develop a theory that encompasses concession behavior, punitive tactics, argumentation, and similar phenomena. Dependence theory provides such an integrated framework by identifying themes common to various tactics and to bargaining context, process, and outcome. The value of our dependence theory as an integrative device is indicated by the breadth of topics to which it can be applied. For example:

1. Our framework offers a multidimensional conceptualization of bargaining power that scholars and practitioners can use to classify and interrelate the disparate environmental and structural conditions that underlie bargaining. The dimensions of bargaining power can be construed as filters through which parties interpret the environmental context and make tactical decisions (see Chapter Two).

2. Our framework adopts a cognitive approach to bargaining power and identifies different ways in which parties might interrelate the dimensions of bargaining power, for example, zero-sum and variable-sum images of power. Bargaining power is a cognitive construct, and bargainers' images of bargaining power determine their lines of tactical action. The subjective nature of bargaining power requires practitioners and scholars to adopt a tactical approach to bargaining (see Chapters Two and Three).

3. The dimensions of bargaining power identify the potential objects toward which bargainers direct their tactics of argumentation and bluffing (see Chapter Six). Through argumentation, bargainers manipulate the operative (subjective) power context that guides the opponent's action, and thus the power relationship is an implicit issue at the bargaining table.

4. Our perspective promotes the analysis of inducements (concessions) and sanctions (punitive tactics) in bargaining. Consistent with the variable-sum assumption of dependence theory, bargainers tend to use the opponent's bargaining power, rather than their own, to make decisions on how tough or soft to be in the offer-counteroffer sequence of bargaining

(Chapter Three). Comparisons between dependence theory and two complementary theories, deterrence and conflict-spiral, elucidate the relationship between punitive capabilities and tactical action and specify conditions under which deterrence or conflict spirals are likely to occur (Chapters Four and Five).

5. The dependence framework emphasizes the role of power convergence in predicting two dimensions of the settlement process: the likelihood and nature of agreement. Power convergence on some dimensions of bargaining power facilitates agreement, while convergence on other power dimensions reduces the likelihood of agreement. Nonconvergent power, regardless of the power dimension, creates greater deviation from split-the-difference principles for constructing an agreement (see Chapter Seven).

Overall, we contend that most facets of bargaining can be cast in terms of a dependence theory of bargaining power. Power is central to bargaining, and dependence theory offers the optimal framework for analyzing bargaining power. Concessions, argumentation, punitive tactics, and the settlement process all involve the dimensions of bargaining power specified by our theory. In this sense, dependence theory offers not just one more theory of bargaining but a general paradigm for bargaining. This claim may appear to be overly bold, but not if one considers two aspects of traditional bargaining theory. First, no other theory has the breadth of our dependence theory, at least with reference to the range of topics that the theory allows one to analyze. Second, the major elements of the theory—the dimensions of dependence—are well documented in bargaining literature. Many theories deal implicitly or explicitly with what we call the alternatives and commitment dimensions of bargaining power, but none has fully recognized the integrative potential of these dimensions or the breadth of their potential application (see, for example, Chamberlain, 1951, 1955; Dunlop, 1950; Pen, 1959). Our theory integrates diverse notions from bargaining literature and yields a framework with considerable breadth and flexibility.

The breadth and flexibility of the dependence perspective

make it a foundation for a general paradigm. Such a paradigm has obvious theoretical merit and is also useful to practitioners who must analyze a particular bargaining setting in detail, considering simultaneously matters that scholars frequently consider in isolation. The dependence framework appears to provide a flexible, heuristic theoretical tool for practitioners to systematically analyze bargaining relationships and to identify analogues between uniquely different bargaining settings. We hope that this book prompts practitioners to be more self-reflective about the subtle (and not so subtle) ways that bargaining power is intrinsic to their activity. Thus dependence theory appears to provide a framework for juxtaposing the concerns of scholars and practitioners.

In this book, we also propose a number of propositions that relate bargaining power and tactical action. These propositions are intended to develop the specific implications of dependence theory and to show that the theory generates testable hypotheses and propositions. We now summarize the theory of tactical bargaining and our core propositions.

Scope of the Theory

Our theory of tactical bargaining applies primarily to conflict settings that meet the following six conditions.

One, there are two parties with a conflict of interest. The parties may be persons or collectivities (groups, organizations, or even societies). For purposes of simplicity, the theory holds constituent-representative relations constant and is limited at this time to two-party contexts. However, the theory could be extended to contexts with more than two parties and to constituent-representative relations. Such contexts are more complex but should not alter the basic patterns or principles suggested by our theory.

Two, the issue or issues embody a continuum of potential resolution points. This continuum may be quantitative (for example, pay in a labor-management context) or qualitative (for example, union security). The existence of a continuum makes compromise possible.

Three, parties mutually consent to engage in bargaining.

The parties acknowledge the conflict of interest, recognize the legitimacy of each other's interests, and make a commitment to consider compromise. The theory does not necessarily apply to pure conflict or to tacit bargaining (see Bacharach and Lawler, 1980; Schelling, 1960).

Four, neither party has complete information on the pay-offs or utilities, the power relationship, or the other's tactical plans. Thus neither party can fully predict or anticipate the action of the other and neither is immune to bluffing and deception.

Five, although the information is not complete or perfect, both parties gather and process information on each other that can be classified under the dimensions of bargaining power (dependence). Parties do not necessarily think in terms of power or dependence, but knowingly or unknowingly they accumulate information relevant to dimensions of bargaining power. Thus the information available to parties can be conceptualized in terms of power, but the quality of the information is imperfect.

Six, parties begin bargaining with an individualistic orientation, taking the form of a maximizing-gain or minimizing-loss approach. An individualistic orientation reflects a primary concern with one's own payoffs or outcomes; for example, parties attempt to maximize their own payoff rather than maximize the difference between their own and the opponent's payoff. The theory assumes that an individualistic orientation is the dominant one through most of the bargaining, although other orientations may be present. Thus, a strict interpretation of this condition is not warranted.

These six conditions describe in general terms the scope of our dependence theory. The conditions are broad enough to subsume most bargaining in international and labor-management settings, as long as such bargaining takes the form that social psychologists have termed *explicit bargaining* (see, for example, Bacharach and Lawler, 1980; Chertkoff and Esser, 1976; Schelling, 1960). At the same time, these conditions indicate areas in which the theory should be elaborated and extended in the future. Most of these conditions can be transformed into variables that affect the bargaining process—for example, the quality and quantity of information can vary, as can the strength of the individualistic orientation or the nature of constituent-representative relations. Our theory of tactical bargaining provides a framework for examining such phenomena.

Core Propositions

One of the basic tenets of our dependence approach is that an analysis of bargaining power should consider three facets of the power relationship: the absolute power of each party, the relative power of the parties, and the total power in the bargaining relationship. The distinction between these facets of power separates our approach from traditional notions of power dependence (Blau, 1964; Emerson, 1962, 1972a, 1972b; Thibaut and Kelley, 1959) and from analyses of power in the collective-bargaining literature (see, for example, Chamberlain, 1951, 1955; Chamberlain and Kuhn, 1965; Dunlop, 1950; Pen, 1959; Stevens, 1963). These other approaches implicitly or explicitly stress relative power and fail to develop the connections between dependence, bargaining power, and tactical action.

Our theory begins with three basic propositions that relate dependence and bargaining power:

Proposition 1. An increase in the dependence of A on B increases B's absolute bargaining power.

Proposition 2. An increase in the ratio of A's dependence on B to B's dependence on A increases B's relative bargaining power.

Proposition 3. An increase in the sum of A's and B's dependence increases the *total bargaining power* in the relationship.

These are the core propositions of a dependence approach to bargaining power.

These propositions do not suggest that all three facets of power are relevant to every aspect of bargaining. Different facets of power may be important for different tactical issues. For example, in Chapter Three, we examine the role of all three aspects of power, but stress those that imply a variable-sum conception of power, that is, absolute power and total power. Absolute, relative, and total power are typically interrelated; to emphasize any one of these aspects is to generate somewhat different, but complementary, implications for tactical concessions. In discussing punitive tactics (Chapters Four and Five), we stress the role of total power as a condition that determines deterrence or conflict spirals. In Chapter Seven, we emphasize the effect of power convergence (or relative power) on the likelihood and nature of bargaining agreements. Overall, it is clear that no one aspect of power is universally the most critical—importance varies with the phenomena of concern—yet all three are crucial to a complete understanding of bargaining power.

Three hypotheses can be derived from the foregoing propositions, based on the assumption that the dependence of A on B is determined by A's alternative outcome sources and A's commitment to the outcomes. The alternative outcome sources refer to the level of similar or substitutable outcomes that A can obtain from other sources or parties, while A's commitment refers to the importance A attributes to the outcomes at stake in the bargaining. Poorer alternatives and higher levels of commitment for A make A more dependent on B. The three hypotheses are:

Hypothesis 1. A decrease in A's alternative outcome sources or an increase in A's commitment to the outcomes at issue increases B's absolute bargaining power.

Hypothesis 2. An increase in the ratio of A's alternatives or commitment to B's alternatives or commitment increases B's relative bargaining power.

Hypothesis 3. An increase in the sum of both parties' dependence along the alternatives and commitment dimensions increases the total bargaining power in the relationship.

The hypotheses and related propositions can be interpreted as divergent perspectives for either investigators or bargainers to analyze bargaining power. Given the subjective nature of bargaining power, the propositions and hypotheses identify the choices available to bargainers. Bargainers may emphasize relative power, as do most researchers, or they may stress the absolute or total facet of bargaining power. Our theory is partially a theory of the choices available to bargainers or investigators and the consequences of choosing to treat bargaining power in a given way. The theory further suggests that the success of an analysis of bargaining power depends on the degree of similarity between the analyst's and bargainer's emphases regarding absolute, relative, and total power. Our interpretation of these propositions, therefore, stresses the subjective side of bargaining power.

Consider each of the propositions as a different perspective on bargaining power. With proposition 1, bargainers view power in individual terms, treating in relative isolation their own power and the other's, either of which could form the foundation for their tactics. In Chapter Three, we present theoretical reasons and empirical data suggesting that bargainers focus on other's power when making tactical decisions. That is, a bargainer's own alternatives and commitment are the foundation for that bargainer's tactical behavior, consistent with hypothesis 1. If bargainers extend this emphasis on absolute power to other tactics, their bluffing would tend to manipulate their own alternatives or commitment; tactics of argumentation (all other things being equal) would be directed at these same dimensions. That is, if bargainers want to change the power relationship (subjectively or objectively), they direct most of their effort at reducing their own dependence on the opponent. Thus, proposition 1 leads to a tactical focus different from those implied by propositions 2 or 3.

With proposition 2, bargainers attend primarily to relative power, rather than individual or absolute power. This approach implies that bargainers equally consider their own and the other's bargaining power and treat the dimensions of dependence in relative terms rather than in isolation. To change the power relationship—defined by the power ratio—bargainers can manipulate any of the four dimensions of bargaining power. From this standpoint, parties' tactical concessions are viewed in relative terms. The ratio of one's own to other's concessions is most salient to bargainers, and they assess their own concessions only in relation to the other's concessions.

The tactical differences of absolute- and relative-power approaches are a matter of emphasis. An absolute-power approach implies not that bargainers ignore the relationship between each other's concessions but that their tactical behavior is primarily grounded in the opponent's power, that is, in their own dependence on the opponent. A relative-power approach does not suggest that parties ignore absolute power but that their cognitive calculus for interpreting and using power stresses its relative quality, and thus concessions are more likely to be treated in comparative or relative terms.

The distinction between relative and individual power can be related to the individualistic and competitive orientations of interest to social psychologists (Rubin and Brown, 1975). Recall that an individualistic orientation implies a concern only with one's own payoffs, whereas a competitive orientation implies a concern with the relationship of each party's payoffs. Bargainers who stress absolute power are concerned primarily with their own situation (their dependence on the other), whereas a relative-power strategy implies a concern with the relationship between the two parties' power situations. This isomorphism between bargaining orientations and approaches to bargaining power suggests the following hypothesis: An individualistic orientation gives rise to an absolute-power strategy, while a competitive orientation engenders a relative-power strategy. In other words, bargainers' orientation partially determines their tendency to act in terms of proposition 1 or proposition 2. These ideas point to a basic theoretical inconsistency in prior work on bargaining. Theorists typically assume an individualistic orientation, while treating power in relative terms. Yet, if bargainers adopt an individualistic orientation, models of relative bargaining power are probably inadequate to depict the manner in which bargainers approach and use power in bargaining.

The third perspective, total power, implies that bargainers are most concerned with the amount of power in the relationship. Knowingly or unknowingly, bargainers are sensitive to the mutual dependence in the relationship, and they adjust their tactical action accordingly. However, action based on total power may be less conscious than action based on absolute or relative power primarily because the idea of total power is likely to be less obvious or salient to bargainers. Total power is best seen as a complement or supplement to absolute and relative power, which are more likely to be explicit elements of bargainers' phenomenological world. In any case, total power is important to tactical action in bargaining and can modify (weaken or strengthen) the tactical tendencies embedded in absolute- or relative-power conditions.

To conclude, our theory identifies how bargainers might approach and use bargaining power. It emphasizes the subjective side of bargaining power, the tactical nature of the bargaining process, and the emergent quality of bargaining outcomes. By distinguishing absolute, relative, and total power, it points to some major practical choices confronted by bargainers and suggests the consequences of making one or another choice or adopting one or another emphasis. We hope that this book encourages theorists and practitioners to think more critically about the traditional ways of analyzing bargaining power and that it facilitates their efforts to analyze this critical dimension of bargaining relationships.

References

▼▼

Adams, J. S. "Inequity in Social Exchange." In L. Berkowitz (Ed.), *Advances in Experimental Social Psychology.* Vol. 2. New York: Academic Press, 1965.

Ashenfelter, O., and Johnson, G. E. "Bargaining Power, Trade Unions, and Industrial Strike Activity." *American Economic Review,* 1969, *59* (1), 35-49.

Bacharach, S. B., and Lawler, E. J. "The Perception of Power." *Social Forces,* 1976, *55,* 123-134.

Bacharach, S. B., and Lawler, E. J. *Power and Politics in Organizations: The Social Psychology of Conflict, Coalitions, and Bargaining.* San Francisco: Jossey-Bass, 1980.

Bacharach, S. B., and Lawler, E. J. "Power and Tactics in Bargaining." *Industrial and Labor Relations Review,* 1981, *34,* 219-233.

Benton, A. A., Kelley, H. H., and Liebling, B. "Effects of Extremity of Offers and Concession Rate on the Outcomes of

Bargaining." *Journal of Personality and Social Psychology,* 1972, *24,* 73-83.

Berkowitz, L. "The Self, Selfishness, and Altruism." In J. Macaulay and L. Berkowitz (Eds.), *Altruism and Helping Behavior: Social Psychological Studies of Some Antecedents and Consequences.* New York: Academic Press, 1970.

Bierstedt, R. "An Analysis of Social Power." *American Sociological Review,* 1950, *15,* 730-738.

Bishop, R. L. "A Zeuthen-Hicks Theory of Bargaining." *Econometrics,* 1964, *32,* 410-417.

Blau, P. M. *Exchange and Power in Social Life.* New York: Wiley, 1964.

Blumer, H. *Symbolic Interactionism: Perspective and Method.* Englewood Cliffs, N.J.: Prentice-Hall, 1969.

Bowlsby, R. L., and Schriver, W. R. "Bluffing and the 'Split-the-Difference' Theory of Wage Bargaining." *Industrial and Labor Relations Review,* 1978, *31,* 161-171.

Braithwaite, R. B. *Theory of Games as a Tool for the Moral Philosopher.* Cambridge, England: Cambridge University Press, 1955.

Brown, B. R. "The Effects of Need to Maintain Face on Interpersonal Bargaining." *Journal of Experimental Psychology,* 1968, *4,* 107-122.

Brown, B. R. "Face-Saving and Face Restoration." In D. Druckman (Ed.), *Negotiations: Social-Psychological Perspectives.* Beverly Hills, Calif.: Sage, 1977.

Chamberlain, N. W. *Collective Bargaining.* New York: McGraw-Hill, 1951.

Chamberlain, N. W. *A General Theory of Economic Process.* New York: Harper & Row, 1955.

Chamberlain, N. W., and Kuhn, J. W. *Collective Bargaining.* (2nd ed.) New York: McGraw-Hill, 1965.

Cheney, J., Harford, T., and Solomon, L. "The Effects of Communicating Threats and Promises upon the Bargaining Process." *Journal of Conflict Resolution,* 1972, *16,* 99-107.

Chertkoff, J. M., and Conley, M. "Opening Offer and Frequency of Concession as Bargaining Strategies." *Journal of Personality and Social Psychology,* 1967, *7,* 181-185.

Chertkoff, J. M., and Esser, J. K. "A Review of Experiments in Explicit Bargaining." *Journal of Experimental Social Psychology*, 1976, *12*, 464-486.

Cohen, B. D. *Developing Sociological Knowledge: Theory and Methods*. Englewood Cliffs, N.J.: Prentice-Hall, 1980.

Cross, J. G. "A Theory of the Bargaining Process." *The American Economic Review*, 1965, *55*, 67-94.

Dahl, R. A. "The Concept of Power." *Behavioral Science*, 1957, *2*, 201-218.

Deutsch, M. *The Resolution of Conflict*. New Haven, Conn.: Yale University Press, 1973.

Deutsch, M., and Krauss, R. M. "Studies of Interpersonal Bargaining." *Journal of Conflict Resolution*, 1962, *6*, 52-76.

Deutsch, M., and others. "Strategies of Inducing Cooperation: An Experimental Study." *Journal of Conflict Resolution*, 1967, *11*, 345-360.

Druckman, D. (Ed.). *Negotiations: Social-Psychological Perspectives*. Beverly Hills, Calif.: Sage, 1977.

Dunlop, J. T. *Wage Determination Under Trade Unions*. New York: A. M. Kelley, 1950.

Edgeworth, F. Y. *Mathematical Psychics*. London: Routledge & Kegan Paul, 1881.

Emerson, R. M. "Power-Dependence Relations." *American Sociological Review*, 1962, *27*, 31-40.

Emerson, R. M. "Exchange Theory, Part I: A Psychological Basis for Social Exchange." In J. Berger, M. Zelditch, and B. Anderson (Eds.), *Sociological Theories in Progress*. Vol. 2. Boston: Houghton Mifflin, 1972a.

Emerson, R. M. "Exchange Theory, Part II: Exchange Relations, Exchange Networks, and Groups as Exchange Systems." In J. Berger, M. Zelditch, and B. Anderson (Eds.), *Sociological Theories in Progress*. Vol. 2. Boston: Houghton Mifflin, 1972b.

Esser, J. K., and Komorita, S. S. "Reciprocity and Concession-Making in Bargaining." *Journal of Personality and Social Psychology*, 1975, *31*, 864-872.

Etzioni, A. *A Comparative Analysis of Complex Organizations*. New York: Free Press, 1961.

Foldes, L. "A Determinate Model of Bilateral Monopoly." *Economics*, 1964, *31*, 117-131.

French, J. R., Jr., and Raven, B. H. "The Bases of Social Power." In D. Cartwright (Ed.), *Studies in Social Power*. Ann Arbor: University of Michigan Press, 1959.

Gamson, W. A. *Power and Discontent*. Homewood, Ill.: Dorsey Press, 1968.

Gergen, K. J. *The Psychology of Behavior Exchange*. Reading, Mass.: Addison-Wesley, 1969.

Gibbs, J. P. *Sociological Theory Construction*. Hinsdale, Ill.: Dryden Press, 1972.

Goffman, E. *Frame Analysis*. New York: Harper & Row, 1974.

Gulliver, P. H. *Disputes and Negotiations: A Cross-Cultural Perspective*. New York: Academic Press, 1979.

Hage, J. *Techniques and Problems of Theory Construction in Sociology*. New York: Wiley, 1972.

Hammermesh, D. S. "Who 'Wins' in Wage Bargaining?" *Industrial and Labor Relations Review*, 1973, *26*, 1146-1149.

Hamner, W. C. "Effects of Bargaining Strategy and Pressure to Reach Agreement in a Stalemated Negotiation." *Journal of Personality and Social Psychology*, 1974, *30*, 458-467.

Hamner, W. C., and Yukl, G. A. "The Effectiveness of Different Offer Strategies in Bargaining." In D. Druckman (Ed.), *Negotiations: Social-Psychological Perspectives*. Beverly Hills, Calif.: Sage, 1977.

Harsanyi, J. C. "Bargaining and Conflict Situations in the Light of a New Approach to Game Theory." *The American Economic Review*, 1965, *55*, 447-457.

Harsanyi, J. C. *Rational Behavior and Bargaining Equilibrium in Games and Social Situations*. New York: Cambridge University Press, 1977.

Heath, A. *Rational Choice and Social Exchange: A Critique of Exchange Theory*. Cambridge, England: Cambridge University Press, 1976.

Heider, F. *The Psychology of Interpersonal Relations*. New York: Wiley, 1958.

Hicks, J. R. *The Theory of Wages*. (2nd ed.) New York: St. Martin's Press, 1963. (Originally published 1932.)

Hirschman, A. O. *Exit, Voice, and Loyalty.* Cambridge, Mass.: Harvard University Press, 1970.

Hopmann, P. T., and Walcott, C. "The Impact of External Stresses and Tensions of Negotiations." In D. Druckman (Ed.), *Negotiations: Social-Psychological Perspectives.* Beverly Hills, Calif.: Sage, 1977.

Horai, J., and Tedeschi, J. T. "Effects of Credibility and Magnitude of Punishment on Compliance to Threats." *Journal of Personality and Social Psychology,* 1969, *12,* 164-169.

Hornstein, H. A. "The Effects of Different Magnitudes of Threat upon Interpersonal Bargaining." *Journal of Experimental Social Psychology,* 1965, *1,* 282-293.

Johnson, M. P., and Ewens, W. "Power Relations and Affective Style as Determinants of Confidence in Impression Formation in a Game Situation." *Journal of Experimental Social Psychology,* 1971, *7,* 98-110.

Johnston, J. "A Model of Wage Determination Under Bilateral Monopoly." *The Economic Journal,* 1972, *82,* 837-852.

Jones, E. E., and Davis, K. E. "From Acts to Dispositions: The Attribution Process in Person Perception." In L. Berkowitz (Ed.), *Advances in Experimental Social Psychology.* Vol. 2. New York: Academic Press, 1965.

Kelley, H. H., and Thibaut, J. W. *Interpersonal Relations: A Theory of Interdependence.* New York: Wiley, 1978.

Kirk, R. E. *Experimental Design: Procedure for the Behavioral Sciences.* Monterey, Calif.: Brooks/Cole, 1968.

Kochan, T. A. *Collective Bargaining and Industrial Relations.* Homewood, Ill.: Irwin, 1980.

Komorita, S. S. "Negotiating from Strength and the Concept of Bargaining Strength." *Journal for the Theory of Social Behavior,* 1977, *7,* 65-79.

Komorita, S. S., and Barnes, M. "Effects of Pressures to Reach Agreement in Bargaining." *Journal of Personality and Social Psychology,* 1969, *13,* 245-252.

Komorita, S. S., and Brenner, A. R. "Bargaining and Concession Making Under Bilateral Monopoly." *Journal of Personality and Social Psychology,* 1968, *9,* 15-20.

Komorita, S. S., and Chertkoff, J. "A Bargaining Theory of

Coalition Formation." *Psychological Review,* 1973, *80,* 149-162.

Komorita, S. S., and Esser, J. K. "Frequency of Reciprocated Concession in Bargaining." *Journal of Personality and Social Psychology,* 1975, *32,* 699-705.

Landsberger, H. A. "Interaction Process Analysis of the Mediation of Labor-Management Disputes." *Journal of Abnormal and Social Psychology,* 1955, *51,* 552-559.

Lawler, E. J., and Bacharach, S. B. "Outcome Alternatives and Value as Criteria for Multistrategy Evaluations." *Journal of Personality and Social Psychology,* 1976, *34,* 885-894.

Lawler, E. J., and Bacharach, S. B. "Power-Dependence in Individual Bargaining: The Expected Utility of Influence." *Industrial and Labor Relations Review,* 1979, *32,* 196-204.

Lawler, E. J., and Mac Murray, B. K. "Bargaining Toughness: A Qualification of Level of Aspiration and Reciprocity Hypotheses." *Journal of Applied Social Psychology,* 1980, *10,* 416-430.

Levinson, H. M. *Determining Forces in Collective Wage Bargaining.* New York: Wiley, 1966.

Liebert, R. M., and others. "The Effects of Information and Magnitude of Initial Offer on Interpersonal Negotiation." *Journal of Experimental Social Psychology,* 1968, *4,* 431-441.

Lindblom, C. E. " 'Bargaining Power' in Price and Wage Determination." *Quarterly Journal of Economics,* 1948, *62,* 396-417.

Lindskold, S., and Bennett, R. "Attributing Trust and Conciliatory Intent from a Coercive Power Capability." *Journal of Personality and Social Psychology,* 1973, *28,* 180-186.

Loasby, B. J. *Choice, Complexity and Ignorance: An Inquiry into Economic Theory and Practice of Decision-Making.* Cambridge, England: Cambridge University Press, 1976.

Luce, R. D., and Raiffa, H. *Games and Decisions.* New York: Wiley, 1957.

Macaulay, J., and Berkowitz, L. (Eds.). *Altruism and Helping Behavior: Social Psychological Studies of Some Antecedents and Consequences.* New York: Academic Press, 1970.

McGrath, J. E., and Julian, J. W. "Interaction Process and Task Outcomes in Experimentally Created Groups." *Journal of Psychological Studies*, 1963, *14*, 117-138.

Magenau, J. M., and Pruitt, D. G. "The Social Psychology of Bargaining." In G. M. Stephenson and C. J. Brotherton (Eds.), *Industrial Relations: A Social Psychological Approach.* New York: Wiley, 1979.

Michener, H. A., and Cohen, E. D. "Effects of Punishment Magnitude in the Bilateral Threat Situation: Evidence for the Deterrence Hypothesis." *Journal of Personality and Social Psychology*, 1973, *26*, 427-438.

Michener, H. A., Lawler, E. J., and Bacharach, S. B. "Perception of Power in Conflict Situations." *Journal of Personality and Social Psychology*, 1973, *28*, 115-162.

Michener, H. A., and Suchner, R. "The Tactical Use of Social Power." In J. T. Tedeschi (Ed.), *Social Influence Processes.* Hawthorne, N.Y.: Aldine, 1972.

Michener, H. A., and others. "Factors Affecting Concession Rate and Threat Usage in Bilateral Conflict." *Sociometry*, 1975, *38*, 62-80.

Morgan, M. P. *Deterrence: A Conceptual Analysis.* Beverly Hills, Calif.: Sage, 1977.

Morley, L., and Stephanson, G. *The Social Psychology of Bargaining.* London: Allen & Unwin, 1977.

Nardin, T. "Communication and the Effects of Threats in Strategic Interaction." *Peace Research Society (International) Papers*, 1968, *9*, 69-86.

Nash, J. F., Jr. "The Bargaining Problem." *Econometrica*, 1950, *18*, 155-162.

Nash, J. F., Jr. "Two-Person Cooperative Games." *Econometrica*, 1953, *21*, 128-140.

Ofshe, R., and Ofshe, S. L. "Choice Behavior in Coalition Games." *Behavioral Science*, 1970, *15*, 337-349.

Pen, J. "A General Theory of Bargaining." *The American Economic Review*, 1952, *42*, 24-42.

Pen, J. *The Wage Rate Under Collective Bargaining.* (T. S. Preston, Trans.) Cambridge, Mass.: Harvard University Press, 1959.

Pigou, A. C. *Economics of Welfare.* (4th ed.) London: Macmillan, 1938.

Pruitt, D. G., and Lewis, S. A. "The Psychology of Integrative Bargaining." In D. Druckman (Ed.), *Negotiations: Social-Psychological Perspectives.* Beverly Hills, Calif.: Sage, 1977.

Rabinovitch, R., and Swary, I. "On the Theory of Bargaining, Strikes, and Wage Determination Under Uncertainty." *Canadian Journal of Economics,* 1976, *9,* 668-684.

Raiffa, H. "Arbitration Schemes for Generalized Two-Person Games." In H. W. Kuhn and A. W. Tucker (Eds.), *Contributions to the Theory of Games.* Princeton, N.J.: Princeton University Press, 1953.

Rapoport, A. *Two-Person Game Theory.* Ann Arbor: University of Michigan Press, 1966.

Raven, B. H. "A Comparative Analysis of Power and Power Preference." In J. T. Tedeschi (Ed.), *Perspectives on Social Power.* Hawthorne, N.Y.: Aldine, 1974.

Raven, B. H., and Kruglanski, A. W. "Conflict and Power." In P. Swingle (Ed.), *The Structure of Conflict.* New York: Academic Press, 1970.

Rubin, J. A., and Brown, B. R. *The Social Psychology of Bargaining and Negotiations.* New York: Academic Press, 1975.

Schelling, T. C. *The Strategy of Conflict.* New York: Oxford University Press, 1960.

Schelling, T. C. *Arms and Influence.* New Haven, Conn.: Yale University Press, 1966.

Schopler, J., and Layton, D. B. "Attributions of Interpersonal Power." In J. T. Tedeschi (Ed.), *Perspectives on Social Power.* Hawthorne, N.Y.: Aldine, 1974.

Shackle, G. L. S. *Expectations in Economics.* Cambridge, England: Cambridge University Press, 1949.

Shackle, G. L. S. "The Nature of the Bargaining Process." In J. T. Dunlop (Ed.), *The Theory of Wage Determination.* London: Macmillan, 1957.

Shapley, L. S. "A Value for N-Person Games." In H. W. Kuhn and A. W. Tucker (Eds.), *Contributions to the Theory of Games.* Princeton, N.J.: Princeton University Press, 1953.

Shomer, R. W., Davis, A. H., and Kelley, H. H. "Threats and the

Development of Coordination: Further Studies of the Deutsch and Krauss Trucking Game." *Journal of Personality and Social Psychology,* 1966, *4,* 119-126.

Siegel, S., and Fouraker, L. E. *Bargaining and Group Decision-Making.* New York: McGraw-Hill, 1960.

Siegel, S., Siegel, A. E., and Andrews, J. M. *Choice, Strategy and Utility.* New York: McGraw-Hill, 1964.

Somers, G. G. "Bargaining Power and Industrial Relations Theory." In G. G. Somers (Ed.), *Essays in Industrial Relations Theory.* Ames: Iowa State University Press, 1969.

Stahl, I. *Bargaining Theory.* Stockholm: Economic Research Institute, 1972.

Stephenson, G. M., and Brotherton, C. J. (Eds.). *Industrial Relations: A Social Psychological Approach.* New York: Wiley, 1979.

Stevens, C. M. *Strategy and Collective Bargaining Negotiation.* Westport, Conn.: Greenwood Press, 1963.

Stinchcombe, A. L. *Constructing Social Theories.* New York: Harcourt Brace Jovanovich, 1968.

Strauss, A. *Negotiations: Varieties, Contexts, Processes, and Social Order.* San Francisco: Jossey-Bass, 1978.

Strauss, G. "Can Social Psychology Contribute to Industrial Relations?" In G. M. Stephenson and C. J. Brotherton (Eds.), *Industrial Relations: A Social Psychological Approach.* New York: Wiley, 1979.

Svejnar, J. "On the Empirical Testing of the Nash-Zeuthen Bargaining Solution." *Industrial and Labor Relations Review,* 1980, *33,* 536-542.

Tannenbaum, A. S. *Control in Organizations.* New York: McGraw-Hill, 1968.

Tedeschi, J. T. "Threats and Promises." In P. Swingle (Ed.), *The Structure of Conflict.* New York: Academic Press, 1970.

Tedeschi, J. T., and Bonoma, T. V. "Power and Influence: An Introduction." In J. T. Tedeschi (Ed.), *Social Influence Processes.* Hawthorne, N.Y.: Aldine, 1972.

Tedeschi, J. T., Bonoma, T. V., and Novinson, N. "Behavior of a Threatener: Retaliation Versus Fixed Opportunity Costs." *Journal of Conflict Resolution,* 1970, *14,* 69-76.

Tedeschi, J. T., Bonoma, T. V., and Schlenker, B. R. "Influence, Decision, and Compliance." In J. T. Tedeschi (Ed.), *Social Influence Processes.* Hawthorne, N.Y.: Aldine, 1972.

Tedeschi, J. T., Schlenker, B. R., and Bonoma, T. V. *Conflict, Power, and Games.* Hawthorne, N.Y.: Aldine, 1973.

Teger, A. I. "The Effect of Early Cooperation on the Escalation of Conflict." *Journal of Experimental Social Psychology,* 1970, *6,* 187-204.

Thibaut, J. W., and Kelley, H. H. *The Social Psychology of Groups.* New York: Wiley, 1959.

von Neumann, J., and Morgenstern, O. *Theory of Games and Economic Behavior.* Princeton, N.J.: Princeton University Press, 1944.

Walcott, C., Hopmann, P. T., and King, T. D. "Role of Debate in Negotiation." In D. Druckman (Ed.), *Negotiations: Social-Psychological Perspectives.* Beverly Hills, Calif.: Sage, 1977.

Walton, R. E., and McKersie, R. B. *A Behavioral Theory of Labor Negotiations.* New York: McGraw-Hill, 1965.

Weber, M. *The Methodology of the Social Sciences.* New York: Free Press, 1949.

Wrong, D. H. "Some Problems in Defining Social Power." *American Journal of Sociology,* 1968, *73* (6), 673-681.

Young, O. R. (Ed.). *Bargaining: Formal Theories of Negotiation.* Chicago: University of Illinois Press, 1975.

Yukl, G. A. "Effects of the Opponent's Initial Offer, Concession Magnitude, and Concession Frequency on Bargaining Behavior." *Journal of Personality and Social Psychology,* 1974a, *30,* 322-335.

Yukl, G. A. "The Effects of Situational Variables and Opponent Concessions on a Bargainer's Perception, Aspirations, and Concessions." *Journal of Personality and Social Psychology,* 1974b, *29,* 227-236.

Zeuthen, F. *Problems of Monopoly and Economic Warfare.* London: Routledge & Kegan Paul, 1930.

Zeuthen, F. "La théorie du monopole bilateral et multilateral toujours à l'ordre du jour" ["Bilateral and Multilateral Monopoly: Still on the Agenda"]. *Economie Appliquée,* 1955, *8,* 331-334.

Index

▼▼

225